Looking In and Speaking Out

Looking In and Speaking Out

Introspection
Consciousness
Communication

Robin Wooffitt
&
Nicola Holt

imprint-academic.com

Published in the UK by Imprint Academic
PO Box 200, Exeter EX5 5YX, UK

Published in the USA by Imprint Academic
Philosophy Documentation Center
PO Box 7147, Charlottesville, VA 22906-7147, USA

ISBN 9 781845 402273

A CIP catalogue record for this book is available from the
British Library and US Library of Congress

To Samuel

NH

For Wendy

RW

Contents

Acknowledgements

The research reported in this book was funded by two Bial Foundation Bursaries for Scientific Research, and an award from the University of York Innovation and Research Priming Fund.

We would like to acknowledge the contribution of Dr Simon Allistone, who worked as a Research Fellow on the first of the Bial funded projects mentioned above. He made a significant contribution to the analyses reported in Chapter Four. We would also like to acknowledge the conference delegate at the 3rd International Conference on Language, Culture and Mind, at the University of Southern Denmark, who, after an early presentation by the first author of the poetics of introspective discourse, drew our attention to the relevance of poetics in Donne's poetry. We would also like to acknowledge the late Professor Robert Morris, the Koestler Chair of Parapsychology at the University of Edinburgh, who encouraged this research and provided the recordings of the ganzfeld experiments analysed in this book. We would also like to thank Dr Caroline Watt of the Koestler Parapsychology Unit for allowing us to continue working on these materials long after the completion of the project for which they were originally provided.

Some of the arguments and analyses presented in this book have been reported in journals in parapsychology, discourse and communication, and social psychology. We would therefore like to thank the Editor and publishers of the *Journal of Parapsychology* for permission to use material from 'Conversation analysis and parapsychology: experimenter-subject interaction in ganzfeld experiments' (vol. 67, 299–324). We would also like to thank the Editor of *Discourse Studies* and Sage publications for permission to use materials originally published in 'Participation, procedure and accountability: reported speech markers in a parapsychology experiment' (vol. 10, 407–427) and 'Silence and its organisation in the pragmatics of introspection' (vol. 12, 379–406).

We would like to thank the Editor and publishers of *Research in Language and Social Interaction* for permission to use materials from 'Introspective discourse and the poetics of subjective experience' (vol. 14, 135–156) that form the basis of the analyses presented in Chapters Six and Seven. We would also like to acknowledge permission provided by Editor and publishers of a special issue of *Qualitative Research in Psychology* to reproduce materials first reported in 'Introspective discourse and the poetics of subjective experience' (vol. 7, 5–20). Finally we would like to thank the Editor and publishers of the *British Journal of Social Psychology* for permission to reproduce arguments first presented in 'Interaction and laboratory experience: observations from parapsychological data' (vol. 46, 477–501). Parts of the argument in Chapter Nine have also appeared in Hutchby and Wooffitt's *Conversation Analysis* (2nd edition, 2008).

Chapter One

The rise, fall and rise of introspection

Introduction

There is renewed interest in introspection in mainstream psychology, consciousness studies, cognitive science and a raft of cognate social science disciplines. This has been stimulated by developments such as the emergence of consciousness studies as an interdisciplinary but discrete area of study, and the realisation that the development of sophisticated machinery to study brain function and brain states invites consideration of experiences that seem to correlate with them. Indeed, it is increasingly recognised that introspection is at the heart of psychological, social scientific and humanistic endeavour. As Jack and Roepstorff write '... introspection is the *sine qua non* of consciousness. Without introspection, we simply wouldn't know about the existence of experience' (Jack and Roepstorff, 2003b: xv).

Introspective reports, though, are discursive events: introspective data are essentially descriptions of inner experiences that rely on the use of everyday communicative skills and practices in institutional settings, such as the psychology laboratory. But while there have been numerous discussions of the different forms of introspective data, and the methodological advantages and problems associated with studying reports of inner experience, there has been — as far as we are aware — no sustained, detailed analysis of the language of introspective description. In this book, we develop and illustrate an empirical perspective on introspective reports of inner conscious experience that draws from social scientific research on language in social interaction.

In this and the second chapter, we review the history of introspection and its use in contemporary research programmes to explore inner experience and consciousness. Although our account predominantly reflects the kinds of methodological and substantive concerns that animate psychologists and researchers in consciousness studies, we try to introduce a broader range of critical points informed by more social scientific concerns, particularly research on the socially organised practices of communication in naturally occurring settings. The empirical approach is outlined and illustrated briefly in chapter three, which also introduces the data for our study: reports of inner experiences generated as part of an experimental procedure to test for parapsychological phenomena. Chapters four and five examine two broad features of introspective reports: the ways in which participants report how they apprehend their inner experience; and, paradoxically, the absence of reports: periods of silence. In both cases, we argue that descriptions of inner experience (or the momentary absence of description) exhibit the participants' tacit orientation to the context of laboratory research on consciousness. Chapters six and seven examine poetic phenomena in our introspective data (particularly acoustic relationships within and between discrete imagery reports), and other poetic relationships, such as puns and category associations. We show how these ostensibly playful communicative practices have serious import in that their operation can impact upon the content of what is being reported.

One key feature of the renewed interest in introspection and introspective data is the use of one-to-one interviews to generate people's retrospective accounts of their inner experiences. In chapters eight and nine we broaden the focus of our analysis and examine the ways in which interactional processes underpin and impact upon attempts to elicit descriptions of conscious experience in retrospective interviews. In chapter eight we raise some broad methodological issues via discussion of the way that data are often presented in formal research articles or books in consciousness studies. In chapter nine, we extend our argument by examining interviews from the parapsychology experiments in which experimenter and participant review the experimenter's record of the prior introspective report. We identify a number of interactional phenomena and show that the organisation of these communicative practices fundamentally shapes what is taken to have been the participant's inner experience. Finally, in chapter ten, we summarise and reflect on the wider implications of the argument developed through the empirical research discussed in this book: that to understand properly the nature of introspective reports, it is essential that we attend to the socially organised communicative competences that inform their production.

The term introspection, or 'looking into one's own experience', comes from the Latin *intra*, meaning 'inward', and *spicere*, meaning 'to look at'. While the notion that the 'mind can reflect upon itself' was first written about by Augustine circa 410, the word introspection is thought to have emerged in the second half of the 17th century, and as a psychological method introspection has been used with varying levels of caution in experimental psychology since the end of the 19th century. At this time William James stated: 'the word introspection need hardly be defined — it means, of course, the looking into our own minds and reporting what we there discover' (1890: 185). Yet, despite the apparently self-evident nature of introspection, operational definitions have varied greatly over the years, as has its use as a method for the study of inner experience, and debates about the limits and problems of introspection are long standing. It was considered a central feature of the earliest psychological research. But since then, discussion of the value of introspection has been stimulated by three key intellectual developments: Watson's (1913) critique of introspection, and the subsequent rise of behaviourism; the rise of cognitive psychology, and particularly, Nisbett and Wilson's (1977) examination of the use of introspection in cognitive psychological research; and calls for the development of first-person methodologies in response to the recognition of consciousness as a topic of philosophical, psychological and neurological inquiry (for example, Chalmers, 1999). In this first chapter, then, we offer an historical review of the emergence and role of introspection in psychology, focusing on why researchers initially advocated introspective methods and then subsequently rejected them.

Consideration of the use of introspection is enmeshed with epistemological and ontological debates concerning the nature of subjectivity and objectivity, consciousness, and the scientific enterprise (for consideration of these issues the reader is referred to Lyons, 1986; Velmans, 2000b). In this chapter, though, we focus on introspection as a method, rather than as philosophical construct (Armstrong, 1968; Gertler, 2001; Shoemaker, 1994). However, it is important to sketch the philosophical intellectual context from which the experimental application of introspection emerged.

Early experimental introspection

Philosophical antecedents of introspection had engendered a degree of epistemological uncertainty over the value of first-person reports of inner experience. While rationalists such as René Descartes and George Berkeley held that subjective experience was irreducible and the basis of all human knowledge, empiricists, such as John Locke and David Hume grounded knowledge in sense impressions. The empiricists were concerned with how we acquire knowledge about the external world. Nevertheless, Locke recognised the faculty of reflection, knowledge based on 'inner sense'; and Hume, while sceptical of the value of subjective reports of 'the mind's operations', did think it possible that direct knowledge of the content of mind was possible (Lyons, 1986). As such, the empiricists made a clear demarcation between 'inner' versus 'outer' sense, a distinction which formed a logical bedrock for the development of an epistemology based on the deliberate observation of inner experience (Boring, 1953). However, empiricist philosophers did not make the crucial distinction between mere awareness of inner states and the analytical observation of inner states (Danziger, 1998). Nor did they consider whether or not 'reflection' might be subject to error (Boring, 1953). These issues were highlighted by Immanuel Kant.

Kant's legacy for introspection was twofold. Whilst he reasoned that it was possible to acquire empirical data from the observation of inner states, he regarded this data as superficial and limited. He distinguished between awareness and the principles of its organisation, which are not available to conscious experience. As such we can only learn about 'phenomena' or the appearances of things, and not about things-in-themselves (noumena). According to this view, subjective experience was not a reliable source of data about objective reality, and the organisation of consciousness, as noumena, was unknowable (Morris, 1991; Tarnas, 1991). Kant did not consider that the observation of inner experience could form the basis of a science. Any data from introspective observations were limited because they were based merely on the observation and classification of the 'appearance of things', akin to botany (Danziger, 1998). This was not scientific due to the method's inability to explain the organisation of the observed parts: it provided no scope for a systematic and mathematical understanding of inner experience.

Despite philosophically grounded concern about the value of reflective reports of inner experience, towards the end of the 19th century at the University of Leipzig, Wilhelm Wundt argued that conscious states were a legitimate subject for scientific analysis and attempted to establish and 'scientize' introspection as a method, developing a rigorous experimental procedure (Coon, 1993). Wundt has been proclaimed as one of the founding fathers of experimental psychology, having established the first official 'Institute for Experimental Psychology' in 1883 (Danziger, 1998). However, he regarded himself foremost to be a philosopher and physiologist and he used knowledge of both fields in his work, applying the empirical methods of physiology to the study of consciousness. Wundt aimed to go beyond philosophical enquiry based on the laws of logic, and instead establish a careful empirical analysis of the elementary contents of conscious experience (Wundt, 2008: 149). For these purposes, he drew upon his precursors Hermann von Helmholtz (with whom he had worked as a researcher, early in his career) and Gustav Fechner, who both practised psychophysics. Helmholtz and Fechner had begun to apply mathematical laws to the relationship between measurable subjective sensations and external stimuli, thereby challenging the notion that 'mind' was beyond the remit of the scientific enterprise.

To ensure scientific credibility, Wundt imposed strict parameters to the study of inner experience. He distinguished between naïve 'self-observation' or 'pure introspection' and trained 'inner perception' or 'experimental introspection' (Wundt, 1897). Experimental introspection was thought to give 'special access' to inner experience, access that was only given to trained psychologists under controlled conditions. This experimental approach countered James's comment that 'If to have feelings or thoughts in their immediacy were enough, babies in the cradle would be psychologists, and infallible ones' (James, 1890: 189). Wundt's distinction between the 'pure introspection' that James describes and experimental introspection placed emphasis not on access to experience as a source of psychological insight, but on the method and attitude by which experience is attended and reported.

Wundt's method of experimental introspection was designed to facilitate exact observation. His introspective observers underwent considerable training; Boring (1953) rehearses the anecdote that observers had to have practised reporting on inner experiences at least 10,000 times before they could contribute to formal experiments. Wundt also insisted on careful timing: attention was paid to conscious experience for a set interval, after which reports were made immediately. Moreover, he focused on simple conscious events, such as the intensity and duration of a stimulus. He was aware, for example, that, as immediate experience was composed of both content and an 'experiencing subject', the latter could influence the prior. This led him to avoid introspecting on complex and dynamic phenomena that might change as a result of observing them analytically, such as intense emotions (Wundt, 1897). He argued that complex psychological phenomena (such as emotions or beliefs) were social in nature, and could therefore only be studied in the context of language, religion, myth and custom, through history and ethnography (Lyons, 1986; Morris, 1991). His research examined experience in relation to carefully measured and controlled external stimuli in order to create simple conditions for observation that had a specific focus, such as tone-sensation, and by systematically changing the properties of the external stimulus in order to explore the

relationship between 'outer' and 'inner' stimuli. Finally, Wundt advocated the need to repeat observations frequently. Implications of this
method were that reports were amenable to statistical analysis and other
investigators had access to the procedure and stimuli, and could therefore
attempt replication of his work.

Wundt developed this methodology from a particular philosophical
standpoint. He wrote 'the expressions outer experience and inner experience do not indicate different objects, but different points of view from
which we take up the consideration of and scientific treatment of a unitary
experience ... the point of view of psychology ... may be designated as
immediate experience' (Wundt, 1958: 386 [1907]), a quote that encapsu-
lates three key features of his approach. (1) He saw 'inner' and 'outer'
experience as complementary, being equally valid viewpoints of the same
experience, and drew no distinction between the experimental observation of 'inner', immediate experience and the observation of external
events (Morris, 1991). In both instances, the scientist was seen as recorder
of sensory information, whether this be reading the temperature on a dial
or noting whether a light has become lighter or darker (Kroker, 2003).
(2) Wundt did not advocate the study of inner experience in isolation. That
introspective reports were supplemented by independent 'objective'
measures was paramount in his approach. He sought to relate contents of
experience, or 'elementary processes' that belong 'to the psychological
sphere' to 'elementary processes' that belong to the 'natural scientific
sphere' (1958: 387 [1907]). For this reason, Coon (1993) describes his
approach as falling in the 'use of instrumentation camp', for example,
reaction times between the presentation of a stimulus and a response
could be measured with a 'chronograph'. (3) Wundt also clearly demar-
cated immediate conscious experience as the focus of psychology's remit.
He argued that the purpose of psychology, as distinct from the natural sciences, was to examine the contents of consciousness. Consequently, he
had three objectives: to identify the basic components of conscious experience; the relationships between these components and external stimuli,
and the laws that underpinned these relationships.

It might be argued that Wundt's approach actually differs little from the
protocols used in some modern neurocognitive research (for example
Libet, Wright, Feinstein and Pearl, 1979). The reports made were not
lengthy verbal accounts, but brief comments, for example, on the relative
intensity of a perceptual stimulus, when one became conscious of a sensation, or whether a pitch was lower or higher than one just heard previously
(Thomas, 2010). Further, Wundt's introspective method did not deviate
very far from that of his precursors (and successors) in psychophysics.
Although rigorous, his approach was restrictive, being limited to studies

of sensation and perception and based on the verbal reports of a handful of trained psychologists.

Wundt's former students extended and developed his work at other institutions. Oswald Külpe (at the University of Würzburg in Germany) and Edward Titchener (at Cornell University in the United States), continued to study thought processes through the analysis of verbal introspective reports from trained research participants. Their goal, too, was to determine the basic elements of thought – to produce a 'periodic table' of consciousness – based on reports of the sensations of immediate experience (Adams, 2000; Külpe, 1895; Titchener, 1898). Following Wundt, introspection was modelled upon observation (or inspection) in the natural sciences, aiming for measurement and control. However, the aims and introspective practice of Wundt's followers deviated from those of Wundt in important ways: the remit of introspection was broadened to include more complex psychological phenomena; correlates with objective measures were no longer seen as essential; and qualitative reports of experience took on greater importance, there was a shift of focus to quality from quantity (Coon, 1993). Titchener described this departure as a movement from a focus on instruments, the 'chronoscope, kymograph and tachistoscope' to a focus on the observers themselves. His approach attempted to 'mechanise' or standardise the 'introspecting tool', that is, the introspecting person (Coon, 1993; Titchener, 1912). Through extensive training, the aim was to describe accurately 'inner experience' in response to a stimulus; thereby to render introspection 'photographic' (Boring, 1953). For instance, Titchener drew the following guidelines in an attempt to control the introspective attitude: be impartial (observe without preconception); be attentive (make no speculations); be comfortable (to minimise distractions); and be alert (to stop if feeling tired) (Titchener, 1898: 34–35). He was quite clear about some of the limitations of this process: 'The ideal introspective report is an accurate description … of some conscious process. Causation, dependence, development are then matters of inference' (Titchener, 1912: 486). Avoiding inference was central to Titchener's method, referred to as avoiding the 'stimulus error'. Rather than meanings of, or knowledge about, the stimulus, attempts were made to elicit details of the experience itself. For example, rather than observing and reporting 'the apple is green' the introspector would report 'there is greenness'.

Likewise, Külpe's method of 'systematic experimental introspection', was intended to 'subject the whole of conscious content to an exact analysis' (Külpe, 1895:19) in order to identify the components that constituted it. He argued that Wundt's focus on simple conscious elements was artificial because it was not possible to separate simple sensations from complex conscious phenomena. Following James (1890), he argued that consciousness was a 'more or less continuous stream of complex processes' (Külpe,

1895:22). He advocated an observational stance characterised by 'attentive experience' (directing one's attention upon phenomena and not upon the act of introspecting), and impartiality (avoiding bias and expectation in one's reports). However, he did not enforce the avoidance of interpretation as stridently as Titchener.

For both Titchener and Külpe, this extension of the remit of introspection, from specific stimuli to the broad content of consciousness, led to greater emphasis on the making of elaborate verbal reports. Kroker (2003) quotes an example of the introspective method from a study on reading comprehension by Edmund Jacobson, who worked at Titchener's laboratory. Observers were asked to read a sentence, apprehend its meaning, and then to close their eyes and provide in as much detail as possible everything that occurred in consciousness. Three observers did this repeatedly, after much training. In the report that follows an observer describes their experience of reading the sentence 'she came in secretly'. (The observer's comments or interpretations are in parentheses; insertions from the experimenter are in square brackets.)

> **Observer F.** Stimulus sentence: *She came in secretly*: 1.25 sec.
>
> 'Purple (from written words) clear. White (from paper) and black (from cardboard) in background, and these were [comparatively] unclear. Simultaneous with the visual clearness, kinaesthetic-auditory images (corresponding to the words); weak intensity, more as if whispered than as if said in ordinary voice; i.e., lacked deeper tones; and slightly faster than I should ordinarily say them. (The words did not come singly, but the sentence as a whole made a single impression on me; e.g., the period at the end was a part of the total impression. [All this was] Perception of sentence as visual and kinaesthetic-auditory impression.)
>
> 'Then vague visual and kinaesthetic image (of Miss X. coming in stealthy position, on tip-toe with legs bent, through the door into the Audition Room from the Haptics Room), i.e., blue visual image (upper left part of skirt) and very vague, featureless image, flesh-coloured (of left side of face). The image (was projected straight ahead of me, to the position in which the door actually is). Kinaesthetic images in own right upper leg (which was directly opposite in position to the image, as if my own leg was bent); also kinaesthetic images or sensation in muscles, probably intercostals, of right side (such as I get when standing and bending right leg). (The sentence meant: Miss X. came over in there, through the door, secretly.)
>
> 'In the fore-period I told myself: Get the meaning, and set myself muscularly to work hard.'
>
> (From Jacobson, 1911: 556).

It is perhaps no wonder that Boring criticised this work for taking 'twenty minutes to describe the conscious content of a second and a half and at the end of that period the observer was cudgelling his brain to recall what had actually happened' (Boring, 1953:174).

Retrospective reports have been associated with failures of memory and inaccurate perception: verbal suggestion, post-event misinformation effects, retrospective bias (such as misremembering), 'imagination inflation' and theory driven interpretations of past events (French, 2003; Loftus & Hoffmann, 1989). Both Külpe and Titchener were aware of potential errors associated with the description and communication of inner experience. Both argued that in order to reach consensus a scientific attitude of observation was needed and an appropriate language, or vocabulary. An example of an attempt to overcome problems of idiosyncratic description comes from Dallenbach (1913) at Cornell, who worked with three introspectionists who, in order to consensually validate their reports, produced a 'language' or meaning system (based on % clarity) between themselves in training sessions prior to the experiment proper. However, no single system was agreed upon (Mandler, 2007). So, whereas Titchener focused on sensations, using predefined terms, others found this too limiting and reductionist, arguing that it destroyed rather than expressed lived experience, and preferred a metaphorical and holistic approach (Danziger, 1998). As such, there was a tension between consensus and phenomenological detail. The introspectionists were left with a dilemma: their data could be immediate, but limited to simple facets of experience, or detailed and rich, but prone to reconstructive errors.

The reliability of experimental introspection was brought into question by the inability of the Würzburg and Cornell schools to agree on fundamental issues. The aim to identify the elements of consciousness led to discrepancies, Titchener's laboratory demarcating over three times as many 'sensations' as Külpe's laboratory (Boring, 1929; Velmans, 2000a). This suggested the possibility that experimental introspection was flawed in its basic assumption that there is a set or minimal number of mental elements (Hatfield, 2005). However, a more controversial debate concerned whether or not all thought involved imagery. Researchers at Würzburg reported the occurrence of 'imageless thought' whilst Titchener reported that images mediated all thought (Boring, 1929; Valentine, 1998). In a series of studies the Würzburg group observed moments of conscious experience that seemed to be 'inaccessible to further analysis' (e.g. Mayer and Orth, 1901). These moments were characterised by an absence of specific conscious representations and were difficult to express in words (Brock, 1991; Mandler, 2007). Titchener (1912) rejected the notion of 'imageless thought' and explained it as an unnecessary inference based on a stimulus error. However, his prior assumption that experience must be reduced into sensations, images or feelings also imposed a theoretical bias on reports. Based on a re-examination of the data, Hurlburt and Heavey

(2001) argue that the introspectionists at Würzburg and Cornell did not differ in their descriptions of subjective experience, but in the *theoretical interpretations* they each drew from their observations. It is, then, a matter of debate whether experimental introspection as a method of attending to inner experience was intrinsically flawed, or whether the discrepancies that arose were social in nature, ensuing from different research communities, with different aims, interpretations and linguistic tools. What was clear, though, was that experimental introspection was open to the criticism that different training methods and attentional stances had led to different findings, and to contradictions, which, due to the privacy of subjective experience, were seen by some as impossible to resolve (Lachman, Lachman and Butterfield, 1979; Locke, 2009). Training methods themselves generated suspicion: 'During Titchener's time, his Cornell colleagues and students were looked on as a "sect" organized around him, as if the whole idea of a mandatory training was unacceptable and could easily be ridiculed as an "esoteric" activity' (Depraz, Varela & Vermersch, 2003:108).

A potential discovery lurking in this dispute also revealed a limitation of the introspective method. The 'imageless thought' debate highlighted the role of unconscious processing in the microgenesis of conscious experience. According to Boring (1953), this was the introspectionists' most important finding; but it did suggest that the entire workings of the mind were not available to introspection. This limited access counted against the use of the introspective method in psychology. For instance, in his research on concept learning, Hull's (1920) participants were unable to explain how this was performed, leading him to rely upon behavioural rather than introspective indices. Intellectual developments outside psychology were also highlighting the importance of hidden processes and forces in the organisation of human behaviour. The writings of Freud, Darwin and Marx alerted scholars to the importance of unconscious processes, natural selection and the history and inherent logic of capitalism — influences not available to conscious reflection (Tarnas, 1991).

Because of the problems associated with introspectionist methods, variability in empirical findings, disputes about the interpretation of data, and perceived limitations of the reach of introspection, many psychologists turned to behaviourism, the principles of which were outlined in Watson's (1913) polemical account. Behaviouristic psychology held no truck with introspection, regarding it as being unreliable, untrustworthy, and non-functional. Watson did not 'trust the subject' to use meanings and words that could be accurately understood by an experimenter (Boring, 1953); and he did not condone the process of treating 'language behaviour' as evidence of other, non-observable, behaviour, such as distractions of attention or acoustic clarity (Washburn, 1922). 'Psychology as the behaviorist views it is a purely objective, experimental branch of natural science. Its theoretical goal is prediction and control of behaviour. *Introspection forms no essential part of its methods'* (Watson, 1913:158, emphasis added). Not only did Watson reject introspection as a method but he also argued for the abandonment of the study of conscious experience. 'Indeed, the time has come when psychology must discard all reference to consciousness; when it need no longer delude itself into thinking that it is making mental states the object of observation' (Watson, 1913: 163). The proper focus of psychological research, he argued, was the publicly observable behaviour of others.

Watson's arguments about what the core goals of psychology should be reflected wider contemporary debates about the development of the discipline, and these too had a negative impact on the perceived value of introspection as a research method. Strategically, there was a desire to distinguish psychology from philosophy as an academic discipline, which had traditionally drawn upon introspective methods (Coon, 1993; Costall, 2006). There was an impetus in academic psychology for order, applicability, measurement, control and standardisation, in line with a rapidly industrialising society and the development of technology, the need for which was thought to be better met by objective, third-person methods (Coon, 1993). Moreover, experimental introspection had no functional use, which did not sit well with the American zeitgeist (Boring, 1953), and it was perceived as lacking ecological validity, being focused on laboratory situations instead of the ways in which people actually behaved in real world contexts (Neisser, 1976, cited by Costall, 2006: 2-3). Even advocates of introspection such as William James, as well as the Gestalt psychologist Wolfgang Köhler, were querulous regarding the merits of the 'mental atomism' of experimental introspection: its artificiality, triviality, and the arbitrariness of controlled observations (Adams, 2000; Costall, 2006; Hatfield, 2005). It was argued that 'the type of tedious, automatonlike, internal observation that was used in the introspectionist school was so boring and unfruitful that even James dissociated himself from such experimental research' (Wallace, 2000: 89). And finally, the radical behaviourist, B. F. Skinner, subsequently went on to argue that it is not possible to attribute causality to inner experiences: they could not influence any other behaviour (Nye, 1986). While not denying the existence of inner states, from this perspective they were useless for understanding behaviour, and thus of little empirical interest. At a time of rising scientism, with a focus on the applied and practical, the study of conscious experience was seen as obscure and obtuse. As a consequence, over a period of time, studies of subjective experience, and the contents of consciousness, were largely abandoned by mainstream psychology, and so ended what has been hailed as the 'golden age' of introspection (Lyons, 1986).

Introspection and cognitive psychology

Although introspection as an explicitly articulated research programme disappeared from psychology, it is clear, as we shall see later, that substantial research in psychology still relied upon research participants providing what were essentially introspective reports. We should be cautious, then, about accepting the conventional wisdom that renewed interest in the limits and potential of introspection followed from the rise of cognitive psychology. However, it is undoubtedly the case that experimental psychology's renewed interest in the kind of imagery and mental content neglected by behaviourism provided a stimulus to the consideration of peoples' accounts of their inner experience.

In a landmark paper, Nisbett and Wilson (1977) examined the limits of introspective access by reviewing empirical work including work on cognitive dissonance, attribution theory, implicit learning, bystander effects and subliminal perception. For example, in an attribution study by Storms and Nisbett (1970), insomniacs were given a placebo pill before going to bed and were either told that this would increase their heart rate and alertness (symptoms of insomnia) or decrease their heart rate and make them feel relaxed. Storms and Nisbett reasoned, and found, that participants who could attribute symptoms of insomnia to the pill, rather than to their own potentially agitating thoughts, would sleep better. However, participants' own verbal reports did not concur — their explanations for better sleep described personal factors such as having completed an exam or resolved a problem. Further, participants reported not having thought about the pill at all after taking it. This lack of awareness of the ostensible cause of their behaviour (better sleep) was one piece of evidence in support of the thesis that cognitive processes are rarely conscious or verbalisable. Taking this further, in some cases, Nisbett and Wilson surmised, there appears to be no access to the stimulus that has led to a behaviour (such as a word association or the presence of bystanders), even if this stimulus has been consciously apprehended. Nor might there be access to the consequent behaviour itself, such as an attitudinal change. Consequently, they concluded that 'there may be little or no introspective access to higher order cognitive processes' (Nisbett and Wilson, 1977:231) such as those postulated to underpin evaluations and decision-making. What, then, are verbal reports based on? Nisbett and Wilson propose that we draw upon culturally endorsed implicit theories or the making of simple judgements based on what seems plausible rather than introspecting. This idea is by supported by the finding that observers, who, when asked to predict what would occur in an experimental situation (such as the attribution study described above) made the same kinds of verbal reports as actual participants (making the same 'introspective' errors), suggesting that responses were drawn from common beliefs rather than actual experience (Nisbett and Wilson, 1977).

Nisbett and Wilson began with the premise that it is intuitively unlikely that introspective reports are *always* inaccurate, and they outlined conditions that might increase 'introspective certainty': the information requested should be accessible and available to memory; and any stimuli to be reported in an experimental context should be salient, few in number and plausibly relevant in that context. They argued that while causal processes influencing experience might evade introspection, the contents of consciousness might not: introspective 'whats', rather than 'whys' or 'hows', might be reliable. Examples of contents given were one's current focus of attention, sensations, emotions, plans and intentions. However, they argued for the empirical testing of the efficacy of introspection under these conditions, querying whether accurate reports in such cases might again be due to accurate implicit theories rather than 'inner awareness'.

In a review of the impact of Nisbett and Wilson's paper ten years later, White (1988) made a number of theoretical and empirical criticisms of this body of work. Importantly, he argued that verbal reports can be inaccurate due to reasons other than a lack of introspective access. White criticized Nisbett and Wilson for assuming that the relationship between verbal report and introspective access is direct, thereby negating participants' role as active agents in the production of verbal reports; and for not adequately considering methodological flaws that might have led to distorted reports. In the first instance, a range of processes might contribute to the making of verbal reports, such as: one's motivation to be accurate, one's recent focus of attention, cultural beliefs, memories, demands of the social context and experimental cues. If verbal reports are 'hypotheses', based on competing sources of information, that may include introspective access on one hand, and other processes, such as inferences drawn from available cues, on the other, then, an inaccurate report does not necessarily indicate a lack of access, but rather, poor hypothesis building. In the second instance, White (1988) noted a number of design flaws that may have increased the likelihood of inaccurate verbal reports, including misleading experimental cues; poor probes that may have elicited irrelevant information; instructions that did not emphasise a need for accurate reports; appraisal processes that may have biased responses; plus evaluation apprehension and demand characteristics. Thus, White argues, an erroneous report that is influenced, for instance, by misleading social cues, with

poor motivation for accuracy, may mislead an experimenter into constru-
ing that a participant has a lack of direct access to their own experience.
Prior to White's paper, Ericsson and Simon (1980) had argued that the
design of the studies in Nisbett and Wilson's paper did not provide optimal conditions for recall: probes were not closely related to specific processes that could be stored in memory; and some studies gave participants
distraction tasks with high cognitive loads prior to the making of a verbal
report, increasing the likelihood of forgetting. Further, they noted that it
has been documented how, in a series of trials, participants' behaviour on
later trials may become 'automated' and thus internal states about the
'why' of the ensuing behaviour is inaccessible. They also pointed out that,
when prompted in such ambiguous circumstances, participants may make
generalized verbal reports, based on elements they remember from particular previous trials or prior beliefs or expectations.

At best then, Nisbett and Wilson's study makes a small inroad into
understanding which internal events can be accurately reported, demarcating what introspection can and can't do, namely the inability to provide
reliable reports on unconscious processes (that which never reached
conscious awareness or has been subsequently forgotten). At worst, it
suggests that the positivistic framework upon which their propositions
are based imposes limitations and biases that obfuscate such an
understanding.

Some attempts were made to develop introspective methods within the
constraints outlined by Nisbett and Wilson, for example, think-aloud protocols (Ericsson and Simon, 1980) and descriptive experience sampling
(Hurlburt, 1979). However, despite criticisms of the paper (Quattrone,
1985; White, 1988) the predominant response was to interpret it as advo-
cating 'anti-introspectionism' and as a reinforcement of the woeful inaccuracy of verbal reports on internal machinations. In a neo-behaviourist
vein, ways to make cognitive processes amenable to objective analysis —
external, public and thus observable by a third party — continued to be
developed, primarily through performance on tests, for example, of memory recall, solution finding, reaction time or physiological measurements,
(Gross, 1996) as well as computer simulations. This perspective is still
upheld in cognitive textbooks today, for example, Sternberg advocates the
avoidance of self-report for the following reasons:

> The reliability of data based on various kinds of self-reports depends
> on the candor of the participants when providing reports. A partici-
> pant may misreport information about his or her cognitive processes
> for a variety of reasons. These reasons can be intentional or uninten-
> tional. Intentional misreports can involve trying to edit out unflatter-
> ing information. Unintentional misreports may involve not
> understanding the question or not remembering the information accu-
> rately. (Sternberg, 2009:21)

This is not to say that no cognitive psychologists drew on introspective reports. In his work on daydreams, Singer (1976) collected descriptions of inner experience and analysed their content, while Kosslyn, Seger, Pani and Hillger (1990) collected unstructured diary reports of participants' mental images in an attempt to ascertain their function in everyday life. But research that explicitly relied on reports of inner experience were the exception.

It has been argued that, although the notion of introspection has courted interest and disfavour according to shifts in the epistemological zeitgeist, experimental psychology has nevertheless been permeated with its use (Laplane, 1992). Boring recognised that introspection, broadly defined as verbal report, had not disappeared from psychology, referring to its use as 'camouflaged introspection' (Boring, 1953:169). Costall (2006) goes as far as to call the statement that introspection was ever banished from psychological enquiry a myth, the propaganda of cognitivist textbook histories. As Velmans (2000a) stresses, the use of introspection is inherent in much of cognitive psychology and neuroscience; for instance, to ascertain the threshold between subliminal and liminal awareness researchers must rely on participants' subjective reports of what they do or do not perceive; likewise, we only know about visual illusions, such as the Necker cube through introspective reports. Even a cursory examination of classic experiments in cognitive psychology reveals the use of verbal reports on inner experience, for example of enjoyment in cognitive dissonance research (Festinger and Carlsmith, 1959) and of emotional states in Schachter and Singer's (1962) research on attribution. For example, in testing the interaction between physiological arousal and cognitive attributions in the production of experienced emotion Schachter and Singer's dependent variable was based upon verbal reports — participants' descriptions of their emotional state. These reports were elicited both through mood scales, asking for example: 'How irritated, angry or annoyed would you say you feel at present?', with responses indicated along a five-point scale from 'I don't feel at all irritated or angry' to 'I feel extremely irritated or angry'; and 'In addition to these scales, the subjects were asked to answer two open-end questions on other physical or emotional sensations they may have experienced during the experimental session' (Schachter and Singer, 1962: 387). Essentially these are both forms of introspective report, which is perhaps unavoidable when seeking to better understand distinct emotional states, which are consciously apprehended.

Introspective methods also continued under the auspices of Gestalt psychology, transpersonal and humanistic psychology, drawing upon the phenomenological tradition (Cardeña, 2004), psychophysics (Boring, 1953), personality research and psychometrics (which rely on the assumption that in questionnaires respondents can adequately reflect on, aggregate instances of and report experiences, attitudes and behaviour), psychoanalysis, clinical psychology, psychiatry and psychotherapeutic intervention. For example, the perceptual field was explored through experiential reports made in states of sensory deprivation (the ganzfeld) by the Gestalt psychologist Wolfgang Metzger in the 1920s and 1930s (Cohen, 1957). The need to examine inner experience is a practical one from a clinical perspective, where illnesses such as depression are both diagnosed and treated through descriptions of inner experience, and psychotherapeutic interventions are based on communication of, and reflection on, experience and behaviour. It is no surprise, therefore, that Costall was able to argue that

> ... the claims about the demise of the introspective method are highly exaggerated. Introspection, even in some of its more full-blown versions, never went away. Some versions of the method along with their results continued — and continue — to be taken seriously within the discipline (Costall, 2006: 659).

In summary, it appears that while psychology as a discipline continued to mistrust and reject introspection, use of verbal reports on inner experience was a routine feature of numerous experimental procedures. Introspection, whilst being shown to be unreliable for the study of the cognitive microgenesis of conscious experience, was still employed, perhaps with more success, for the study of conscious events for which no other indices were available.

Introspection and the emergence of consciousness studies

With increasing attention being given to a science of consciousness (Chalmers, 1996; Crick, 1994; Dennett, 1991; Velmans, 2000b) the nature and mechanisms of subjective experience returned to the focus of mainstream psychology and neuroscience (Jack & Roepstorff, 2003). Elicitating reports about what people feel, think and see would seem unavoidable in a science of consciousness that includes the experience of consciousness. How else would non-synaesthetic neuropsychologists learn about the occurrence of colour-taste cross-modality and its correlates, or neuropsychiatrists about the nature of inner voices and when they are being experienced?

Assessment of the use and value of introspection in consciousness studies has occurred in the context of wider debates about the precise nature of consciousness. Consciousness has many definitions (Natsoulas, 1987). While it is assumed that all sentient human beings experience 'what it is like to be conscious', the very use of the term consciousness has been critiqued for being too broad, leading to muddled, incoherent usage (Young and Block, 1996). Nearly fifty years ago Miller (1962) warned that 'consciousness is a word worn smooth by a million tongues' (cited in Velmans, 2000:5), suggesting that even then, before the advent of the systematic study of consciousness, the term was used so promiscuously that it impeded scientific research.

In terms of introspective access, consciousness has been defined in terms of 'self-consciousness', a special kind of reflective awareness where the 'self' may be the object of consciousness (typically in retrospect as a constructed model). Young and Block (1996) describe this as 'monitoring and self consciousness', involving thoughts about one's own actions, their effect, the monitoring of perceptual information in coordination with plans, and a concept of the self which is used in thinking about the self. This 'awareness of self' is experienced immediately as an ongoing, subjective, holistic, seamless and integrated impression of being. Natsoulas describes this in terms of a 'personal unity' referring to the 'totality of the impressions, thoughts, and feelings, which make up a person's conscious being' (1987: 912), perhaps akin to James' (1890) metaphor of a stream of consciousness, an enduring, flowing, fluctuating continuum. Within this 'unitary' phenomenological self, which has been described as an emergent gestalt (Greenfield, 1995), there may be an awareness of particular dimensions of consciousness, or aspects of self, such as emotions, inner speech, ideas, sensations, perceptions (Pekala, 1991; Walsh, 1995), and the phenomenal 'qualia' of experience (Chalmers, 1996). Searle (1997) argues that conscious states have two fundamental properties, subjectivity and 'intrinsic intentionality' which refers to the representational nature of consciousness, its 'aboutness', or the awareness of mental contents. This complexity within unity, where a unified field of awareness co-exists with a continuously fluctuating multiplicity of mental contents is one of the paradoxes of human consciousness (Edelman and Tononi, 2001). Thus, introspective consciousness may be defined as the awareness of the contents of consciousness, which are amenable to self-reflection, and which arise within a field of existential-phenomenological awareness that is unitary, holistic, continuous and uniquely private. However, the existence of this introspective faculty is contentious: the notion of a 'split' between 'self' and the contents of experience is controversial, as is the issue of the unity or disunity of consciousness (Carruthers, 2009; Englebert and Carruthers, 2001; Dennett, 1991; Greenfield, 1995; Damasio, 1992; Parfit, 1989; Pekala, 1991; Pronin, 2009; Schwitzgebel, 2008; Velmans, 2000b; Young and Block, 1996).

Chalmers (1999) identifies a number of problems with introspective methods in consciousness research: it is not possible to gain 'pure' access to the first-person experiences of another; introspection changes the experience that is the focus of observation; access to the contents of consciousness is selective (it can't all be accessed or reported at once); reports may be susceptible to 'grand illusions' (introspective experience may not concur with objective reality); and experience is difficult to report linguistically. In the following paragraphs Chalmers' five problems, and attempts to overcome them, will be considered further.

A private view

The 'pure access' problem questions whether, because subjective experience is private and unique, it can be verified objectively. If its epistemic status obscures subjective experience from observation by independent observers, how can it be included within the remit of science, with its emphasis on third-person methods through the verification of 'public' events? This problem is exemplified through Nagel's (1974) question 'what is it like to be a bat?' — we only have direct access to our own phenomenal experience. Moreover, in Levine's terms, there is an 'explanatory gap' between subjective conscious awareness and its observable correlates, between 'mind' and 'brain' (Levine, 1983). Knowing exactly how the brain produces the visual representation of a green apple will not enable one to know what 'greenness' is like; for this, one simply has to *see* green (Chalmers, 1996).

One attempt to resolve this difficulty is to challenge the foundation of this problem, arguing that there is no difference between public and private events in terms of epistemic status. Advocates of this perspective may obviate the public/private dualism either by treating all data as subjective or first-person data (for example, Wallace, 2000), or by treating introspective data as objective or third person data (for example, Piccinini, 2007). The prior reduction puts 'trust' in subjective experience, pointing out that the observations of the individual 'third-person scientist' are also subjective, and as such, are prone to the same errors as introspection (Wallace, 2000). Alternatively, Piccinini (2007) argues that the introspective method requires first-person, private data to be observed from a third-person perspective by a 'scientist', and thus to be treated as 'facts' which are no longer private, but public and observable. In this way, he describes introspection as a data-yielding instrument, and the introspector as a 'self-measuring instrument', which is limited, as are all instruments. Dennett's heterophenomenology also treats the point of view of the subject as third-person data; verbal reports are treated as speech acts that reflect, not conscious experience, but the reporter's *beliefs* about their conscious experience (Dennett, 1991, 2003, 2007).

The problem of the 'mental eye'

Two problems arise with the notion of the 'mental eye': first, whether it is possible to observe one's own experience at all; and second, if it is, whether is it possible to do so without changing an experience in the process, thereby invalidating the method.

Rather than questioning the scientific status of introspection, the first problem questions whether introspection is conceptually possible: can the 'observer' observe the observer? If introspection is perceived as a form of 'inner observation', then who is doing the seeing? This potentially introduces dualism, where a special and separate observer or homunculus is watching the Cartesian Theatre (Dennett, 1991). Auguste Comte argued that introspection is *a priori* impossible because 'the thinker cannot divide himself in two, of whom one reasons whilst the other observes him reason' (cited in James, 1890: 188): one would always find oneself introspecting and not doing anything else.

There are two responses. Mill (1882) and James (1890) both argued that immediate retrospection eradicates this problem (Hatfield, 2005). The 'Mill-James view' suggests that the stream of consciousness can be 'frozen' in memory and then immediately reported upon. This retrospective solution potentially overcomes both problems, although it is recognised that describing and 'rebuilding' the sequential process of this now 'static' memory may lead to distortion (Lyons, 1986). Immediate retrospective reports may avoid problems associated with retrieval from semantic long-term memory, which is conceptual, abstract and belief based, but they remain subject to fallibilities associated with episodic memory, which is experiential, contextualised and quick to decay (Tulving, 1972). The pitfalls of short-term memory include limited capacity (Miller, 1956), limited duration (Atkinson and Shiffrin, 1971; Frederickson & Kahneman, 1993) and primacy and recency effects (Murdock, 1962). Advocates of the retrospective accounts of introspection admit that the method is fallible, but suggest that errors can be limited through appropriate practice, and, following Mill, training (Boring, 1953).

Alternatively, we can question Comte's notion that a split between consciousness and awareness is unfeasible by drawing on contemporary models of meta-awareness to argue that it is possible to observe one's own subjective experience (Adams, 2000; Lyons, 1986). The meta-awareness or 'metacognitive awareness' solution is supported by evidence suggesting that experience and reflective awareness are not necessarily unified, as well as work on differing levels of awareness (Lambie and Marcel, 2002; Overgaard, Koivisto, Sørensen, Vangkilde & Revonsuo, 2006; Teasdale *et al.*, 2002). For instance, Pinku and Tzelgov (2006) argue that there are different states of 'consciousness of self' and that certain states are characterized by an awareness or observation of ongoing experience, while others are not. The implication is that we can have experiences upon which we do not introspect and experiences which are inherently introspective.

Assuming that 'meta-awareness' is possible, this solution still needs to resolve the problem of distortion. James (1890) used the metaphor of shining a light in order to see what darkness looks like to describe the second danger of introspection: that experience might be altered through the very process of observing it. Schooler and Schreiber suggest that the danger for introspection as meta-awareness is that the latter is pervaded by representations and beliefs about the contents of consciousness (including 'self'). Any 'dissociation' between content and beliefs about content may lead to inaccurate introspective reports. They argue that this renders the efficacy of introspection an open and empirical issue, and that introspective practices that eliminate such need to be developed (Schooler and Schreiber, 2004).

A limited view

The third problem is that introspective access is selective. Introspective access depends on the information required: it has to be amenable to conscious processing (Wilson, 2003). If a signal is weak or subtle, introspective access may also be weak and unreliable (Schooler and Schreiber, 2004). Introspection is limited by what reflexive awareness has access to, the amount of detail that it is possible to observe (or recall) and report. Ericsson (2003) identified that accuracy of verbal reports diminished when participants were asked to give more information than could confidently be remembered or that could be retrieved from memory. Introspective techniques can not study: unconscious and subliminal processes (Dixon, 1971), limitless detail (as shown by research on eye witness reports, Loftus, 1996), or give reliable reasons for the microgenesis of experience (Nisbett and Wilson, 1977). Further, Haybron (2007) and Wilson (2002) document how common it is for people to demonstrate a lack of insight into their implicit motives or embodied states. For example, a person may become habituated to background mood/arousal, and may therefore not report, when asked, that they are unhappy or stressed. Indeed, Haybron (2007) argues that salience is required for valid introspective reports. Whilst we may have difficulties describing a diffuse background mood, we might not struggle to the same degree with an intense feeling of grief and sadness or an overwhelming feeling of joy.

A number of studies support the accuracy of introspective reports, which have converged with behavioural and neurological indices, for example: of attention wandering, affective responses to stimuli (Quattrone, 1985; Wilson and Schooler, 1991), social distress and pain (Baars, 2009; Zimbardo, Cohen, Weisenberg, Dworkin, and Firestone, 1969), and the time and effort spent on a task (Corallo, Sackur, Dehaene and Sigman, 2008; Martia, Sackurd, Sigmane and Dehaenea, 2010). Schooler and Schreiber (2004) review the literature on introspection and emotion, visual imagery and mind-wandering, and argue that in certain contexts introspection is accurate. For example, reports of when participants are daydreaming have been found to relate to indices of validity, such as being more frequent during boring tasks, fluctuating as a function of stress and with decrements in performance, as well as corresponding with changes in physiological measures. They concur with the position that reports about the content of experience may be possible, while reports about the whys of experience are not (Ericsson, 2003). For instance, Wilson and Schooler (1991) found that reported liking of jam (introspective report) was related to jam quality (objective measurement), but reasons for liking or not liking the jams were not related to jam quality.

Introspection may give access to the *products* of unconscious processes only (Hatfield, 2005), and then under optimal conditions for recall (such as the report of salient stimuli, and without delay). This suggests the value of introspection is limited to the contents of conscious awareness (to the 'conscious self' rather than the 'adaptive unconscious' Wilson, 2002). Dual-process models of cognition have been applied to this problem, where it is argued that we only have introspective access to the products of slow, controlled cognition, held in working memory (such as perceptions, emotions, the focus of attention), but not to fast, implicit, preconscious processes (Evans, 2009; White, 1988). The solution to this is relatively simple: that introspective methodologies should only focus on the window of experience, not asking for the impossible. Introspection may only be useful to study the contents of immediate awareness, the Jamesian stream of consciousness (Hurlburt, 1990, 1993).

A deluded view

Proponents of the 'deluded view' argue that introspection does not give accurate reports of inner experience; that we may be unaware of this inaccuracy, and are thus deluded; and that it is not possible to tell the difference between reports that are 'veridical' and reports that are confabulatory. Conscious experience and/or verbal reports may be susceptible to illusions (Gregory and Gombrich, 1973), delusions and hallucinations (Bentall, 1990), misinterpretation (Harvey, Richards, Dziadosz and Swindell, 1993), belief-based reconstruction (Barret, Robin, Pietromonaco & Eyssell, 1998), confabulation (Gazzaniga, 1992) or ignorance/lack of awareness (Haybron, 2007). Considering such examples of glaring error, it is no wonder that Schwitzgebel (2008) questions the 'infallibilism of conscious experience', noting reports of phantom limbs, alien hand syndrome and the confabulations of split-brain patients.

This fallibility argument is far removed from everyday assumptions where human communication is underpinned by trusting (or testing, if suspicious of fallaciousness) others' reports of subjective experience (Piccinini, 2003). For this reason, one might argue that such examples are rare or pathological. However, confabulation may operate amongst the non-clinical population and may do so pervasively. For example, Wegner (2002) found that people would confabulate reasons for performing an action that was the outcome of hypnotic suggestion — suggesting that we do not always give accurate reports of why we are doing what we are doing — constructing an 'illusion of control'.

Johansson, Hall, Sikström, Tärning and Lind (2006) developed a procedure called 'choice blindness' to extend Nisbett and Wilson's work on the reliability of introspection. They sought to compare 'veridical' with confabulatory introspective reports. On repeated occasions they asked participants to explain why they had chosen one of two female faces as being the most attractive. In fact, in half of these cases participants were shown the face that they did not prefer in reference to this question, an occurrence that was only commented upon by approximately 25% of participants. Thus, in 75% of cases, participants constructed an explanation for a preference that they had not made. Johansson et al. report that there was no statistical difference between the features of these confabulatory reports and the supposed veridical reports (eliminating responses where participants noticed that their choice had not been maintained). They extrapolate from this that introspective reports are commonly confabulatory, and further, that confabulatory reports and veridical reports are indistinguishable. Thus, introspection is seen as an unreliable tool: not only are reports often invented on the spot, rather than being based on actual experience, but it is not possible to identify and eliminate erroneous reports. Likewise, in her work on 'the introspection illusion' Pronin (2009) argues that our reliance on introspection is misplaced. Introspection, she argues, contributes to a number of illusions about one's self and environment based on blindness to unconscious bias and implicit social influences. For example, research on the 'planning fallacy' suggests that we are unable effectively to predict our future behaviour based on current introspective access (being misled by current feelings, such as optimism). Based on her studies, Pronin concludes that introspection does not provide an accurate or unbiased representation of the 'workings of the mind' (Pronin, 2009: 55). Reliance on it in everyday life, she suggests, is unwarranted and based on a culturally endorsed 'introspection myth'.

The deluded view perspective, then, rests on the idea that introspective reports might be inaccurate. But that misses a crucial point: the very nature of some experiences is that they occur despite apparent contradictions with external reality, such as amputee's experience of moving an arm which has been amputated. Hence, one retort to the deluded view argument is to state that reports of experience are of value in their own right, revealing the gap between subjective experience and objective reality, and therefore, that introspection can assist in understanding the nature of such experiences. Thus, we may question the assumption that providing an objective and unbiased report is a necessary criterion for the value of introspective reports.

The problem of the translator

Inner experience need not be communicated verbally. For example, one's experience of which way round one perceives a Necker cube may be indicated by pressing an appropriate button (Piccinini, 2007). However, in the vast majority of cases, introspective data come in the form of people's verbal descriptions of their inner experience. In introspective methodologies any phenomenologically irreducible conscious experience (such as the holistic, unique, subjective experiencing self), encapsulating the 'what it is like to be' criterion of consciousness, and the qualia of inner experience, have to be communicated in a verbal report.

Psychologists have identified a number of factors that might interfere with the production of introspective reports, even if there is accessibility, and no delusion. First, experience may be ineffable: it may be impossible to capture or convey the sensual richness or essence of experience in words (James, 1902). Second, the process of word-finding means that 'additional processing is required to find understandable referents', thus altering concurrent experience (Ericsson and Simon, 1980: 219). Third, language is a 'system of successive happenings' in contrast to a moment's experience where many things occur simultaneously (Washburn, 1922: 98). As such, selectivity is likely, as language cannot capture the richness of what is occurring moment-by-moment. Fourth, attention might be given to aspects of experience that are easier to communicate than others. Fifth, an additional problem, as we have already seen, is that saying too much can lead to extrapolation based on belief rather than experience (Ericsson, 2003), leading us to 'create' rather than report experiences. Sixth, talk might limit introspective access. Schooler and Engstler-Schooler (1990) empirically tested the impact of verbalisation on introspection. They found that when individuals are asked to describe complex non-verbal images (such as a face), recognition of the face was subsequently impaired. They suggest that 'verbal overshadowing' of conscious experience can disrupt introspective access to non-verbal aspects of experience, and further, that words fail to do them justice. Finally, verbal accounts arise in a social context and are likely to be created with an orientation to the particular demands of this context. This final problem, however, has not been sufficiently explored within the psychological literature; as we shall see in subsequent chapters, sociological studies of talk and verbal interaction have revealed a hitherto unexamined degree of orderliness in the way that descriptions are produced as social activities designed for interactional and interpersonal contingencies.

One potential solution to the problem of the translator has been to help reporters produce categories, and to use metaphors, to facilitate description (for example, Hurlburt and Heavey, 2006a; Varela, 1996). Through training and practice, a 'special vocabulary' may be developed to describe the richness of experience and its nuances. As such, language might fruitfully act as 'pointers', discriminating between and amplifying elements of experience (Petitmengin and Bitbol, 2009). This is analogous with the vocabulary developed to describe fine aromatic distinctions amongst wine tasters. However, such a prepared vocabulary might distort reports, leading to categorization based on expectation, due to the awareness of these pre-existing possibilities increasing conceptual overlay. Indeed, this was one explanation for the failure of agreement between experimental introspectionists in the last century. An alternative suggestion has been to limit verbal reports to experiences that are easily vocalised (Schooler and Engstler-Schooler, 1990), such as the working through of arithmetical problems (Ericsson, 2003). Another approach has been to treat untrained verbal reports as interpreted events that arise in the context of the experiment and to make no assumptions about their transparency (Dennett, 2003). Finally, methods of conversation analysis may be used to examine reports as social acts, through which participants' understandings are exhibited and negotiated in talk, without making assumptions about inner experience (Barnes and Moss, 2007).

The current status of 'looking inward'

Our review of the history of introspection and debates about its value as a method for the study of inner experience has identified a number of key themes. First, it is clear that the potential and limits of introspection have been primarily addressed as a topic in psychological literature. The key issues have been: how can this method help understand inner experience and consciousness? Of what benefit is it to *psychological* science? There is a paradox here, of course, because introspection is absolutely central to research in *social* sciences. For example much qualitative sociological research is based on the analysis of verbal accounts generated in one-to-one or group interviews. Insofar as those interviews invite respondents to reflect on their experiences, consider their feelings and emotions, report their opinions and how they arrived at them, explain their reasoning and interpretations of the world, attribute causal relationships between events, and so on, they are vehicles for the production of introspective accounts. There is a similar reliance on introspective reporting in market research and studies of consumer choice and preference, for example, through the use of narrative storytelling to explore how people think about a brand, and in 'action research', which involves reflection on one's own experiences of consumerism (Gummesson, 2005; Wallendorf and Brucks, 1993). Unlike in the social sciences generally, in market and consumer research, there is more explicit recognition that investigation of consumer behaviour relies upon introspection by research participants (for example, Gould, 1995; Woodside, 2004). However, in the social sciences, there has been relatively little controversy about the role of introspection when compared to the sometimes-polemic positions adopted in academic psychology. Social scientists have, by and large, just got on with generating and analysing data that is essentially introspective, much like their colleagues in psychotherapy, psychoanalysis, counselling, humanistic and transpersonal psychology, and medicine.

A second theme of the psychological literature on introspection is, paradoxically, a recurrent and noticeable absence: there is hardly any systematic discussion of the fact that introspection is ubiquitous in social life. But it is an obvious condition of human existence; it happens all the time, and it is a fundamental part of mundane social activity. We talk to each other and report a range of ostensibly private or inner experiences to which our interlocutors have no access, except through our descriptions of them. That is introspection in its most common form. But introspection is not just found in everyday social interaction. Talk in institutional or work related settings also requires people to engage in introspection: how otherwise could an architect understand the wishes of a client, or a teacher grasp a pupil's confusion, or a doctor a patient's pain? It might be argued that the sensible starting point for any academic reflection on introspection would have been its use in social life, given that it is the home environment for introspective activity, and in which it is ubiquitous. Of course, psychologists would argue that such naturalistic investigations could offer no purchase on the important issue of the accuracy and reliability of introspection. But introspection is not just a research technique: its home environment is not the psychology laboratory, but the discourse of everyday interaction; and in this context, accuracy and reliability may be of less concern than the social and communicative functions it performs in the fabric of social interaction. Perhaps psychology's concern with scientific criteria (and scientific credentials) has led it to miss the deeper importance of introspective discourse: its role in social life.

A third conclusion from our historical survey is that debates and considerations of the limits of introspection have been repeated from the experimental introspectionists onwards, and yet understanding has progressed relatively little (Frith and Lau, 2006). There are, for example, no commonly agreed upon solutions to disagreement about the efficacy of reporting sensations and phenomena versus making reports made on inference, or how to overcome the limitations of memory, or how to address the distorting nature of language. There is no current consensus on how introspective reports should be made and analysed. There is also a lack of agreement about the extent to which introspective reports should be relied upon, how they can best be integrated with objective data such as third-person reports (Overgaard, 2006), and even about exactly what introspection as a process consists of (Petitmengin and Bitbol, 2009). It seems that, in Lakatos' terms, there has been no systematic problem shift in the last one hundred years (Lakatos, 1978).

This is a pressing concern because, in addition to greater use of introspection in the study of consciousness, there are contemporary calls for a return to introspection in neuroscience and medical research. For example, neuroscientists Corallo, Sackur, Dehaene and Sigman (2008) recommend the use of 'quantified introspection', where they correlate introspective reports with chronometric, objective variables (reaction time) in a way that is reminiscent of Wundt's experimental introspection. Delamillieure et al. (2010) have developed an 'introspective questionnaire' to better assess the resting or baseline state in magnetic resonance imaging (fMRI) research. And it is recognised that in medical practice there are no recommended objective criteria for the discernment of pain, necessitating reliance on forms of introspection (Nahmias, 2002; Price and Aydede, 2005). Support for the greater use of introspection also comes from evidence that refutes the behaviourist argument that inner states have no causal role or function. For example, introspective awareness has been used to train epileptic patients to predict and control their seizures (Petitmengin, Navarro and Queyen, 2007), and has been used therapeutically to increase awareness of symptoms that precede intense emotions, enabling intervention in their subsequent development (Philippot and Segal, 2009). And attempts to train people with obsessive compulsive disorders (OCDs) in techniques of mindfulness, so as better to equip them to anticipate and deal with specific compulsive reflexes, have not only been successful, but seem to result in neural restructuring in the orbital frontal cortex, that part of the brain associated with OCDs (Schwartz and Begley, 2002).

Within the methodological literature on the value and use of introspection, there has been considerable discussion of a range of basic problems and difficulties: people forget; they confabulate, and make and errors based on reconstruction; there is reporting based on beliefs about experience rather than experience itself; descriptions of inner experience may be based on inference rather than observation; participants may censor sensitive details; they may tailor their accounts to seek social desirability; there may be basic deception; and there are experimenter effects (Chalmers, 1999; 2004; see also Cardeña, 2004; Conner *et al.*, 2007; French, 2003; Pekala and Cardeña, 2000). However, comparatively little attention has been paid to the demand characteristics of the experimental setting (Orne, 1962). Demand characteristics are 'the totality of cues and mutual expectations which inhere in a social context (e.g., a psychological experiment or therapy situation), which serve to influence the behavior and/or self reported experience of the research receiver or patient' (Orne and Whitehouse, 2000: 469). It is perhaps no surprise that demand characteristics have not been explored in greater detail in the introspection literature (and in experimental psychology more generally): they are an ever-present threat to the ecological validity of an experimental setting. This is because, unlike experimenter effects, which can be controlled for, for example through the use of double blind experimental procedures, demand characteristics are omnipresent. They arise from fundamental human processes of inference and reasoning. Orne explored demand characteristics primarily in terms of expectations associated with the roles of experimenter and subject or participant. There are, however, other features of the setting of experimental research that may inform a participant's tacit interpretation and understanding of activities in an experimental trial, such as wider culturally based knowledge about the processes the experiment has been designed to investigate, and normative conventions that underpin discourse and communication. It is not just that demand characteristics need to be more fully addressed when we evaluate the production and analysis of introspective data; it may also be necessary to extend the concept to include a range of interpersonal and social influences that hitherto have not been considered.

Finally, across a range of disciplines in the social sciences in the last quarter of a century, there has been a turn to language as the topic of analysis. A core feature of research in this tradition is that discourse is seen as a form of social action, and not merely as a means of exchanging information between individual brains. Consequently in philosophy (Austin, 1962; Wittgenstein, 1953), sociology (Garfinkel, 1967; Sacks, 1992), social psychology (Potter and Wetherell, 1987; Edwards, 1997), linguistics (Levinson, 1983) and anthropology (Moerman, 1988), research has focused on the way that people use language to perform interpersonal activities, and the communicative competences that underpin discursive action. It is clear, though, that the action orientation of language use has not been addressed in the psychological literature on introspection. Researchers have relied on what might be termed a more common-sense approach to the relationship between language and the world, treating it as a channel through which salient aspects of experiences and events can be recovered, as long as intervening and confounding variables and problems such as memory distortion, confabulation and self censoring can be tackled. This observation is not, however, intended as a criticism of psychologists conducting introspection research. The interest in language use as social action has emerged relatively recently, and has primarily been stimulated by intellectual developments in social sciences, particularly sociology, and so it is no surprise that researchers have not considered introspective accounts as distinctly social activities. However, what we now understand about language, and the way it is inextricably tied to social actions, does have important implications for the way we think of introspection and the data about inner experience it yields. This is because introspection is primarily a discursive process: with the exception of studies in which participants register their inner experience by some mechanical means such as button pressing, introspective research relies on practices of description, and the use of language in interviews. We return to this issue in the next chapter, in which we review contemporary methods for the collection and analysis of introspective data.

Chapter Two

Contemporary methods for the collection of introspective data

In this chapter we examine a range of key contemporary approaches towards the use of introspection in studies of mind and consciousness: think-aloud protocols (Ericsson and Simon, 1993), phenomenological approaches (Giorgi and Giorgi, 2003; Smith, Flowers and Larkin, 2009); neurophenomenology (Varela, 1996), and experience sampling (Hurlburt and Heavey, 2006a; Hektner, Schmidt and Csikszentmihalyi, 2006). Our overview identifies links and departures between different approaches, thereby providing a map of the contemporary terrain of introspective research. However, unlike other reviews (for example, Overgaard, Gallagher and Ramsøy, 2008, and Cardeña, 1994), we also examine these approaches from the perspective of developments in the study of discourse, description and communication in sociology. We argue that contemporary approaches to the study of introspective data overly emphasize cognitive and psychological factors, and systematically ignore the situated, practical, communicative skills involved in producing reports of inner experience.

Think-aloud protocol, or protocol analysis

As the name suggests, in the think-aloud protocol participants are asked to vocalise their thinking whilst completing a specific task, and is associated with the work of Ericsson and Simon (1980, 1993). Beginning with the basic postulate that 'verbal reports are data', they sought to develop a theory of the 'introspecting measuring instrument', by which they meant verbal reports, and how they are made. They attempted to evaluate the cognitive processes involved in verbalising, and outlined implications for the elicitation of reliable and valid data. So they were focused on issues such as 'in what memories the response information has been stored, what demands the response makes on short-term memory, whether responses can go on in parallel with other behaviors, and so on' (1980: 216). This think-aloud procedure is based on the assumption that what people say during the protocol is an expression of inner speech, rather than a reported analysis of inner experience. In this, the method is informed by the argument of the behaviourist J. B. Watson, that thinking was accompanied by subvocalization, to which thinking aloud might give direct access (Ericsson, 2003, 1993).

In think-aloud experiments, tasks are chosen which involve cognitive processes that are amenable to verbalisation (Schooler and Schreiber, 2004), allowing the 'verbalization of heeded information already generated by the task directed processes' (Ericsson and Simon, 1980: 218). For example, during a mathematical problem-solving task, one participant, asked to think aloud whilst mentally multiplying 36 x 24, reported:

> OK, 36 times 24, um, 4 times 6 is 24, 4, carry the 2, 4 times 3 is 12, 14, 144, 0, times 6 is 12, 2, carry the 1, 2 times 3 is 6, 7, 720, 144 plus 720, so it would be 4, 6, 864. (Ericsson, 2003: 10)

Or, during an experiment of reading comprehension in which participants were required to read a vignette and then articulate their understanding of it, one participant reported:

> Even after the boom days were over, farmers and ranchers still found a profitable Canadian market.
>
> > 'Just saying how even after the gold was gone people could still make a living on the land.'
>
> In 1866, the United States customs office at Little Dalles reported $507,479 worth of goods exported over the line.
>
> > 'Back in those days that would have been an awful lot of money, worth a couple million today, so that was an awful lot of money.'
>
> Of this sum nearly $350,000 was in livestock, beef cattle, sheep, and pack animals.
>
> > 'Just saying how more than half was in animals so the farmers were doing good.'
>
> (Crain-Thoreson, Lippman and McClendon-Magnuson, 1997: 584)

Ericsson and Simon argue that the think-aloud protocol offers the closest possible match between inner experience and verbal report by limiting introspection to the immediate contents of awareness, thus eliminating problems associated with memory and translation, based on the assumption that existing inner speech is simply being verbalised. In their model 'inconsistent' or invalid introspective reports are likely to be made when retrospective probes are too general, leading to answers being based on averaged or typical scenarios drawn from long-term memory; or, when participants are asked to infer missing information, which, again, may be filled in from long-term memory. Similarly, participants are not asked to explain how they are solving a problem, nor do they attend to the process of reporting and observing, but are only required to solve a problem and report as they are doing it. Thought sequences are not 'introspectively ana-lysed', for example, into visual or auditory mental elements but merely expressed (Ericsson, 2002). Accordingly, the think-aloud protocol is con-current, thereby designed to avoid problems associated with memory retrieval, and undirected, with no probes for missing or general information.

It is claimed that the think-aloud protocol allows the researcher to over-come problems associated with other forms of introspective data. For example, Ericsson (2003) argues that, as each verbal report is associated with a task that has a correct answer, the consistency between the report and the outcome can be checked. Thus, there is no need to rely on blind 'trust' in the accuracy of these reports. Indeed, the protocol has been described as 'a highly constrained measurement situation where trust is not an issue' (Ericsson, 2003: 3) because when verbal reports are collected concurrently with other records of behaviour, it becomes possible to check the consistency of the reports with this behaviour. The think-aloud proto-col has been used to study individual differences in learning, such as reading comprehension (Crain-Thoreson, Lippman, and McClendon-Magnuson, 1997), spatial awareness, such as the effects of test anxiety on spatial tasks (Kelly, 1996), and in applied settings, such as human-computer interaction to understand users' current work practices, and to identify problems with usability (Haak, Jong & Schellens, 2002).

However, within psychology, the think-aloud protocol has been criti-cised for being too constrained in scope (Jack and Shallice, 2001). It is lim-ited to verbal reports of tasks, the performance of which is not disrupted by the cognitive processes involved in vocalisation of associated inner speech. It is not suitable for the study of spontaneous experiences or open reports on experience, and therefore it is lacking ecological validity. Eco-logical validity is also an issue when we consider some of the kinds of tasks participants have been required to report upon. For example, in an age when calculators are available on a range of new media technologies, such as computers and mobile phones, it is not clear what is to be gained from asking people to report on mental arithmetic tasks. There have also been critiques of the use of vignettes in psychological research; for exam-ple in their assessment of attribution research from the perspective of discourse analysis, Potter and Edwards argued that researchers do not recognise or take account of the moral and evaluative work that is unavoidably embedded in stories or narratives designed to elicit attributional reasoning (Potter and Edwards, 1990).

Further, the method has been criticised for an over-reliance on verbalisation (Schooler and Schreiber, 2004). It only reveals information about verbalizable thought sequences, rendering affect and imagery obscure. Schooler and Schreiber argue that there are inherent difficulties in describing non-verbal experiences and that protocol analysis forces individuals to attempt to do so, possibly leading to distortions or omissions.

Some researchers have developed more sociological themes in their critical appraisal of think-aloud protocols. For example, Cotton and Gresty (2005) argued that the method does not take account of potentially biasing effects of instructions or the influence of observers. Their research suggested that without explicit instructions on what to attend to, participants were unsure of which thoughts to attempt to vocalise. (Indeed, even Ericsson and Simon, 1993, found evidence that performances differed according to how participants were told to verbalise.) Further, being video-recorded or observed by an experimenter may increase reactivity. Finally, they report that, in retrospective interviews, some participants claimed not to have interacted as they normally would on the required tasks because of the self-consciousness this engendered. It is clear that the think aloud protocol significantly underplays the role of context in the elicitation of verbal reports and the potential role of demand characteristics.

These criticisms reflect the kinds of concerns that resonate in methodological discussions in the psychological literature, and raise doubts about the claims to objectivity that have been made on behalf of data derived from the think-aloud protocol. There is, though, a more serious problem, which draws from a more social scientific perspective: in the think-aloud protocol there is the assumption that any kind of language use can be a mere expression of mental states or inner experience; and there is now a substantial set of empirical and philosophical arguments that challenge this assumption (for example, Austin, 1962; Coulter, 1979, 1989; Edwards, 1997; Harré, 1995; Heritage, 1978; Sacks, 1992; Wittgenstein, 1953). The communicative competences that inform description of inner experience, and the participants' understanding of the requirements of the setting in which introspective reports are being produced, will significantly shape the way that any actual description is produced. The extent to which descriptions can be treated as providing access to experience which is independent of its expression must be framed by recognition that descriptive activity is always situated.

Phenomenological approaches

The term phenomenology derives from the Greek word *phainomenon*, meaning that which appears or is seen. Phenomenology is not a unified theoretical or methodological approach, but rather, a collection of theories and practices. However, the broad aim of phenomenology as a psychological method is to explore subjective experiences of events as 'lived', as they appear in conscious experience, without reducing them to theoretical components or seeking to manipulate or control their expression in an artificial context. The emphasis is upon being faithful to experiential evidence, referred to as attending to 'the things themselves' (Merleau-Ponty, 1945). It is concerned with 'presences not realities' (Giorgi and Giorgi, 2003), for example, what an illusion or hallucination is like to the percipient, its structure and content.

Emerging within continental European philosophy in the late 19th century, phenomenology took two routes: transcendental phenomenology, which explored consciousness in an attempt to uncover human biases that obviate the apprehension of reality; and existential phenomenology, which focused phenomenological attention on existence itself (Spinelli, 2005). Initially, this existentialism influenced humanistic and transpersonal psychology (for example, Rogers, 1951; Tart, 1975) and schools of psychotherapy (for example, Binswanger, 1958) rather than mainstream psychology. However, in recent years phenomenology has been increasingly used in health and clinical psychology, for example, to explore the experience of addiction (Shinebourne and Smith, 2009) and the impact of Huntington's disease on families (Brewer *et al.*, 2008).

As a philosophical endeavour, phenomenology emerged contemporaneously with introspection. Both Wundt and Brentano (a key influence on the phenomenological movement) published key texts in 1874 (Boring, 1929). Brentano argued that consciousness always has intentional relation towards objects in the world; that one is always conscious of something, and that consciousness has 'aboutness'. This has been described as the central assumption of phenomenology (Spinelli, 2005). He supported the development of a scientific psychology as a 'descriptive psychology': one that describes this 'aboutness', and the content of consciousness, which was deemed to be self-evidential. Brentano did not advocate a psychology that began with causal explanations, as description of a phenomenon precedes theories of causality.

Edmund Husserl founded phenomenology, drawing upon Brentano's work, under whom he had studied. Both Brentano and Husserl advocated the description of 'mental phenomena' as they appear to the experient (Sajama and Kamppinen, 1987). For Husserl, conscious experience is fundamental, primary, irreducible, and the foundation of all knowledge. However, due in part to the intentional nature of consciousness, where stimuli are translated into known objects and referents, appearances are shrouded with layers of interpretation (Spinelli, 2005). Thus, around 1905, Husserl proceeded to develop methods of 'phenomenological reduction', with the goal of gaining unbiased, clear access to experiential reality. 'Reduction' derives from the Latin *reducere*, meaning 'to lead back', the return being, ultimately, to the transcendental, the essence of subjectivity or 'pure consciousness', stripping away all interpretative bias, although Husserl held that this 'complete reduction' was not possible in practice (Moran, 2000).

As a practice, Husserl's phenomenological reduction consists of a number of steps that aim to facilitate a reflective awareness that brings us closer to 'lived experience'. First, an attempt is made to recognise and suspend assumptions, biases, preconceptions, presuppositions, interpretations and pre-givens (whether based on theory or common sense), and to direct attention to 'the things themselves' (a process referred to as bracketing or *epoché*). By so doing, it is thought that one is able to connect with the 'givenness' of subjective experience, beyond beliefs about what an experience should be like. In effect, this involves a shift in attention. One where, while it is not possible to eliminate assumptions and preconceptions, they are acknowledged and 'looked past', refraining from being 'drawn in' to them. The aim is to attend to 'essential' contents of consciousness as they appear. Such presuppositionlessness is thought to enable 'a new aspect or insight into the phenomenon to unfold', through intimacy with the 'lifeworld' or pre-theoretical experience (Varela, 1996: 339).

> Husserl characterised the practice of *epoché* in many different ways: 'abstention'... 'dislocation' from, or 'unplugging' or 'exclusion' ... of the positing of the world and our normal unquestioning faith in the reality of what we experience. He speaks of 'withholding', 'disregarding', 'abandoning', 'parenthesising'... 'putting out of action' and 'putting out of play' (Moran, 2000: 147).

As such, Husserl thought that experience is 'given', while interpretations of it are fallible (Moran, 2000). Fallibility arises from either misinterpretation, poor reflective awareness, or, as we shall see below, inadequate description.

Next, begins a process of careful identification and description of phenomena. This stage is crucial because the description that is chosen 'incarnates and shapes what we experience' (Varela, 1996: 337). The process of careful identification of the contents of consciousness and translation into communicable form enables the discernment of 'essential' experiential contents, or 'invariants'. Husserl's goal was 'eidetic description' — to uncover the non-varying essence of experience (Stevens, 1999). Invariants are those elements which distinguish or define the phenomena, and occur in different incidences of the same type of experience, such as the essence of 'redness' common to both a strawberry and a post box. Reflection at this stage was guided by further principles, such as imaginative variation and horizontalisation. Imaginative variation is a technique to clarify the core essence of a phenomenon, for example, by subtracting features and varying frames of reference. Horizontalisation refers to the equality of all descriptions and the avoidance of ordering these in terms of any perceived relative importance, significance or ontology (Spinelli, 2005). However, this very process of identification and translation potentially introduces bias, selectivity and distortion. For instance, Husserl noted that a potential pitfall was automatically to label a phenomenon in accordance with already known phenomena, rather than being open to the experience and its unique intricacies.

Subsequent phenomenologists have taken both an existential turn and a hermeneutical turn. Husserl's approach was seen as too abstract, not recognising experience as contextualised and complex, embedded in a world of objects, relationships, language, social, emotional and situational events. Further, Husserl did not emphasise the temporality and 'specificity' of the lifeworld, which is experienced from a particular viewpoint — 'my point of view' — at a particular point in time. Consequently, both Heidegger and Merleau-Ponty advocated a movement from the transcendental to the concrete and worldly, from essence to existence, from being, to being-in-the-world and embodiment. The hermeneutic turn developed out of Heidegger's reflections on the word *logos* in the etymology of phenomenology, which means discourse, account, reason or judgement. He asserted that description without interpretation was not possible: we interpret everything in terms of our language and experience. As such, access to 'being' is always through discourse. It is a form of sense making, driven by human concerns (Moran, 2000).

The later phenomenological interest in the way that language interprets experience recognises the complexity of the relationship between language and the objects or processes it describes. However, there is still insufficient attention given to the ways in which reports of inner experience are mediated by the interactional context in which they may be solicited. This is especially clear in contemporary phenomenological methods, which have moved away from examination of philosophical and epistemological concerns, and which instead focus on the exploration of other people's consciousness and their concrete lived experiences (Smith *et al.*, 2009).

Phenomenologically informed research proceeds through analyses of collections of experiential reports, usually gained through semi-structured interviews; and it may be the researchers themselves who employ the attitudinal stances advocated by phenomenological reduction, rather than those reporting on experience. Thus, the focus is not upon consciousness as directly experienced, but upon meaning-making, how people interpret, recall and make sense of and integrate experiences. In practice, therefore, phenomenological methods reveal insight to reconstructed beliefs about experiences rather than immediate conscious experience. A diverse array of phenomenological methods are used in psychological research today, including hermeneutic phenomenology (van Manen, 1990), existential phenomenology (Eckartsberg, 1998), interpretative phenomenological analysis, or IPA (Smith and Osborn, 2003), 'scientific phenomenology' (Giorgi and Giorgi, 2003) and critical phenomenology (Velmans, 2007). An important distinction according to which these methods vary is the relative emphasis they place on the description and interpretation of experience (Langdridge, 2007). In this section scientific phenomenology and IPA will be focused upon due to their rising popularity, and the way that they illustrate the differing emphases on interpretation and the researcher's role in the construction or co-construction of reports.

Giorgi and Giorgi (2003) advocate a scientific phenomenological method to gain perspectives on 'how persons actually lived through and interpreted situations' in which the goal of analysis is 'to capture as closely as possible the way in which the phenomenon is experienced within the context in which the experience takes place' (2003: 28). They describe the analytical process as intersubjective, a dialogue between the reported subjective experiences and the researcher's own subjective interpretations (the stages of which are laid bare for examination by peers). This is gained through the analysis of documents, either written testimonies or, more usually, the transcripts of semi-structured interviews. Giorgi and Giorgi describe four steps by which their scientific phenomenological method is claimed to uncover and elucidate psychological meanings inherent in these reports. Firstly, researchers adopt the attitude of *epoché*, and then read the transcripts, thereby gaining a holistic overview. Secondly, they note 'transitions of meaning' and 'meaning units', in each document, which mark ways in which participants interpret an experience. The third step is to transform these meaning units into statements that mediate between the raw data and psychological theory and explore how the meaning units relate to each other. For example, transformations might make meanings explicit, might articulate the meaning in more detail, making it salient. The fourth step is to examine variation to see what different reports have in common, and through this comparative process, to identify the invariant or essential components and describe a structure, if possible, that determines the relationship between these invariants. This approach emphasises description and aims, drawing on Husserl, to uncover invariant themes in the experiences of participants.

Interpretative phenomenological analysis (Smith and Osborn, 2003; Smith, 2008) stresses the active and dynamic nature of the interpretative process; thus accepting that even meanings, let alone experiences, are not transparently available, but are 'worked up' by the researcher, through an 'interpretative relationship with the script'. IPA uses semi-structured interviews, and through analysis seeks to elucidate beliefs and constructs. In the analysis, IPA advocates switching between empathic understanding (of meaning-making) and critical analysis (of interpretations drawn). The analysis is essentially a thematic analysis, where the researcher reads through documents, marking interesting points, and clustering these together to form recurrent themes. Connections are then made between themes, and themes are linked to theory (as well as being linked back to data in the transcripts). Convergences and divergences across reports are noted, drawing upon idiography to emphasise unique elements of experiences, again taking Heidegger's point that experiences are from a particular person's perspective, rather than focusing on invariants alone. These themes are then converted into a 'narrative account' for a research paper. As such, the emphasis is upon examining how people make sense of their experiences.

Both methods, through different procedures, aim to produce a structure of psychologically insightful and theoretically relevant key meanings or themes that represent the complexity of the experience that is the focus of the research. However, phenomenologically inspired approaches have been criticised. For example, Piccinini (2007) argues that, because biases are always inherent in observation, the experiencing 'instrument' (the person making reports) needs to be 'calibrated', or trained in methods such as phenomenological reduction in order to reduce such distortion; and neither the approach of IPA nor scientific phenomenological method seeks to establish such 'calibrations' in their 'instruments'. In addition, phenomenological approaches are said to be overly individualistic; they do not consider the unconscious processes that produce 'meaning' (Moran, 2000); and they rely on retrospective reports, often of events and experiences that may have occurred years or months before the interview, and which may thus be prone to belief based reconstruction. Further, they do not acknowledge the processes by which resultant themes are socially constructed and are influenced by the situation and personalities of the individuals involved in the research process (Stevens, 1999). Indeed,

Stevens questions the notion that 'themes', 'invariants' or 'essences' of experience exist at all, suggesting that they are not there to be uncovered and that the outcomes are rather generalised abstractions, created through the analytical process, which rests 'on general and unsystematic reflection on the part of the theorist or at most the use of verbal self-report from others' (Stevens, 1999: 107). As such, it is suggested that commonalities of experiences are not discovered, as phenomenological approaches assume, but are constructed or invented.

These are familiar criticisms, and have been levelled at many kinds of introspective data collection processes. But there are other issues that need to be addressed, the most pressing of which is that phenomenological methods give scant attention to the active role of talk in interviews, for instance, how the interactional and communicative practices through which the interview is conducted may constrain, shape or facilitate what the participant says, and how they may say it. It is not uncommon, then, to find phenomenologically informed analysis of interview data in which interviewee's accounts of their experiences are extracted from the context of their production and examined without reference to the interviewer's turns which solicited them, and to which they are a response (Wooffitt and Widdicombe, 2006). This is not just a rehearsal of the argument that the design or delivery of a question can lead or influence a respondent, resulting in biased or distorted responses. It is based on the recognition that talk in research interviews is a site of, and vehicle for, social action, and not merely a passive medium by which experiences can be expressed and thereby collected by the researcher. The communicative competences through which participants in an interview collaboratively coordinate their discursive activities may also generate tacit understandings and interpretive frameworks which can significantly inform respondents' contributions (Drew and Heritage, 1992; Heritage, 1997).

Neurophenomenology

Varela's (1996) neurophenomenology draws directly on Husserlian phenomenology, as well as on Buddhist philosophy (Thompson, 2007). The working hypothesis of neurophenomenology is that 'phenomenological accounts of the structure of experience and their counterparts in cognitive science relate to each other through reciprocal constraints' (Varela, 1996: 343). Introspective methods are rigorously employed and subjective experience is given equal status with physiological measurements. Thompson *et al.* (2005) emphasise the heuristic strategy of neurophenomenology, enabling the collection of rich introspective data through disciplined phenomenological reduction, which may in turn uncover new objective data about the physiological underpinnings of conscious experience. Thus, they stress the potential exploratory nature and originality of the method.

In neurophenomenology the participants take part in the process of phenomenological reduction: they are 'active agents' in the constitution of meaning (Varela, 1999). In methodological terms, neurophenomenology consists of four aspects of phenomenological reduction: attitude, intuition, invariants and training; followed by testing of the correlations and feedback between invariants and physiological correlates. The phenomenological attitude follows the principles of phenomenological reduction advocated by Husserl. With its suspension of habitual beliefs and assumptions (bracketing), it is thought to enable observations of 'the arising of thoughts themselves' (Varela, 1996: 337). As such, neurophenomenology seeks to develop a disciplined exploration of 'the structure of nowness', developing awareness through observation of the distinction between language-based categorisation and phenomenal experience (Ginsburg, 2005). This process is described as leading to 'intimacy' with experience, making it vividly immediate, with an awareness of variation (Varela, 1996). Such familiarity leads to insights about the experiential components of the phenomenal area of investigation (Rudrauf, Lutz, Cosmelli, Lachaux and Quyen, 2003). As described in the previous section on phenomenology, through a process of careful demarcation and description of these insights, phenomenological invariants are exposed. As Varela does not envisage consciousness as uniquely private, but rather as 'inextricably linked to those of others and the phenomenal world (1996: 340), these invariants are concretised through intersubjective validation. Through a process of 'communal validation' phenomenological reports can be verified in the same way as reports of objective phenomena, developing consensual, accurate and refined descriptive categories (Thompson *et al.*, 2005). Skill is required to 'stabilize and deepen one's capacity for attentive bracketing and intuition, as well as the skill for illuminating descriptions (Varela, 1996: 338). Thus, neurophenomenology advocates training in order to 'increase sensitivity to lived experience'(Lutz and Thompson, 2003: 32). Training involves both attentional and self-regulation strategies and the ability to give clear verbal reports. Such training, Lutz and Thompson (2003) argue, not only generates more refined reports but renders the introspective process less intrusive, so that it does not modify the experience being observed.

The remaining methodological stage involves taking and comparing verbal reports with physiological measurements — the quest of neuro-

phenomenology being to forge links between 'two irreducible phenomenal domains' (Varela, 1996: 340). However, this is not simply a quest for
mental correlates:

> What is different in the research strategy proposed by neuro-
> phenomenology is that these bridges are not of the 'looks like' kind but
> they are built by mutual constraint and validated from both phenome-
> nal domains where the phenomenal terms stand as explicit terms
> directly linked to experience by a rigorous examination (e.g., reduc-
> tion, invariance and intersubjective communication). (Varela, 1996:
> 345).

That is, knowledge gained from meanings and observed physiological
correlates reciprocally moderate each other. The neuroscientist is guided
by the first-person data in their interpretation of physiological data and
this data may feedback to the phenomenological accounts, leading to
refinements, for example, in descriptive categories, or facilitating
increased awareness of experience. Through such a dynamic intertwining
of lived experience and its physiological underpinnings, it is hoped that
neurophenomenology can help to resolve the 'hard' problem of consciousness: how subjective experience is mechanistically linked with neurology
(Rudrauf et al., 2003).

Neurophenomenology aims to keep neurocognitive science
contextualised in actual experience that is recognisable, and not based on
abstractions or hypothetical accounts of inner experience. In practice,
Varela (1996) suggests that neurophenomenology enables experiential
counterparts to be accurately identified. For example, he discusses the
neurophenomenology of time consciousness. He argues that we automatically assume that time is experienced in a linear fashion, 'like an arrow',
based on analogies in Western culture and the assumptions of classical
physics. However, phenomenological reduction shows that time is actually experienced with a 'complex texture', consisting of a centre with a
horizon that is already past and an intended future projected to the next
moment — which he describes with William James's metaphor of the
'specious present' (Varela, 1999). More recently neurophenomenology has
been applied to the study of self-consciousness (Lutz, 2007), mental imagery (Thompson, 2007) and anticipation of epileptic seizures (Petitmengin,
Navarro and Quyen, 2007).

Of course, neurophenomenology falls prey to the same criticisms as
Husserlian phenomenology, which were discussed in the previous section. For instance, the method assumes that there are invariants of consciousness, the nature of which can be communicated, and which are
independent from this process of communication. As such, the method
does not take account of the active role of talk and the social context in the
shaping of reports.

. The method can also be criticised for its reliance on training, and training that is led and cued by researchers. This may lead to the transformation of the experience being inwardly observed and reported upon; a related problem is that introspective training may lead to theory-led reporting (Chalmers, 1999, 2004).

For example, in one of the earliest studies, Lutz, Lachaux, Martinerie and Varela (2002) used neurophenomenology to study visual illusions. In the first stage, participants practised an illusory depth-perception task. This constituted the training, where each participant identified and distinguished aspects of their phenomenal experience (improving their 'perceptual discrimination') and honed their vocabulary to identify these categories. Following is an extract describing the training process, in which it becomes clear that this occurred with probes from an interviewer to help participants attend to 'things in themselves':

> To train the subjects, open questions were asked to try to redirect their attention toward their own immediate mental processes before the recordings were taken. For example: Experimenter, 'What did you feel before and after the image appeared?' Subject S1, 'I had a growing sense of expectation but not for a specific object; however, when the figure appeared, I had a feeling of confirmation, no surprise at all;' or subject S4, 'It was as if the image appeared in the periphery of my attention, but then my attention was suddenly swallowed up by the shape.' Subjects were reexposed to the stimuli until they found their own stable experiential categories to describe the main elements of the cognitive context in which they perceived the 3D shapes. (Lutz, Lachaux, Martinerie and Varela, 2002, p. 1587).

Subsequently, participants made verbal reports on their experience using these pre-defined categories whilst recordings were made of brain activity (with an electroencephalogram). The importance of this approach was seen to be that the EEG recordings differed according to the experiential nature of the trials (in this case, a key phenomenological category was types of 'readiness'), suggesting that internal states affect the outcome of such studies, accounting for some variation in response across participants. The correspondence between experiential categories, both across individuals, and with EEG profiles, further reinforced the reliability of the introspective reports made.

As we observed in the last chapter, introspection is a form of descriptive activity that takes place in everyday life: in numerous circumstances we report phenomena that are entirely private and subjective. The formalisation of introspective practice in psychological research on consciousness, then, is a transformation of a set of competences and skills that have their home environment in everyday discourse and social interaction. This has an important implication for our appreciation of the degree to which researchers in the neurophenomenological tradition require research participants to undertake training to provide introspective reports. The idea is, of course, that training leads to refinement of skills, thereby ensuring more accurate or comprehensive reports of the fundamental of consciousness. There are two issues. First, given that the home environment for introspective description is everyday life, there remains the argument that analytic attention should be on the way that people use language to report on inner experience in naturalistic settings, as part of their everyday activities. Second, and more important: if we accept that language use is fitted to the setting in which it is produced, and reflects the participants' interpretation of relevant interactional contingencies, such that the design of descriptions are shaped by tacit reasoning about the requirements of the context in which a report is produced, there is the argument it is misplaced to try to train people to produce refined or expert reports. If all descriptions are to some degree interactionally generated and shaped, then introspective reports produced after or through training are not necessarily guaranteed to deliver better or more accurate access to independent inner experience: what they will deliver is merely another *kind* of descriptive account, one that is fashioned in relation to the participants' orientation to the contextual requirements of 'being trained', or producing reports that are 'precise', 'complete', and so on. Put bluntly, it may be, then, that training does not deliver better accounts, but merely facilitates another kind of descriptive activity, which should not enjoy a privileged status in relation to everyday or naturalistic introspection.

Experience Sampling

Descriptive experience sampling, or DES (Hurlburt and Heavey, 2004, 2006) and experience sampling methodology, or ESM (Hektner, Schmidt and Csikszentmihalyi, 2006) both seek to capture regularities in and dynamic fluctuations of the phenomenological content of everyday life, through reports that are assumed to reveal 'online conscious experience'. Both methods involve repeatedly 'beeping' participants at randomly selected times and asking them to report on their conscious experience immediately before they heard the beep. Both methods propound the value of collecting situated, contextual, and thus (it is claimed) ecologically valid, experiential reports. As such, experience is reported in response to triggers *in vivo*, in interaction with meaningful life events rather than in constructed laboratory scenarios or in response to hypothetical questions. Proponents of both methods argue that, by immediately

recounting experiences, reports will be less tinged by retrospective falla-
cies and biases, such as theory-led recall, misinformation effects or 'imagination inflation', which are considered to be problematical in diary reports
and phenomenological interviews (for example Bolger, Davis and Rafaeli,
2003; French, 2003). Both extol an 'idiothetic' approach (Lamiell, 1981)
nesting the idiographic within the nomothetic — attempting to understand
the meaning of contingent, subjective phenomena embedded within laws
that explain objective phenomena. And both methods are described as a
form of phenomenology: ESM is characterised as 'systematic phenomenology' through the repeated process of 'foregrounding' the stream of consciousness (Hektner *et al.*, 2006: 4), while proponents of DES use the
metaphor of 'freezing' a moment of the stream of consciousness (Hurlburt
and Heavey, 2006). The two approaches differ primarily in that ESM asks
participants to fill in a brief experience sampling questionnaire (ESQ) after
each beep and analyses data quantitatively, while DES is qualitative, asking participants to provide open reports on the contents of consciousness,
which are discussed in a subsequent interview. DES strategically
addresses and attempts to overcome the limitations of introspective methods that were outlined in the previous chapter (Hurlburt and Heavey,
2006), while ESM sidesteps these issues, aligning itself with multi-level
modelling and quasi-experimental research rather than with introspection
(Hektner *et al.*, 2002, 2006). For this reason we will focus on DES in this
review of experience sampling.

Descriptive experience sampling was developed by psychologist Russel
T. Hurlburt, and although he has worked with numerous colleagues, it is
fair to say that he has been the principal proponent and practitioner of this
method. His work, and the DES approach, have been widely recognised
within the field of consciousness studies as a serious and sustained
attempt to study inner experience. The methods of DES and Hurlburt's
own analyses of his data have been widely debated: he co-wrote a book
with a philosopher who is sceptical about many aspects of DES (Hurlburt
and Schwitzgebel, 2007); and this collaboration inspired a recent special
issue of the *Journal of Consciousness Studies*, in which psychologists and
philosophers evaluated various aspects of DES and Hurlburt's work, and
on which he and Schwitzgebel subsequently reflected in a series of single
authored or collaboratively produced rejoinders (Weisberg, 2011). DES
has been applied in the study of the inner experience of psychology under-
graduates (Heavey and Hurlburt, 2008), individuals with schizophrenia
(Hurlburt, 1990) and individuals with 'disturbed affect' (Hurlburt, 1993).
Hurlburt has focused on three research issues. First, he has tried to discover what it is like to be a specific kind of person. Second, he has explored
how the typical features of inner experience of one group of people compare to those of other groups, for example, people with schizophrenia and

'normals' (Hurlburt, 1990). Finally, he has tried to identify the contents of conscious experience, seeking to demarcate generic properties of inner speech, visual images, pristine experience, and so on (Heavey and Hurlburt, 2008; Hurlburt, 2009; Hurlburt, Heavey and Bensaheb, 2009).

In the DES procedure, participants, or co-researchers, wear a beeper in an earpiece for a minimum of three to four continuous hours each day, choosing a period during which they expect that their activities will vary. They are instructed to respond to randomly triggered beeps and record their inner experience at that very moment, where inner experience refers to anything that is going on in awareness. Recordings are made in a note-pad or recorded vocally on a separate voice-recorder. In this way, partici-pants are asked to 'freeze' the stream of inner experience occurring just prior to interruption by the signal—a brief moment only, described as analogous to a light being switched on and off—and asked to record the contents of their consciousness at that time, not their reaction to the signal or extraneous observations about their current environment. At the end of each DES day, participants discuss these reports in an interview, where the inner experience associated with each beep is examined and clarified. Thus, practice with this signal-reporting-interview procedure constitutes a training process through which the participants' introspective observa-tional skills are refined.

In the subsequent interviews, descriptions of inner experience arise through a process of phenomenological co-enquiry, where experimenter and participant work together until they feel that they have adequately and clearly described the content of a representative sample of experi-ences. The content of these open-ended descriptions may be coded accord-ing to the prevalence of emerging categories of experience across all samples, for example, inner speech, inner hearing and feeling (Hurlburt and Heavey, 2006b; Heavey and Hurlburt, 2008). Analysis is not driven by particular theories of consciousness or the nature of experience, thus allowing for the possibility of unexpected or counterintuitive findings. For instance, Hurlburt (1990) reports that schizophrenic participants reported very clear emotional experiences that were associated with particular bodily locations; mental images that were often 'damaged' in some way (for example, being partially obliterated by black splotches or being tilted); and inner speech or words that had visual or spatial presences (for exam-ple, words experienced as flying past or through their head).

As with neurophenomenology, training is a key component in the DES method. Through practice (and detailed and repeated discussions with the researcher), it is argued that participants' ability to differentiate between aspects of their inner experience can be improved, minimising the inter-pretation of experience, and allowing them to communicate their inner experience accurately. Such training in the making of introspective reports finds parallels with neurophenomenology (Lutz and Thompson, 2003). However, unlike neurophenomenology, Hurlburt (2009) emphasises the open nature of the focus of attention in DES, rather than focusing on the development of specific categories in the training process. It is argued that this unconstrained focus minimises conceptual overlay and distortion which may arise when monitoring awareness for a specific purpose. Nevertheless, the impact of reactivity in DES, where the intrusive nature of the procedure upon one's everyday subjective experience and inherent alterations in one's attention and behaviour change the very focus of enquiry is an unavoidable problem, remains unclear. And the argument that training simply yields a different kind of introspective activity, rather than qualitatively superior reports, is also relevant.

In descriptive experience sampling participants are not asked to make causal attributions, but to describe the content of 'inner experience'; neither are participants required to provide interpretations of their experience. According to Hurlburt and Heavey (2001), this means that DES overcomes some of the key difficulties associated with introspective data. They also argue that by minimising introspection to specific epochs of conscious experience, which is reported immediately, that both the filtering of reports through self-theories and the selective aggregation of memories into a constructed narrative are minimised (Hurlburt and Heavey, 2006). Further, through the techniques of 'bracketing' assumptions and awareness training they assert that reports of the contents of consciousness will contain less interpretation and fewer confabulations—less extrapolation of hows or whys, but more accurate reports of what—the contents themselves. Hurlburt optimistically suggests that by following the procedures of DES online inner experience can be reliably mirrored (in Hurlburt and Schwitzgebel, 2007). Experience sampling addresses additional problems with the generation of first-person reports posed by Chalmers (1999). By asking participants to retrospect on experience that has just occurred, the problem of the 'inner eye' is avoided, as participants do not deliberately introspect on the now, thereby altering ongoing experience. By introspecting on a snapshot of experience only, problems with selectivity are minimised. Through both repeated sampling of many moments of consciousness to gain a representative collection of experiences, and by focusing on contents only, without interpretations or extrapolation, 'grand illusions' should not present a problem. Perhaps the most significant methodological contribution, though, is that DES seeks to capture naturally occurring inner experience: the participants go about their everyday business, and so, when they are randomly beeped, they introspect on real life inner experience. In this, Hurlburt's approach makes a serious attempt to generate ecologically valid data, although, as we argue later, there are

problems with the assumption that a report of inner experience can be considered naturalistic if it is solicited in everyday life.

Introspection and the dependence on language, descriptions and communication

The four broad approaches reviewed in this chapter all rely upon the provision of verbal reports, where participants attempt to communicate their
inner experience (or, in the case of think aloud protocols, inner vocaliza-
tion) to a co-present researcher, or for the subsequent attention of a
researcher, or for the purposes of discussion with the researcher in a subsequent interview. These approaches to introspective data collection,
however, may be compared in relation to the following range of issues: the
broad aims and assumptions (whether the intention is to uncover experiential invariants or patterns in lived experience); the time delay between
an experience and the participant's report of it; the degree of training
required; the frequency of reports; the setting in which the report is produced; the ways in which the data collection procedures constrain the
degree and nature of the participant's verbal contribution; and the degree
to which the reports of inner experiences are regarded as trustworthy or
transparent expressions of inner experience. These comparative dimensions reflect a concern to identify the best way to ensure that people's
introspective reports capture or reflect their conscious experience; or may
be elicited so as to minimise the extent to which intervening variables may
degrade recall, or lead to confounding interpretation. As such these are
eminently reasonable concerns relevant to the broader psychological project: ensuring the accuracy and validity of data, the efficiency and reliability of data collection procedures and so on. There are, however, a range of
other factors relevant to our understanding of introspective data and its
production that are rarely considered in methodological discussion within
psychology. We raise some key points here, and thereby begin to sketch
the character of the empirical perspective we develop in subsequent chapters, and the methodological foundations on which it rests.

Description: from representation to action

The contemporary approaches to introspective data outlined above share
the assumption that, in principle, and if due regard is given to the various
ways in which introspective reports might be obscured or distorted, participants can use language to reveal the phenomena of inner experience.

This assumption is enshrined in other forms of psychological research on, broadly, the causal influence of mental states, or the basic properties of cognitive entities. For example, in research on autobiographical memory, the content of reports of past experience are taken as more or less accurate indicators of what information is actually stored in the head (for example, Brown and Kulik, 1977; Gold, 1992). And in research informed by the theory of social representations, it is assumed that talk can be examined to investigate the expression of underlying cognitive representations (for example Jodelet, 1991). Thus, traditional cognitivist psychology regards language as a potential window on, or expression of, the workings of cognitive procedures.

(Of course, this view of language as a representational medium is not restricted to psychological sciences, but is prevalent in social sciences also. Social scientists collect people's accounts and narratives in semi-standard and informal interviews, and from focus group discussions. Although social science methodology texts recognise the various difficulties in using qualitative data from interviews, it is fair to say that, on the whole, sociologists treat participants' descriptions as 'good enough' representations of either an external social reality, or an inner mental realm of attitudes and opinions.)

As we noted at in the last chapter, however, across a number of social science disciplines, there is widespread and growing recognition that language use is a form of *social action*, and not just a medium of information exchange. It is not merely the site of interpersonal conduct, but the vehicle in which social interactions are initiated, and through which their consequences and trajectories are mediated and developed. In this perspective, the act of describing is not regarded as a passive mechanism for conveying information about inner realities or social experience. Instead, description is regarded as being action oriented, in that it is both embedded in and a contribution to the interplay of on-going social actions constituted in talk and interaction. Description, then, is a dynamic process. We should therefore be cautious about assuming that descriptions of inner experience can, in principle, provide access to the properties of consciousness, or allow such properties to be inferred, as the content and structure of a report of an account may be shaped by the participant's tacit understanding of the discursive activity that description has been designed to perform. Introspective descriptions of inner experience are actions, designed for the 'here-and-now' of their production. The dynamic and action oriented features of descriptions of inner experience have not been sufficiently considered, even with respect to data from retrospective interviews, in which the accounts of inner experience are solicited in and mediated through interaction between researcher and participant.

Social interaction, normative structures and description

Perspectives which focus on the dynamic, action oriented properties of language use do not merely examine what, for example, a turn in interaction is doing. The empirical focus is broader, in that there is also a concern to identify the framework of normative understandings that inform the ways in which people use discourse to perform social actions. That is, there is an interest in the broadly evaluative and inferential dimensions of language use: the ways that the structures of communicative activity shape the participants' expectations or understandings about their ongoing interaction with others. The ways in which the people produce descriptions of experiences, even in formal and constrained settings, will reveal their sensitivity to expectations about appropriate courses of discursive action, or may exhibit an awareness that some activity is inappropriate, or accountable, or absent.

In some sense, a concern with the normative and inferential aspects of language use is echoed in the way that the concept of demand characteristics draws attention to how participants may behave according to what they infer is really going on in experimental settings, even if that interpretation runs counter to the official statements about the purpose of the experiment, or indeed, what the experiment is in reality designed to investigate. However, the kinds of interpretations identified by the concept of demand characteristics are restricted to gross or obvious specifics of the setting. So it is proposed that participants may fully embrace the role of subject in an experiment in anticipation of the real purpose of the tasks they are performing, thereby behaving systematically in a way that is actually unconnected to the processes the experiment is designed to explore. But people's interpretative and inferential skills are not focused solely on easily observable aspects of a setting, and expectations which may be attendant on role identities of 'research participant' and 'experimenter', but inform the very communicative competences which underpin any kind of social interaction, be that in a formal laboratory setting, where roles such as experimenter and participant are clearly defined, and transparently related to the task that the participants are to perform, or in more mundane conversational settings where it is not so easy to identify any overarching and fixed purpose or goal to any spate of interaction.

People are sense making and interpretive creatures, tacitly aware of the web of normative conventions, expectations and obligations that shape and inform how language is used. This means that, if we are to fully understand introspective descriptions of inner experience, it is necessary to explore the underlying normative and inferential communicative competences that shape them.

Communication in work related or institutional settings

Introspection researchers are fully aware of the importance of the relationship between an introspective report and the setting in which it is elicited. It is recognised that the generation of verbal reports is nested within social contexts, in which, for example there may be co-present researchers, or that retrospective reports may be discussed in semi-formal research interviews. However, the focus has been on the way in which the various settings in which introspective accounts are elicited might hinder the researcher's access to the 'raw data' of inner experience. So, for example — and setting aside for the moment the questionable assumption that raw or pristine experience is in principle expressed through peoples' reports — it is recognised that participants in a laboratory setting may be influenced by the environment: they may be anxious or apprehensive, and report 'artificial' or contingent inner experiences simply because they are in the unfamiliar setting of a psychology laboratory. Researchers have tried to address these concerns in various ways. In experience sampling methods, for example, participants carry a beeper about with them in their everyday lives, and record accounts in their own naturalistic environment, without the physical presence of a researcher. It is argued that this produces ecologically valid data, in that it allows the capture of naturalistic 'lived experience'.

Methodological reflections on the impact of the setting have been framed in terms of primarily psychological variables, such as experimenter effect on performance, where participants' accounts may vary according to the skill, behaviour or attitudes of researchers, the elicitation of socially desirable responses, participants' 'reactivity', such as feeling self-conscious when an interview is audio-recorded, and the impact of theoretically loaded instructions as to how to attend to experience. What is absent from all these discussions, though, is recognition that the collection of any kind of introspective data is mediated by ordinary communicative skills put to work to address a particular of work or institutionally related tasks. The psychology laboratory is a social setting in which experimenter and participant interact through their talk to address a range of tasks connected to the formal work of psychological research; as such, the laboratory may be regarded a site in which researcher and participant communicate collaboratively to accomplish *institutional* or *work related* activities.

Within the sociological tradition that treats talk as social action, there has been considerable research on communication in institutional settings, such as doctors' consultation rooms, police interrogations, political rallies, aeroplane cockpits, calls to emergency services, surgical theatres, therapy and counselling sessions, or broadcast news interviews. This research has revealed how everyday discourse practices are modified or amended to address specific activities relevant to that setting (for example, Boden and Zimmerman, 1991; Drew and Heritage, 1992). Thus, procedures for turn taking in unconstrained conversational interaction might be adapted to reflect particular work related identities of the participants; turn design may reflect an institutional orientation, for example, through particular syntactic constructions or lexical choices; or distinct sequences of discursive action might be associated with specific work related requirements, and so on. Moreover, the particular characteristic of interaction in an institutional setting will embody the participants' understanding of those normative inferential or evaluative frameworks that underpin their contributions to that setting. These contingent and localised normative frameworks will thereby shape the participants' verbal conduct in institutional settings (Heritage, 1997).

It is important to explore the discourse of the psychology laboratory as a form of institutional interaction. This is because participants will be relying on ordinary communicative practices to accomplish specific tasks; and institutionally relevant normative frameworks will inform their verbal contributions. With respect to studies of introspective description, then, what participants say may not merely reflect their inner awareness, but will be shaped by their tacit understanding of work related tasks and requirements, and what counts as appropriate forms of participation in that setting. It is therefore, necessary to examine the ways in which language is put to work to produce introspective accounts in the formal setting of a psychology laboratory.

But what of those methods that merely require people to record their inner experiences in everyday life, such as descriptive experience sampling? Do these methods produce data that are independent of work or institutional contexts? A first point is that even in this method, people's 'on the spot' accounts are then subject to intensive reflection and elaboration in interviews with researchers, such that what is taken to be the final record of the experience is clearly the outcome of a sustained period of social interaction within a clear institutional context. A second point is that even asking people to produce introspective reports in their everyday lives will not generate data which are exempt from the constraints of institutional requirements. People's orientations to the institutional character of their activities is not determined by reference to recognisably institutional settings, such as a university laboratory or a researcher's office. There is nothing natural about wearing, for a substantial portion of the day, an ear piece which will randomly make a noise, thereby requiring the wearer to describe at that moment their awareness just prior the signal. This is quite simply a work related task: eliciting descriptions of inner experience in this way clearly resonates with the requirement of formal scientific research. The way that any account of a moment of consciousness is constructed is just as likely to reflect the research participant's tacit understanding of particular work related requirements as any contribution elicited the more recognisable, formal constraints of, say, a university setting.

When people take part in research on consciousness, and produce introspective descriptions of their inner experience, they are performing social actions, designed with respect to the institutional or work related setting in which they are produced, and informed by normative frameworks that shape interpretations of their conduct and the conduct of the researcher, and which furnish a set of inferential and evaluative resources by which they can make sense of their ongoing involvement in the research procedure. As such, introspective descriptions of inner experience are socially organised, interactionally oriented communicative events.

Chapter Three

Analysing the language of introspective reports

Methodological considerations

The key argument of this book is that it is important to recognise that introspective reports are communicative events that display an order and organisation that embody the interpersonal and interactional orientation of language in use. Consequently, we argue that it is necessary to employ empirical methods that are sensitive to the complexity of everyday communication, and which can also illuminate the ways in which routine discourse competences may be oriented to the requirements of formal or institutional contexts, such as laboratory based experiments on consciousness and introspection. Our empirical analyses are informed by conversation analysis, a qualitative method for the study of naturally occurring interaction that emerged initially in sociology, but which has been adopted by scholars across a range of social science and cognate disciplines. Our data are introspective descriptions of inner experience that come from ganzfeld parapsychology experiments. Parapsychology is widely perceived to be a controversial discipline, and there may be reservations about the value of arguments about discourse and introspection based on examination of data from a laboratory-based experiment to test for parapsychological phenomena. However, our interest in these data is not motivated by the extent to which they cast light on ostensible parapsychological phenomena. The procedure of the ganzfeld extra sensory perception experiment often requires the research participant to spend a period of time describing out loud the phenomena of their own consciousness and inner experience. This experimental procedure for studying ostensibly parapsychological abilities, then, just so happens to generate verbal reports on consciousness that are suitable data for the study of the communicative practices of introspection. We begin with a brief account of parapsychology, and the specific experimental procedure from which our data were collected.

Introspection in ganzfeld parapsychology experiments

Parapsychology is the study of experiences that suggest some form of extrasensorimotor communication between humans and their environment, such as telepathy, extra sensory perception and precognition. Although stimulated by anecdotal reports of premonitions, ghosts and apparitions, clairvoyance and contact with spirits, it has adopted a distinctly scientific approach, reflecting the way that the parent discipline of psychology modelled itself on the methods of the natural sciences. Thus the vast majority of parapsychological studies have been conducted in laboratories, involving many experimental trials with ordinary subjects, the results of which are analysed using rigorous statistical techniques. The objective of these experiments has been, first, to find evidence for *psi*, the mental facility that is taken to underpin various forms of ostensible parapsychological phenomena, such as mind-to-mind communication or the ability of the mind to influence the external physical environment. The second objective has been to examine the physical and psychological factors that influenced the operation of psi. (Introductions to parapsychology can be found in Broughton, 1991; Edge, Morris, Palmer and Rush, 1986; Irwin, 1997; Radin, 1997).

The psychological community has been largely sceptical about the existence of paranormal phenomena; indeed, there is evidence that psychologists are the most sceptical members of the scientific community (McClenon, 1982). Amongst psychologists it is largely assumed that parapsychological abilities do not exist; consequently, much psychological research on paranormal experiences has focused on the cognitive or perceptual errors or distortions which lead people to believe they have experienced some kind of extraordinary phenomena (Forer, 1949; Hyman, 1977; Jones and Russel, 1980; Singer and Benassi, 1981; Zusne and Jones, 1982). And because of its controversial nature, parapsychological work, and parapsychologists themselves, have been the subject of intense — sometimes overtly hostile — critical scrutiny by sceptics and debunkers (for example, Alcock, 1981; 1987; Hanlon, 1974; Kurtz, 1985; Randi, 1988; see also the journal *The Skeptical Enquirer*). The sceptics' position is that parapsychology is a pseudo-science; and a key part of their argument is that it has failed to produce cumulative and replicable evidence of the existence of anomalous communication (Alcock, 1981; 1987; Hyman, 1995).

Sceptics often portray parapsychology as a controversial discipline, but it is not clear how controversial it actually is. Should parapsychological abilities exist, their confirmation will be a significant scientific discovery with implications for our understanding of the physical world. But our understanding of the physical world is routinely challenged by scientific advancement, and it is not clear why parapsychological phenomena would be more difficult to assimilate into scientific canon than many other theoretical or empirical claims. In a review of the history of scepticism to parapsychological research, Charles Honorton, an innovative experimental parapsychologist, stated that 'I believe in science, and I am confident that a science that can boldly contemplate the origin of the universe, the nature of physical reality 10^{-33} seconds after the Big Bang, anthropic principles, quantum nonlocality, and parallel universes, can come to terms with the implications of parapsychological findings — whatever they may turn out to be' (Honorton, 1993: 211). Moreover, the kinds of experiences that parapsychologists study seem to be a fundamental aspect of human experience. William James wrote of extraordinary experiences: 'The phenomena are there, lying broadcast over the surface of history .... Look behind the pages of official history, in personal memoirs, legal documents, and popular narratives and books of anecdotes, and you will find that there never was a time when these things were not reported as abundantly as now.' (James 1979: 223 [1897]). Anecdotal evidence is supported by survey data that suggest up to a third of sampled populations report having some kind of paranormal experience (Castro, Burrows and Wooffitt, in preparation; Haraldsson, 1985; Haraldsson and Hootkooper, 1991). Some have gone as far as to argue that the paranormal is normal (Greeley, 1975, 1991). And there is little that is controversial in what parapsychologists actually do. From the perspective of the sociology of scientific knowledge, parapsychologists conduct their work like other scientists (Collins and Pinch, 1979). There is a willingness to explore the possibility of parapsychological abilities via experimental research, but no overriding commitment to advocacy other than that supported by evidence. Moreover, parapsychologists have attempted to conduct experimental research to high scientific standards, often refining procedures in response to criticisms of experimental methods (Honorton, 1993) and sometimes even in consultation with trenchant sceptics (Hyman and Honorton, 1986). And, finally, parapsychologists have produced statistically significant experimental results that suggest the operation of extrasensorimotor communication — some of sufficiently strong to merit publication in prestigious, mainstream, peer reviewed academic journals (Bem 2011; Bem and Honorton, 1994). After reviewing the statistical evidence from a range of parapsychological experiments from the United States and Europe conducted over a period of approximately 25 years, the statistician Jessica Utts wrote:

> This is a robust effect that, were it not in such an unusual domain, would no longer be questioned by science as a real phenomenon. It is unlikely that methodological problems could account for the remarkable consistency of the results …. It is clear to this author that anomalous cognition is possible and has been demonstrated…. The phenomenon has been replicated in a number of forms across laboratories and cultures. (Utts, 1995: 310–311)

Some of the evidence Utts considered came from ganzfeld ESP studies (Honorton *et al.*, 1990). The ganzfeld is an experimental procedure in which research participants are in a relaxed state, in an environment that minimises variations in sensory input. The rationale for this is that previous experimental research and anecdotal evidence suggest that psi, if it exists, is a weak signal that can be best detected during reduced brain activity and arousal. There are numerous variations in the ganzfeld procedure, but, typically, a sender (usually an experimenter or a friend of the participant) tries mentally to send or project images of a target: usually a video clip from a large database chosen randomly by specifically modified software. This clip will be shown several times during the 'sending' part of the experiment. After the sending period the participant is shown four video clips: the target and three others. On the basis of the images and sensations experienced during the sending phase, she or he has to nominate which clip they think the sender was trying to project. Therefore, there is a 25%, or one-in-four probability of a correct identification of the target clip by chance alone.

Introspection in the Edinburgh ganzfeld studies

The data for this study are transcripts and audio recordings of ganzfeld ESP experiments conducted during the mid 1990s at the Koestler Parapsychology Unit in the Department of Psychology at the University of Edinburgh (Honorton *et al.*, 1990; Morris *et al.*, 1995).

In preparation for the experiment, research participants were seated in a room alone, and they listened through headphones to a relaxation tape. When this was completed, white noise was played through the headphones. Masking over the eyelids ensured a homogenous light distribution on the retina. This was designed to ensure that the participant was in a highly relaxed state. There were three participants (but see below): the experimenter, the research participant, who was target of the mentally transmitted images (a volunteer member of the public), and the sender (either another experimenter or friend/relative of the participant).

(But note: The Edinburgh ganzfeld experiment was designed in part to investigate the extent to which ostensible psi communication could occur in the absence of a sender. The reasoning was that, if an above chance number of hits declined when the sender was absent, there was evidence for the operation of some distinctly *telepathic* communicative process. If the number of above chance hits seemed remained constant regardless of whether there was a sender or not, then some form of more general *extra sensory* or *clairvoyant* ability was being employed. Consequently, there were experimental trials in which, unknown to the participant, a sender was absent: during the period of the mentation when the research participant was describing their imagery, the target video clip was playing on the computer screen to an empty room. The authors do not know which, if any, of the recordings that form the data corpus for this research come from trials designed with the no sender conditions. As we are focussing on the language of introspective reports, rather than their parapsychological significance, we do not consider this relevant to our analyses.)

The experimenter, participant and sender (if there was one) were located in separate rooms designed to prevent sensory leakage. At an appointed time, a video monitor in the room in which the sender was located began to play a short video clip, chosen randomly by computer from a large data base of clips of a similar length. The experimenter was unaware of the target clip for any specific trial. The sender was required to concentrate on any aspect of the images on the clip, or the narrative or story if one was discernible, and mentally to project to the participant the images or impressions of the clip. This was called the sending period.

During the sending period, the participant was required to describe out loud the images, thoughts and experiences that impinged upon their consciousness. This introspective report is known as the *mentation narrative* and it is extremely valuable to the parapsychologist. This is because the participant's descriptions of their experience of their own consciousness may reveal clues about the ways in which anomalous cognitive processes (if they exist) interact with known cognitive mechanisms. Because of the importance of the mentation narrative, during the pre-experiment briefing, the participants were explicitly encouraged to report out loud every and any image that comes to mind during the sending period (Morris, personal communication). The experimenters could hear the mentation narrative via an intercom system, but they did not interact with the other participants unless explicitly required to intervene to assist the participant or safeguard the procedure. As they overheard the mentation narrative being produced, the experimenters made hand written notes. If there was ambiguity as to what the participant had said, the experimenter did not interrupt the mentation to clarify his or her understanding, but made a best guess in their notes as to what was said. The experimenter's notes became the basis for a subsequent review (to allow clarification or correction of the record) prior to the judging phase, in which the participant viewed the target video and the three decoys.

After the sending period, the experimenter made contact with the participant via the intercom system and the *mentation review* commenced. In the review the experimenter read through his or her notes of the images and sensations reported by the participant during the sending period. The mentation review is also an important part of the ganzfeld procedure. In the subsequent judging phase, the participant is expected to draw on their experiences during the sending period to identify which of a series of video clips the sender was trying telepathically to project. The review provides an opportunity for the participant to survey their impressions, which also serves to refresh their memory about images that seemed vivid, unusual, dramatic, and so on. Moreover, it is assumed that the mentation imagery may provide clues as to how psi processes interact with more routine psychological processes. The review allows experimenters to ensure that their record of the participant's imagery is accurate and complete.

During the judging phase, the participant is shown four video clips: the target and three others. On the basis of the images and sensations experienced during the sending phase, the participant had to nominate which clip they though the sender was trying to project, or to rank each clip in terms of the likelihood that it was the target clip and therefore the object of the sender's mental projections.

In total, there were 97 discrete trials (no participant undertook more than one trial), from which a subset of recordings of 24 experiments were made available to the authors. Each individual experimental trial was tape recorded in full, thereby generating two kinds of data relevant to an examination of communication and introspection: mentation narratives, and mentation reviews.

Mentation narratives

The sending period lasted approximately thirty minutes, during which the participants were required to describe out loud any imagery, thoughts or sensations that came to conscious awareness, in as much detail as they could, using whatever language that seemed appropriate.

There is substantial variation in the way participants produced their mentation narratives. Some participants reported very little imagery, and remained silent for lengthy periods of time, and then offered only one word or short descriptions of their imagery. This kind of mentation is illustrated in extract 3.1 in which brief reports are punctuated by periods of silence (all periods of silence over a second are recorded in brackets), and which comes from the start of the mentation.

(3.1) (01-05: E3/F) ('P' is the research participant. All extract headings contain the following information: the code of the trial provided by the KPU experimenters; E + number indicates which of the three experimenters conducted this trial; and the following letter designates the gender of the participant. Prior to discussion of transcription, standard orthographic transcription is used.)

1 P: um (2.4) something about butterflies (3.8) and there's somebody swimming
2   (27) um (2.6) an engine (25.5) way in the horizon far away (1.3) just a dot
3   (19.4) a doorway made of stone (15.4) things seem to be- um passing (2.4)
4   going past (28) a picture in a frame (11.3) um (8.0) a shoe (10) might've
5   been a footprint cos' there's some sea (11.3) something in the air as well
6   (12.4) apple (34) 'n there's a tunnel (2.2) going into a tunnel (6.2) there's
7   a present (4.6) and a cable car (1.2) going down (45) Christmas tree well a
8   fir tree (50) um (1) a boat in the water leaving a wake (31) 'n a pile of
9   something (36.5) a frog, (5.5) big one

There are minimal descriptions of imagery: 'an engine' (line 2), 'a shoe' (line 4) and 'apple' (line 6), in which even the definite or indefinite article is absent. There are slightly more complex reports, such as 'a doorway made of stone' (line 3) and 'a picture in a frame' (line 4). In addition to these reports of imagery, there are other kinds of discursive activity. For example, the participant seems to engage in clarification or correction: in line 7 and 8 there is a report of a Christmas tree that is then amended to a fir tree. There is also an instance in which a minimal imagery report is subsequently expanded: in line 9 the report of a frog is amended by the report of its dimension. Finally it is noticeable that there are lengthy periods of silence between the discrete imagery reports. The longest in this brief sequence is 50 seconds, but it is routine in this narrative for the participant to remain silent for over 20 or 30 seconds.

Other participants produced much a much more extensive report of their imagery. For example:

(3.2) (01-82: E1/M)

1 P: the first thing I notice is um for a start that my body doesn't feel (1.3) quite as
2   though I'm sitting in a chair it- it's as though my arms feel this uh they were
3   the other way up than they were to start off with and bu- I'm I'm not sort've
4   sitting in the same position (1.5) that almost as though it e- the feeling that
5   you might get if you're sort've drifting in space (20.3) there seems to be
6   some sort've impression of um: (1.3) I mean maybe it's the it's the noise
7   that's reminding me of the sea but s'rt've sitting on a- a- a- a- cliff on on on
8   the top of a hill an- (1.3) not so much hearing the sea as j'st s'rt've staring
9   out at a big expanse of of of sea (70.2) somehow I get the idea of a lot've uh:

10   colours uh I don't know (2.3) uh I don't know what colours or anything but
11   s'rt've uh or whatever the other they're reasonably bright they're not um s-s-
12   s'rt've um (1.5) um (.) psychedelic they're not um they're not natural (1.4) uh
13   something like on a- a- a- a- s'rt've a unreal like a gameshow or something or
14   or um (2) on these these adverts uh (45.6) I also get the impression of feeling
15   um quite opposite s'rt've isolated a- as though um (2.7) I dunno uh very
16   different as as though you you're in a a yu- uh big long tunnel or in an ice
17   cave or something like that where where n- n-n-not- that- you're the only one
18   that just that there's ur you're surrounded by by (1.6) um uh something
19   something very big um um something that you can't touch maybe that sort've
20   thing ((continues))

In this sequence, the participant describes three discrete kinds of imagery: the sensation of the body, colours, and feeling isolated or in a long tunnel. The imagery reports are considerably more extensive than the reports from the previous extract, and stretch over several lines of transcript. The participant's speech also shows a considerable degree of dysfluency or perturbation: there are numerous hesitations, repeats of words, repeat of the initial sound of a word, and exclamations of doubt about the nature of the imagery being reported. It is difficult to state with confidence that these features of the participant's speech are idiosyncratic speech patterns, such as a stammer, or reflect the participant's slightly altered state of consciousness following the preliminary relaxation period prior to the start of the experiment. Curiously though, despite the differences between the mentation reports in extracts 3.1 and 3.2, it is apparent that in both, reports of discrete imagery are punctuated by extensive periods of silence. In the case of extract 3.2, there is a silence exceeding 70 seconds between the first and second imagery reports, and a silence exceeding 45 seconds between the second and third.

Mentation reviews

The mentation review is designed to ensure that the experimenter's hand written record of the mentation is accurate, and to allow the participants to elaborate or expand upon their imagery before the judging phase of the experiment. However, there are several procedural stages prior to the commencement of the review. First the experimenter has to initiate contact with the participant via the headphones to inform them that the sending/ mentation period is over. As the participant may have been in a mildly altered state of consciousness, or at least highly relaxed, experimenters routinely inquire about the participants' well being. For example:

(3.3) (01-81: E1/M. All names are anonymised.)

1   E: Jonathan?

2   P: mhm,
3   E: hi how do you feel?
4   P: *((Heavy breathing))* um okay
5   E: okay?
6   P: yeah
7   E: okay, good

(3.4) (01-29: E2/M)

1   E: hello Miles?
2   S: hello
3   E: how are you doing?
4   S: I'm fine
5   E: you feel okay
6   S: yeah

(3.5) (01-31: E3/M)

1   E: okay Roger? That's uh completes the impression period how did that
2   feel?
3   S: uh, it's quick—I felt quite confused

The experimenter then asks the participant to estimate how long the sending/mentation period lasted. Often participants are able to estimate the duration quite accurately; others are less accurate, often markedly so: it is not uncommon for participants to estimate that the 30 minute sending period lasted only 10 minutes.

The experimenter then proceeds with the review proper. This consists of a series of stepwise phases in which the experimenter reads out his or her record of the reported imagery for the participant's confirmation or correction. Routinely, the participant confirms the report with a minimal response token, such as 'yes', 'yeah' or 'mm', and the experimenter moves to the next item in their record.

(3.6) (01-29: E2/M)

1   E: woman in white
2   P: mm
3   E: snake with a head
4   P: mm
5   E: um: a carpet surrounded by people
6   P: mhm
7   E: violin someone eating the violin
8   P: mhm
             ((continues))

Some participants remain silent after the experimenter's report, and this is also routinely taken as confirmation that the record was accurate, and the experimenter proceeds to the next imagery.

(3.7) (01-47: E1/F)

1	E:	next an apple
2		*((Silence))*
3	E:	and then a hand again.
4		*((Silence))*
5	E:	a strange face with bulging eyes and teeth grinning
6		*((Silence))*
7	E:	next you had the impression of a magazine and the edge of the magazine
8		*((Silence))*
9	E:	next a toadstool
10		*((Silence))*
11	E:	and then an underwater scene,
14		*((Silence))*
15	E:	and there were worms heading towards a chest?

At the completion of the review, the experimenter asks a further series of questions about the participant's imagery (if they felt that there were persistent themes, or surprising imagery, or unclear imagery, and so on), and whether or not they thought that there was a sender or not in their trial. The experiment then moves to the final judging stage. A monitor in the participant's room is activated, and they are shown the target clip and three decoys, and, on the basis of their imagery and in consultation with the experimenter, they are invited to identify which of the four they think was the target.

The mentation review is clearly interactional, in that experimenter and participant collaboratively ensure the smooth progression of the encounter as a formal check on the experimenter's written record of the mention. But there are some interesting analytic features of these encounters. For example, in mundane conversation, periods of silence are often problematic and lead participants to attempt to identify or repair what is inferred to be the problem (Jefferson, 1989). Yet here, however, it is normal for the participant's silence to be interpreted as an unproblematic confirmation that the experimenter's prior turn was a correct record of the participant's imagery. This suggests that in this setting everyday conversational competences may be suspended or amended to ensure the institutional 'business' of the review — to check the experimenter's record — can be accomplished smoothly. The ways in which everyday competences are marshalled in the service of the review, and the consequences this may have for the trajectory of interaction, will be discussed in chapters 8 and 9.

In this section we have described the parapsychological data for this study. Although parapsychology may be regarded as a contested discipline, we have tried to demonstrate that there is nothing controversial about the mentation narratives and the mentation review data from the Edinburgh ganzfeld experiments. Whether or not an individual trial resulted in the participant identifying correctly the target clip is irrelevant for our purposes, as, regardless of the outcome of the trial, they still had to spend time reporting their experiences, and then going through the mentation review prior to the judging phase. To this extent, then, the narratives and the reviews are non parapsychological by-products of a procedure for testing for parapsychological abilities; periods of introspection and interaction that require the participants to use everyday communicative competences to engage in mundane activities, such as describing, checking, affirming, clarifying and correcting. In this sense, they are naturally occurring communicative events within the context of the experimental procedure. They are verbal activities produced in, and with respect to the requirements of, an institutional or work related setting.

The study of talk-in interaction

Our analysis of mentation narratives and mentation reviews is informed by the assumptions and methodological principles of conversation analysis, or CA.

Conversation analysis is a formal, qualitative method for the analysis of talk in collaborative, naturally-occurring social interaction. It developed out of the pioneering studies of Harvey Sacks and his colleagues Emanuel Schegloff and Gail Jefferson, and is now widely acknowledged as the pre-eminent method for analysing the socially organised communicative competences through which participants in all kinds of verbal interaction produce intelligible, meaningful conduct. Although known as *conversation* analysis, its methods can be applied to the analysis of any unscripted, naturally occurring verbal communication, including that which occurs in formal or institutional or work based settings. Consequently, it is now common for CA to be referred to as the study of *talk-in-interaction* (Schegloff, 2007) to capture the wide variety of forms of talk that have been studied using CA methods. Although emerging from sociology, conversation analytic methods and findings have had significant impact on research in a number of cognate disciplines and related methodological approaches, such as discourse analysis in social psychology (Potter and Wetherell, 1987), discursive psychology (Edwards, 1997; Potter and Edwards, 1992), linguistics (Levinson, 1983), anthropology (Moerman 1988), human computer interaction (Luff, Glbert and Frohlich, 1990; Wooffitt, Gilbert, Fraser and McGlashan, 1997) and speech therapy (Wilkinson 1995; Wilkinson, Bryan, Lock, Bayley, Maxim, Bruce, Edmundson, and Moir, 1998).

(Introductions to CA can be found in Heritage, 1984a; Hutchby and Wooffitt, 2008; ten Have, 1999. Sacks developed the style of analysis that grew into CA in lectures given during the 1960s and 1970s; these were published as Sacks, 1992. Some notable early papers in conversation analysis were published in Lerner, 2005. Collections of CA papers can be found in Atkinson and Heritage, 1984; Boden and Zimmerman, 1991, and Drew and Heritage, 1992.)

Research in this tradition is characterised by distinctive methodological procedures concerning data collection, transcription, and the development of empirical findings. But we begin first with a discussion of assumptions about the nature of language and interaction that inform CA studies. These assumptions reflect CA's origins in sociology, but are also supported by cumulative findings from empirical research in this tradition.

The orders of social actions: sequentially organised patterns of talk-in-interaction

Conversation analytic research recognises and prioritises the action orientation of language: we use utterance to perform actions, such as greetings, invitations, complaints, offers, accusations, promises, reportings, and so on. Talk is treated is both a vehicle for interpersonal social actions and the site in which social actions may be performed. An initial step in empirical research is to try to identify the kind of activity an utterance is accomplishing. In this, there are similarities between CA and speech act theory associated with J.L. Austin (1962) and John Searle (1969). An important difference though, is that CA seeks to examine how utterances perform actions in relation to the context of utterances in which they are produced. Research has identified that talk-in-interaction exhibits robust and highly regular patterns: *sequences* of speech acts in interaction, such as greeting–greeting, offer–acceptance/refusal, invitation–acceptance/decline, question–answer, and so on. These kinds of activity sequences — and others that are much more complex — display recurrent properties. These sequences are taken to be the site in which participants manage interpersonal activities collaboratively.

The emphasis on sequential analysis is not theoretically motivated but reflects the result of extensive empirical research that shows that the design of turns at talk is highly sensitive to the immediate interactional environment, such as the prior turn; and that the production of an utterance, while being intimately responsive to prior utterances, also constitutes the immediate interactional environment for any subsequent turn. In this sense CA treats each discrete contribution to interaction as being context shaped and context renewing (Sacks, Schegloff, and Jefferson, 1974). It is for this reason that analysis does not consider utterances extracted from the context of their production. The consistent finding from cumulative studies that utterances cohere into larger sequences (the organisation and properties of which are impossible to anticipate intuitively or theoretically) ensures that empirical research prioritises the turn-by-turn unfolding of interaction *in which* any particular turn might be produced, and *to which* it is designed as a contribution.

Normative dimensions of talk-in-interaction

Conversation analytic research shares many assumptions with ethnomethodological studies of social action (Garfinkel, 1967; Heritage, 1984a). Ethnomethodological sociology examines how the immediate and ongoing understanding of social action is accomplished through the participants' use of tacit, practical reasoning skills and competences. These skills are referred to as 'tacit' and 'practical' because, by and large, they are not the kinds of 'rules' or norms of behaviour that are available to conscious articulation. Instead, they inhabit the very fabric of social life, and thereby become invisible and unnoticeable, except on occasions here they are breached or challenged. These tacit frameworks have an implicitly normative or moral character, in that they guide tacit interpretations as to what should be happening at any moment, such that certain courses of action can be are seen to have deviated from expectations, and subsequently become accountable, requiring explanation or redress. Goffman's pioneering studies of everyday life also identify the powerful normative and inferential concerns that underpin the presentation of self in social settings (Goffman, 1959; 1961, 1971). Conversation analytic research departs from ethnomethodological and Goffmanesque studies of social action in that it has developed a much more formal set of methodological procedures. However, it retains an interest in the way naturally occurring verbal interaction is underpinned by a web of normative and interpretative frameworks that shape and inform co-interactants' inferences about the ongoing interaction, and which demonstrably impinge upon the trajectory of that interaction. For example, many simple interactional sequences have two action parts, such as in greeting–greeting sequence, or invitation–acceptance/refusal sequences. In these paired action sequences (Schegloff and Sacks, 1973), there is the normative assumption that the issue of the first part of the pair generates an expectation that the second part is forthcoming, or that an account for its absence is produced. That is, the second part is *conditionally relevant* on the production of the first (Schegloff, 1968). Evidence for this normative framework emerges when an expected second part is not produced. We do not simply record such absences as statistical anomalies, but treat them as normatively accountable departures from tacit expectations. To illustrate this, consider the following extract that comes from talk between a child and her mother.

(3.8) (From Atkinson and Drew, 1979: 52; simplified transcription.)

1	Child:	Have to cut these Mummy
2		(1.3)
3	Child:	Won't we Mummy
4		(1.5)
5	Child:	Won't we
6	Mother:	Yes

After the child's initial question there is a 1.3 second silence. The child's second and third versions of the initial question display her orientation to the normative expectation that an answer should follow a question: the absence of the answer is not regarded as happenstance, but a *noticeable* absence that motivates her subsequent turns (Heritage, 1984a: 247). The subsequent truncated attempts to solicit an answer display the child has inferred that the mother heard the initial question, but is at that point not answering (a verbatim repeat of the question would demonstrate that the had she assumed the mother had simply not heard the question).

The social organisation of word selection and turn design

It is a common sense assumption that the words we use broadly reflect the 'idea', 'intentions', or 'goals' of the speaker; and that, consequently, word selection reflects cognitive processes, or seeks to express and make public psychological or personal realities. This assumption is enshrined in numerous psychological writings on language in interpersonal action. A related position is that our descriptions of events or objects in the world reflect the properties of those events or objects. In this perspective, our descriptive utterances are in large measure determined by the properties of the things to which they refer. This realist or representational under-standing of language is enshrined in many psychological perspectives on introspective descriptions, in which at its core, language is viewed as a means of information transfer, rather than a medium through which social activities are conducted. These theories about meaning and representation have been critiqued by philosophers (Austin, 1962; Wittgenstein, 1953; Waismann, 1965) and social scientists (Coulter, 1979; Gilbert and Mulkay 1984; Heritage, 1978; Potter and Wetherell, 1987). But CA has a particular contribution to the critique of naïve representational theories of language and description. This is because CA research strongly suggests that word selection and utterance design involve a complex set of communicative competences that are highly sensitive to the immediate social context. To explain we can consider the very basic practice of describing something utterly mundane.

With regards to the formulation of location, or 'place', Schegloff has written:

> Were I now to formulate where my notes are, it would be correct to say that they are: right in front of me, next to the telephone, on the desk, in my office, in the office, in Room 213, in Lewisohn Hall, on campus, at school, at Columbia, in Morningside Heights, on the upper West Side, in Manhatten, in New York City, in New York State, in the North east, on the Eastern seaboard, in the United States, etc. Each of these terms could in some sense be correct ... were its relevance provided for. (Schegloff 1972b: 81)

Schgloff's example illustrates how the description of any state of affairs in the world — however mundane or 'obvious' they may seem to be — requires a degree of selection from the range of possible words phrases that could have been used. This means that no actual description can exhaust the properties of the state of affairs it describes, as any description could be extended or revised; furthermore, the end of any actual description is therefore a *practical* termination, not a logical one. By the production of a descriptive utterance built from a range of potentially usable words and phrases, speakers 'bracket in' or index certain particulars of the referent of the description, and, at the same time, 'bracket out' other aspects of the referent. Thus, any description is a selection that brings into play to a set of specific particulars of the state of affairs being described (Garfinkel, 1967; Heritage, 1984a; Heritage and Watson, 1979). Descriptions, then, have inferential consequences, in that their design can shape co-partici-pants' understanding of any aspect of the ongoing interaction: what is being talked about, why it is being talked about, the motives of the speakers, and so on. This is true whether the referent is a person, or a place, or an object, or a memory, or any other kind of entirely private mental experience (Edwards, 1997; Wooffitt, 1992).

In everyday communication, there are numerous interactional contingencies that may come into play, and these can all inform word selection and utterance design. A turn may be constructed to offer a particular kind of response to the prior turn; it may be designed with respect to the kind of next turn the speaker seeks to elicit from a co-participant; it can be designed in relation to the kind of activity that utterance is required or intended to perform; it can be constructed with respect to the range of normative conventions that are in play; and it may be designed to address the range of inferential concerns relevant to the talk at that moment. These are sociological concerns, in that they arise from and are intimately connected to the normative and sequentially structured production of talk on a turn-by-turn basis. As such, turn design and word selection are socially organised, practical matters, not merely the externalised expression of internal mental phenomena such as intentions or goals, nor the reflection of objective properties of the world being described.

Attending to the detail of interaction

In the social sciences, qualitative analysis of verbal or textual data very often proceeds via the identification of broad thematic consistencies, which in turn are then categorised to reflect the theoretical, ethical or moral concerns that motivated the research in the first instance. This reflects two key characteristics of mainstream qualitative research: broad description or glossing of the data; and the imposition of analytic categories or empirical schema that reflect the analysts' theoretical or empirical positions. In conversation analytic research, analysis of data is conducted differently. First, analysis proceeds by close description of the data. No aspect of talk is assumed *a priori* to be unimportant. This is because research has shown that even apparently inconsequential contributions to interaction, such as inbreaths, words cut off in mid production, and minor pauses, may have demonstrable impact on the trajectory of the subsequent interaction.

Relatedly, CA research rejects the imposition of broad analytic categories of classificatory schema that reflect theoretical perspectives, or embody quasi scientific hypotheses. This is because talk-in-interaction is viewed as a domain of activity in its own right: it is not regarded as a simple expression of psychological idiosyncrasies or personality, nor as a canvas which reflects the influence of overarching sociological variables, such as the participants' relationship, class, ethnicity, gender, status, and so on. The analyst does not, therefore, begin research with a series of pre-established and theory-led questions to be explored in the data. Instead, analytic priority is given to the examination of speakers' own interpretations of what is happening in, and relevant to, any interaction to which they contribute (Sacks *et al.*, 1974; Schegloff, 1997). It is taken that participants' understanding of ongoing interaction is exhibited in the design of their turns at talk. So, in response to a turn like 'come over and see me sometime': an *acceptance* will display that the speaker heard this as an invitation; *laughter* will exhibit the speaker's inference that the turn was humorous; and an *apology* will show that the speaker understood the turn to be a complaint. Every turn at talk unavoidably exhibits some understanding of the prior turn. The turn-by-turn unfolding of interaction is, therefore, an on-going and public display of the participants' tacit reasoning about what is happening at that moment in interaction. As such, it constitutes a 'building block' of intersubjective understanding (Heritage, 1984a: 255–6).

Analysis of naturally occurring data

In the early development of conversation analytic research, data came from recordings and transcripts of telephone conversations. While telephone data are still used, analysts also examine data from audio and video recordings of other kinds of everyday social activities, such as family dinners, as well as data from more institutionalised or work related contexts. Regardless of the kind of data, though, there is an unyielding commitment to the analysis of real life or naturally occurring interaction: talk that is unscripted, and not solicited for the purpose of studying talk. The emphasis on naturally occurring data reflects the empirical finding that the organisation of talk-in-interaction exhibits robust properties that are either counter intuitive, or which would be difficult to anticipate based on what the analyst 'commensensically knows' about the logic of language or how people use talk in social life (Levinson, 1983). Intuition alone does not equip us to deal formally with the full range of empirical phenomena in spontaneous communication, nor at the level of detail at which participants in interaction manage talk. This is a major departure from speech act theory, in which the analyst seeks to identify theoretically the circumstances under which utterances achieve the status as a particular kind of speech event, and in which there is strong reliance on many philosophically informed intuitions about how language works (Schegloff, 1982).

This emphasis on naturally occurring data also demarcates CA research from experimental social psychological investigations of communication, in which it is routine for research participants to be invited into a formal setting, such as a laboratory, and then asked to engage in some form of interaction to generate data that has a bearing on a particular theoretical position or hypothesis. These kinds of artificially generated data are rejected, because it is unclear to what extent interactional phenomena generated in artificial environments relate to the communicative competences that inform naturally occurring communication. Neither is it always apparent that the communicative skills and organisations that inform talk solicited for a purpose have any relationship to the theories that motivate the collection of such artificial data in the first place. It is important to stress that the introspective narratives generated in the ganzfeld experiments are unlike talk produced in social psychological research in order to test theories about interpersonal communication. The mentation narratives are naturally occurring form of institutional interaction, in that they are by-products of the experimental procedures to test for the operation of parapsychological abilities, rather than discourse elicited for the purpose of studying introspective reports.

Empirical claims and the examination of collections of cases

Although there are some notable analytic papers that provide a detailed analysis of a single case, such as a particular stretch of interaction (Goodwin, C., 1987; Schegloff, 1984, 1988/9; Tainio, 2003; Whalen, Zimmerman and Whalen, 1988), the vast majority of conversation analytic research is directed to identifying and describing the properties of generic communicative practices and competences based on analyses of collections of instances. For example, one of the earliest published studies in CA was an analysis of the sequential organisation of beginnings to telephone calls, which was based on examination of 500 cases (Schegloff, 1968). The openings to telephone calls are easy to collect, as by definition they occur in every telephone conversation. Other kinds of interactional phenomena may not be implicated in the structure of the interaction and may therefore occur less frequently. Even in these cases, there is an attempt to build collections of instances, often culled from a range of available corpora, such as British and US English telephone calls. The development of empirical claims from the analysis of collections of cases is one of the key methodological procedures by which research findings are advanced and warranted.

Transcription

Conversation analytic research is the study of audio or video recordings of interaction, assisted by detailed transcripts. To those unfamiliar with its practices, transcripts may seem unnecessarily elaborate. It is therefore important to explain why such care is taken, and to emphasise the benefits from careful transcription.

  Conversation analytic research has shown that even apparently minor or trivial aspects of interaction have a significant impact on its subsequent development. Transcriptions therefore try to capture characteristics of verbal interaction omitted from transcripts that merely record the spoken word. This means not only transcribing what was said, but the way it was said, and making sure that things that might seem messy, 'accidental', or ungrammatical are recorded in the transcript and not filtered out in some form of 'tidying up' process. To capture these routinely overlooked features of interaction, analysts use a distinctive transcription system, based on symbols available on conventional typewriter and computer keyboards. This transcription system was developed by Gail Jefferson, and is now widely recognised in a range of social science disciplines: it is often the standard system required by academic journals in communication and discourse studies. The system focuses on, first, the properties of turn taking, such as the onset of simultaneous speech and the timing of gaps within and between turns; and second, it exposes features of the production of talk, such as emphasis, volume, the speed of delivery and sound stretching. The main transcription symbols used in the analyses that follow are explained below.

(0.5)   The number in brackets indicates a time gap in tenths of a second.

(.)   A dot enclosed in a bracket indicates pause in the talk less then two tenths of a second.

.hh   A dot before an 'h' indicates speaker in-breath. The more 'h's, the longer the inbreath.

hh   An 'h' indicates an out-breath. The more 'h's the longer the breath.

(( ))   A description enclosed in a double bracket indicates a non-verbal activity. For example ((banging sound))

–   A dash indicates the sharp cut-off of the prior word or sound.

:   Colons indicate that the speaker has stretched the preceding sound or letter. The more colons the greater the extent of the stretching.

( )   Empty parentheses indicate the presence of an unclear fragment on the tape.

(guess)   The words within a single bracket indicate the transcriber's best guess at an unclear fragment.

.   A full stop indicates a stopping fall in tone. It does not necessarily indicate the end of a sentence.

,   A comma indicates a continuing intonation.

?   A question mark indicates a rising inflection. It does not necessarily indicate a question.

Thaght   A 'gh' indicates that word in which it is placed had a guttural pronunciation.

Under   Underlined fragments indicate speaker emphasis.

↑↓   Pointed arrows indicate a marked falling or rising intonational shift. They are placed immediately before the onset of the shift.

CAPS   Capital letters indicate a section of speech noticeably louder than that surrounding it.

° °   Degree signs are used to indicate that the talk they encompass is spoken noticeably quieter than the surrounding talk. If the talk is especially quiet, double symbols are used.

> <   'More than' and 'less than' signs indicate that the talk they encompass was produced noticeably quicker than the surrounding talk. If the talk is especially quick, double symbols are used.

=   The 'equals' sign indicates contiguous utterances.

[   ]   Square brackets between adjacent lines of concurrent speech
[   ]   indicate the onset and end of a spate of overlapping talk.

Detailed transcription of this kind yields substantial amounts of paper data: once transcribed, the 24 mentation narratives (approximately 12 hours of recorded data) produced a corpus of exactly 100 pages of single lined, A4 sized pages of transcript. The transcripts of the mentation reviews generated substantially more. (A more detailed description of these transcription symbols can be found in Hutchby and Wooffitt, 2008.)

The relevance of CA to the study of interview interaction in which the researcher seeks to establish retrospectively the nature of conscious phenomena will be apparent. But it may seem an unusual method to adopt in the study of introspective reports that are essentially monologic narratives on inner experience. In the next section, then, we make some preliminary empirical observations to illustrate the kinds of issues that can be examined via the application of a 'conversation analytic mentality' (Schenkein, 1978) to introspective descriptions of inner experience. This also allows us to sketch some of the analytic themes that will be explored in more detail in subsequent chapters

Preliminary observations

In this section we illustrate some basic features of the introspective data via a consideration of a single stretch from one of the mentation narratives. This is not chosen because it is in some way special or remarkable, but precisely the opposite: it exhibits a range of features found in numerous mentations in the corpus. This extract comes from the start of the mentation.

(3.9) (01-18: E1/M)   (From this point on, conversation analytic transcriptions will be used. 'P' is the research participant.)

1   P: anima:ls: °it's° a– (.) a dogs a horse
2   (5.4)
3   white noise is making me think've (.) trains and planes:, °but uh(h)
4   ʰhh (0.6) °(hh) >I c'n see-< u:: I c'n see° a book
5   (6.6)
6   OLD lady passing (2.8) >'s a< walking stick (2.3) 'er's an indian dancer
7   (6.7)
8   >there's a< old lady walking towards me now

9   (6.9)
10   song::, called tw(r)igs and see:ds,
11   (14.0)
12   a <u>song</u> called (pink pig slats)
13   (6.6)
14   °>I c'n<° see things (.) <u>pa:</u>ssing >sort've< (2.4) <u>patterns</u> in the dogs 'n
15   co:nes,
16   (33.0)
17   ˙hh there's a ri<u>ver</u> (0.6) a waterfall (4.5) th's a big <u>like</u> <u>a</u>:: (.) >nuclear
18   explosion reflected,< ˙hh in the wat°er.°
19   (93.0)
20   >something< on the white noise:, sounds like a ban::d ˙h (.) play:ed
21   backwards.
22   (14.0)
23   ba<u>lloon</u> >I feel like< (.) hh (2.5) ˙h feel like I'm inside a big balloo:n
24   (33.5)
25   ˙hh feel like I'm >wobbling< from side to si::de
26   (4.4)
27   cycling (0.5) >cycling< down north bridge
28   (6.1)
29   the big issue.
30   (2.0)
31   cold, (.) wind,
32   (11.0)
33   >feel like< I'm much bigger:, (.) feel like °I'm:° (0.3) ˙h >hundred foot<
34   <u>tall</u> 34>u- feel< °u:::° (0.2) ˙hh my hands feel SO LIGHT that they're very
35   >heavy< (6.7) >feel like there's uh< <like <u>I'm</u> inflated from::. °eh° ˙hh
36   I'm:: >s't've< one big balloo::n
37   (21.5)
38   ˙hhh feel a bit °of a° <u>pain</u> in my lower stoma:ch, (.) °like° >my lower
39   gut< (5.6) °>u: yu-<° <u>feel</u> <u>like</u> I'm::, ˙hhh e:r::: >could be something<
40   like aeroplane:? °>t- uh,<°
41   (58.8)
42   now I manage to- (1.4) l <u>leave</u> my body a bit (2.3) °>uh bu-<° I feel
43   less:, (.) °u-° inside my head (5.3) °be°gin to feel s'r'ta higher?
44   (35.8)
45   I'm going upwards
46   (13.0)
47   °m-° (.) piece of tchaikovsky's fifth symphony:: (1.7) ˙h I think, (2.0) yeah?
48   (9.7)
49   >another °piece of the° same< symphony:, ˙hh <u>roof</u> (0.6) BEAMS (.)
50   ><u>GIR</u>ders on a< roof:: (0.9) ˙hh um, seeing it from underneath:: the

51	WHIte roof with black (.) black <u>bea</u>:ms: (0.2) like top've a::: (.) barn
52	(2.6)
53	a <u>horse</u>:
54	(59.5)
55	>°uh something° I can't quite make out< °uh° like a- u:- u:- u:: °>th- th-
56	th's a<° tee shape (.) °there's a° ˙hhh semi circle:: s'rt've °uh:° going up at an
57	angle.
58	(16.1)
59	°uh u:(h)° (4.2) there's >something< like a::: 's like an ironing board
60	having >epileptic< fi:t.
61	(11.4)
62	°I:° c'n see a <u>slope</u> with a::: °with some° sort've doorway at the top,
63	(30.1)
64	<u>eyes</u> are beginning to ache a little bit ·
65	(27.2)
66	˙hh roof again:. (0.6) > ˙h< looking straight up at it,
67	(27.0)
68	˙hhh toothbrush, >it's s'rt've< wrapped up in it's package ˙h <u>spin</u>ning
69	round between somebody's finger and thumb (2.8) I think it says >big<
70	toothbrush with blue letters on it,
71	(7.0)
72	°u° mickey mou:se,
73	(15.5)
74	˙hh it's in slow motion like a::, (0.6) ˙h <u>oh</u>? i's: like a <u>drill</u> like a:, (1.4) ˙h I
75	see the threads of a drill spinning roun:d.
	((Continues))

This extract confirms observations reported earlier: imagery reports may be minimally designed, such that they are constructed out of one or two words, or may be extended by the addition to an initial imagery report of further descriptive components. In addition, it highlights how participants' reports may be clear and articulate, or they may exhibit dysfluencies and speech perturbations, as in the report of bodily sensations in lines 33 to 36. Utterances are marked by a wide range of pronunciation characteristics: on occasion, participants momentarily speak faster than normal; sometimes they stress words; some sounds are elongated and stretched; intonation can vary, as can volume.

The content of the discrete reports is extraordinarily varied. In this one relatively short stretch the participant reports imagery relating to people (an old lady, line 6), iconic cultural figures (Mickey Mouse, line 72), everyday objects (a toothbrush, line 68 to 70; the *Big Issue*, a magazine sold on the streets of UK cities to assist homeless people, line 29), activities (cycling, line 27), sensations (wobbling, line 25, sore eyes, line 64), music (popular music in lines 10 and 12, and classical music in line 47), vague shapes (the 'T' shape and semi circle in lines 55 and 56), and reflections on the immediate environment of the experiment (reporting how the white noise is bringing imagery to mind, line 3). There are some images so odd that they seem to defy categorisation (for example, something that is 'like an ironing broad having an epileptic fit', lines 59 and 60). Most images are reported once, but some reoccur, such as the imagery of a roof, first reported in line 50, but which is reported as appearing again in line 66. Some reports are un-modulated, and suggest the participant's imagery is unambiguous; while other reports suggest that the participant has some doubt as to what exactly they are experiencing; compare the report of the horse (line 53) with that of the 'T' shape/semi circle (lines 55 to 56).

As noted earlier, it is very common for participants to describe a specific image or sensation, or a discrete set of related images or sensations, and then remain silent for sometimes very long periods of time before reporting the next imagery. So, after the report of something passing/patterns (line 14), over half a minute elapses before the participant speaks again. This next utterance reports imagery associated with, and reflections in, water (lines 17 to 18); this is new imagery and appears unconnected to the imagery of things passing. After this, 93 seconds pass before the participant embarks on a report of the next imagery, something audible on the white noise being played through the headphones (lines 20 to 21). The periods of silence between discrete imagery reports may vary, but in the vast majority of cases, they are far longer than those that appear in mundane conversational interaction. Moreover, they are also usually longer than the relatively short periods of silence that appear embedded within imagery reports. We examine silences between discrete imagery reports in more detail in a later chapter. It is sufficient for present purposes to note that mentation introspective narratives are composed of two phenomena: talk, and silence. They are series of discrete imagery reports, punctuated by periods in which the participant says nothing.

One of the difficulties with many forms of qualitative analysis is that they permit — or indeed require — a degree of interpretative licence on the part of the analyst that can seem unprincipled, contingent or even idiosyncratic when set aside the kinds of formal methodological steps associated with quantitative approaches. However, the report — silence — report — silence structure that is intrinsic to the mentation narratives provides a framework which shapes and guides our analytic efforts, and which thereby acts as a safeguard against loosely formulated claims or interpretive excesses. First, we can identify the discrete report as an unambiguous unit of analysis, which provides a broad locus for analysis that reflects objective structural properties of the data. This parallels CA studies of talk-in-interaction, in which the primary unit of analysis is the turn and its relation to the prior turn (or stretch of talk) to which it is serially or sequentially positioned. Second, because each discrete report is bounded by a period of silence, it has a beginning and an end. This is an obvious statement, but it raises several issues that can guide analysis.

How do participants begin their reports? That is, what communicative resources are used in the *turn initial* position? Do participants terminate the on-going silence with words or some non lexical components, as in the use of 'uh' (lines 55 and 72)? And what consequences do these have for the trajectory of the subsequent report? Do they establish for that report a particular quality, such as certainty, hesitancy or circumspection? Further, is it the case that the first components of a discrete report display a relationship to some feature of the prior report? Do they recycle images from prior reports? Are there any other kinds of relationships that are mobilised through the selection of turn initial components? For example, is it the case that turn initial components pick up on and thereby recycle acoustic properties of prior reports? A related set of empirical issues concern the final component — the *terminal position* — of each discrete report. What resources are used in terminal positions? Do participants simply report their inner experience and then fall silent, or do they then reflect on what they have described, and offer an assessment or evaluation? How do these turn terminal components retrospectively change the shape or trajectory of the report? How do terminal components relate to turn initial components (if at all)? What kinds of relationships between initial and terminal components can be identified? These are empirical questions that unfold from recognition of the selection of words and phrases in the design of turns.

The beginnings of discrete reports are, in a sense, unambiguously apparent, in that they are the words that break the silence. We can examine which words are used, and how they are pronounced; and we can reflect on the length and import of silence before they are uttered. But the beginnings of discrete reports are an unavoidable acoustic fact of the mentation. The same cannot be said, however, of the end of reports. Like turns at talk in interaction, discrete imagery reports can be constructed in various ways. As extract 3.9 illustrates, they may be built from single words, a word with a definite or indefinite article, simple phrases and clauses, more complex compound clauses, or complete grammatical sentences. And, as with turns in ordinary conversation, arriving at the end point of an imag-

ery report is a practical matter, as an initial imagery report could, in principle, be extended indefinitely.

In their study of the turn taking system in conversation Sacks *et al.* (1974)
identified that turns at talk are built out of turn construction units, or
TCUs; these are syntactically bounded lexical, clausal, phrasal or
sentential units. A property of any turn construction unit is that, at its completion, another speaker may begin. At the end of a turn construction component, then, is a transition relevance place. The phrase 'transition
relevance' is key here, as Sacks *et al.* do not claim that any next speaker *will*
necessarily begin at the end of a turn construction unit, or that a next
speaker *has* to begin. Their analyses show that speaker exchange *may* be
initiated: turn transfer is normatively appropriate in these structural locations. Indeed, ongoing turns can arrive at a TCU and then continue.
Numerous studies of interaction have shown the various procedures
available to current speakers to retain speakership at transfer relevance
places so as to produce lengthy turns. Similarly, there is a range of ways
that potential next speakers can 'gear up' to launch a turn in anticipation of
a forthcoming transfer relevance place, especially if there may be more
than one possible next speaker.

In the mentation narratives, there is no other speaker who may seek to
initiate a turn: the participant produces what is effectively a monologue
for the overhearing but non-participating experimenter. Consequently,
the participant does not have to safeguard their on-going speakership in
the way that is required if a speaker wishes to extend their turn in ordinary
conversation. But some basic principles of utterance design for social
interaction still operate in the mentation narratives. There are various
ways in which an imagery report can be extended. For example consider
the utterance that begins in line 55 with the report '>°uh something° I can't
quite make out<'. This could be a complete turn—stand alone reports of
highly ambiguous sensations are common. But immediately after, the participant says 'uh' quietly. This small particle does two tasks. It occurs at the
end of the initial imagery report; therefore it is an audible continuation of
that report. But it is also a display of ongoing uncertainty, which in turn
suggests that further attempts at clarification can be anticipated. Alter-
nately, an initial imagery report can be extended into a syntactically complete sentence. For example, the first word of the imagery report on line 64
is 'eyes'. This one word utterance could stand as a complete imagery
report: many participants report seeing eyes or eye like imagery; and there
is no indication at this point that the participant is referring to *her* eyes,
which would grammatically imply a continuation of the description.
However, the description is extended with the phrase 'are beginning to
hurt'. Again, at the end of this additional component, the utterance could
stand as a complete imagery report. However, there is a further additional

component, 'a little bit', that qualifies the degree of physical sensation. The incremental extensions transform the utterance into a near complete sentence — only the pronoun 'my' is absent.

Extensions to initial imagery reports can be accompanied by slight increase in the speed at which the talk is produced. In line 68, for example, the initial component of the utterance is 'toothbrush'; again, this could stand as a complete imagery report. The start of the extension '>it's s'rt've<' is produced faster than the surrounding talk, and thereby could be said to 'rush through' (Schegloff, 1982) into the post initial imagery space.

The additional turn components in extended imagery reports invariably deal with epistemic matters, in that they provide further information about the experience and the participant's understanding of it, or their attempts to interpret it. This may come in the form of a simple addition of detail, for example, the extension to the report of a toothbrush (line 68) reveals related information about colour and size. The extensions can reveal how it is that the imagery has come to the participant's awareness; the extension to the report of a roof (line 66) reveals that the participant is 'looking straight up at it', thereby establishing a mode of apprehension (that the imagery was visual, as opposed to merely being a concept or thought that came to mind) and the participant's point of view with respect to the roof in her imagery. Extensions can also be used to mark the participants' circumspection or doubt about what the imagery is, or to disclose their uncertainty about their account of the imagery. An example can be seen in the report of the slope (line 62), in which the participant uses the phrase 'some sort've' to qualify the additional information that there is also a doorway in the imagery.

Every discrete description of conscious sensations, experiences or imagery will be a practical accomplishment, in that any report involves tacit selection from the indefinitely extendable ways in which any state of affairs can be reported. Analysis of the design of imagery reports can yield insight as to communicative competences that inform their initiation, subsequent production and eventual termination. It is important to bear in mind that use of 'design' to capture the detail of imagery reports is not to imply that participants are deliberately or consciously articulating accounts of their conscious experiences. Rather, it points to the way in which everyday, tacit communicative competences are being marshalled with respect to the requirements of the setting. We develop this theme in the next chapter, in which we examine in more detail how participants' reports of their imagery display an epistemic stance or position towards the status of their experience.

Chapter Four

Epistemics and the organisation of introspective reports

During introspection, when people describe their conscious experiences, they are making *epistemic* claims: that they are aware of or can apprehend in some way a sensation or imagery; or that the imagery is about a specific object or event; or that they have confidence (or doubt) about the clarity of the imagery, and so on. In this chapter we explore how these kinds of epistemic matters are handled in the design of descriptive utterances that serially constitute the mentation narratives. We focus on the ways in which a tacit concern with epistemic matters inform the pragmatics of word selection, utterance design and speech production.

In conversation analytic research, there is a long-standing interest in the ways in which epistemic matters inform everyday talk in interaction. The focus of research, though, is not on how people express or represent cognitive states or knowledge, but how claims to knowledge (or its absence) could be marshalled as a resource in the service of an interactional goal. For example, Harvey Sacks' first analyses (that subsequently developed into the kind of analysis associated with contemporary CA research) concerned audio recordings of calls to a Los Angeles suicide prevention agency. At the start of each call, the agency's staff stated their name. In one call, Sacks observed that the caller said 'I can't hear you', thereby displaying that he had not heard the staff member's name. Instead of treating this statement as literal expression of a hearing problem, Sacks examined it as strategic resource used by the caller to accomplish an action: in this case, not giving a name. Sacks' argument was that by doing 'not hearing' (and thereby demonstrating 'not knowing'), the caller was able to change the course of the interaction. Where there had been a slot in the call in which name exchange is routine and normatively expected, the caller had initiated a sequential trajectory in which the agent had to repeat his name, and this in turn meant that the agent's opportunity to establish the caller's name without explicitly asking for it was minimized. In this way, the caller could avoid both giving their name *and* having to state explicitly that they did not wish to give their name (Sacks, 1992, vol. I: 3–7). Critical to Sacks' analysis was the insight that utterances are objects that perform actions in talk; and that this is true also for utterances that appear merely to express some cognitive state, such as a claim to knowledge or the absence of knowledge.

Subsequent research has developed Sack's insight, and has begun to identify how knowledge claims are made or implied, warranted, resisted and negotiated in interaction. This in turn has led to investigation of how the management of epistemic issues inform interpersonal dynamics in establishing who has 'rights to speak' on particular topics (Pomerantz, 1980, 1984; Raymond and Heritage, 2006; Sacks, 1979; Stivers, 2005), authority and expertise (Clift, 2006; Heritage and Raymond, 2005; Pomerantz, 1986; Raymond, 2000; Wooffitt, 1992, 2006), argumentation and disputes (Clayman, 2002; Dersley and Wootton, 2000, 2001; Hutchby, 1996a, 1996b), and remembering and forgetting (Drew, 1989; Goodwin, C., 1987; Wooffitt, 2005). A concern with epistemics has also been the focus of research in cognate disciplines strongly informed by conversation analytic findings and methods, such as discursive psychology. In discursive psychology, research has focused on the ways in accounts of events or opinions can be formulated so as to be authoritative, persuasive, factual, or resistant to alternative or sceptical counter formulations (Edwards, 1997; Edwards and Potter, 1992, 2005; Potter, 1996; Potter and Hepburn, 2003; Stokoe and Hepburn, 2005; Wiggins, 2001; Wiggins and Potter, 2003). A key finding of these studies is that epistemic authority is not a given in social interaction, an invariant feature which simply reflects the participants' roles, relative status or identities, but an achievement, the outcome of verbal and textual activities embedded in routine communicative procedures.

In this chapter we examine epistemic claims in the mentation narratives, and look to see the work that they do in the social context of a laboratory experiment. We focus our analysis on two forms of what we call perceptual markers: phrases that portray how conscious imagery comes to the attention of the participant as they concurrently monitor their inner phenomenal experience. Specifically we focus on visual markers, such as 'I see…', 'I can see…', and 'I'm seeing…', and cognitive markers, such as 'I think…', I'm thinking…' and 'I thought'. We focus on perceptual markers because they are massively common throughout the corpus. In the corpus used in this analysis, there is only one mentation narrative in which no perceptual markers occur. However, it is important to stress that our use of the term 'perceptual markers' should not be interpreted as a commitment to some ontological position on the existence of inner mental processes. In keeping with conversation analytic and related traditions, we ask: what kinds of work do these imagery formulations do? We begin by examining references to 'sight', 'seeing', and 'looking'.

Visual perceptual markers

The most commonly used perceptual marker within the corpus relates to visual imagery, with participants often stating that they can see something. An initial examination of the data appears to indicate that the use of such markers is not linked to any specific type of imagery, such as specifically seeing figures or colours. Moreover, the prevalence of perceptual markers relating to sight certainly indicates that participants are prone to formulating imagery descriptions in visual terms.

As in ordinary conversational interaction, perceptual markers are often formed as part of the participant's personal experience, as can be seen in the following two extracts. In both cases, the participants locate themselves in the first person position, stating 'I see and 'I'm seeing'.

(4.1) (01-69. E2/M)

((Mentation starts))

1   P: u::m (8.3) I see a::: (.) a man? in a:: (2) yello:w (0.5) ma:cintosh? (.)
2   and a:: (4.1) a lighthou:se (0.8) s::sorta thi:ng ˙hhh (0.5) e- on a::: (1.2) a
3   (0.4) pier? (0.5) of (0.3) made o:f (.) s:: (0.4) stone?

(4.2) (01-25: E1/M)

((Mentation starts))

1   P: I:'m seeing::, (.) eagles: °(h)a° a little bit hh (5.6) but they're::,
2   they're very (.) vague
3   (11.4)
4   °bur:° *(swallows)* just kinda birds

The first person nature of the mentation narrative during these extracts is highlighted by the verb tense of 'see' and 'seeing', which position the imagery as being a 'live' or concurrent experience. Both participants thereby present themselves as delivering a commentary on concurrent cognitive/perceptual events. It is also worth noting that in both cases, the combination of explicitly marked first person perspective, and the visual nature of the mentation experience, takes place during the delivery of the first imagery item in the mentation. The 'live' ongoing character of the

experiences is established at the outset. This acts as a normative interpretative frame through which the status of subsequent imagery can be interpreted, much in the same way in which the initial components of other
kinds of largely monologic accounts have been found to circumscribe a
range of inferential possibilities for the hearing or reading of subsequent
components (Smith, 1978; Wooffitt, 1992; Woolgar, 1980).

The ongoing live nature of the experience can be further underlined via
turn components that reinforce the immediacy of the events being
reported.

(4.3)(01-91:E2/F) (To establish that the descriptions are produced as discrete clusters, we will occasionally include in the transcript the period of
silence that has elapsed prior to the first reproduced report.)

```
1          (11.9)
2    P:    >I suddenly see a< rocket (.) (n)hh (1.5) like that bit at the E:nd (2.3) which
3          shoots out fire as it- (0.2) (n)HHh (.) ˙Hhh (0.4) >°s'rt've° goes u:p< (4.4) like a
4          jet ca:r
5          (10.4)
```

(4.4)(01-94:E2/F)

```
1          (12.7 )
2    P:    ↑flying °like° (2.7 ) >no:w what I see: are< sha:pes like (2.5) TRIangle:s (.)
3          or (2.4) ˙hh (.) as if the ↑shape of a ba::t but it ver::y >tis very< (0.8) stylisti:c
4          hhh (4) like POI:nts
5          (7.2)
```

In extracts 4.3 and 4.4, the use of 'suddenly' and 'now' depict the participants as capturing their conscious experiences 'in flight', an inference
which is supported by the increase in the speed of delivery of that part of
the description in which the participants establish how it is they come to be
aware of the imagery.

Participants may orient to and exploit different kinds of sight based perceptual markers in extending an initial imagery description. However, the
shift between ostensibly synonymous terms may initiate and constitute
subtle changes in the very nature of what it is that is being reported.

(4.5)(01-80: E1/M)

((Mentation starts))
```
1    S:    I see a bridge (7.5) I'm looking down on a bri:dge (5) large (6)
2          silver (5.4) bri:dge
3          (35.6)
```

In this descriptive unit, the participant's initial turn component is 'I see a bridge'; and in the same way as in the previous two extracts, implies the participant's first person perspective and live nature of the imagery. Having established in such a straightforward way what is being experienced and how the imagery is being obtained (that is, through some form of 'inner eye'), the participant extends this first imagery report. In this extension component, the participant shifts from using a direct perceptual marker to a more activity based one: 'I'm looking down'. In itself this is hearable as an upgrade from the original report, since the participant is now providing more information about how exactly he is currently 'seeing' the bridge. But it also highlights the wholly different emphasis that such lexical changes can bring about, since the upgraded description of the bridge imagery places the participant into a very specific relationship physically with what is being visually apprehended in consciousness. So, from simply stating that he can see the bridge, the participant now establishes that his point of view places him above the focus of the imagery. In this sense, the epistemic business of the first extension component — the perspective on the focus of the imagery — now shapes a more ontological concern: the content of the imagery.

The use of 'looking' does similar work in the following extracts. In each case, it is produced as a subsequent commentary on the imagery, and it establishes the participants' perspective, thereby subtly shaping the nature of what the imagery is.

(4.6)(01-05: E3/F)

```
1        (17.6)
2    P:  h(h)uh, ˙hh a t- (.) a foot (0.3) can see the toe::s (1.4) 's a big foot (2.2)
3        got white toenail:s (3.3) I'm looking down on it like it was my, foot ˙hh
4        but it's no::t (0.4) 's too b(h)ig
5        (9.0)
```

(4.7)(01-82: E1/M)

```
1        (19.2)
2    P:  I can see: some u::m (.) I'm looking at the whee:ls 've and it seems
3        to be: (0.2) ˙hhh (0.3) that- it's going along some sort've concrete tra:ck
```

(4.8)(01-52: E1/F)

```
1        (1)
2    P:  an um:::: (1.5) an a bus? (2.7) looking at (0.4) travelling
3        alo:ng (1.2) on a bu:s
4        (9)
```

In extract 4.6, the participant initially reports the appearance of a foot, which is then verified by the report of seeing toes. After more detail on the nature of the imagery the perceptual marker 'looking' establishes a perspective on the imagery, which in turn subtly constitutes how the imagery is being experienced, and indeed, of what it consists. In 4.7, the participant initiates a turn with an 'I see' component, in this case, 'I can see'. The turn projected by this component is abandoned after 'some', and it is self repaired (Schegloff, Jefferson and Sacks, 1977) and restarted with a significantly different turn initial component in which 'looking' is used to introduce the focus of the imagery. Finally, in 4.8, a 'looking' formulation extends a description of imagery which is initially not reported via a perceptual marker, but is simply announced with a questioning intonation.

It would seem, then, that word selection to capture the participants' apprehension or perspective on the imagery is not merely a choice between synonyms with little consequence for the content of the report. The way that the participant describes their mode of apprehension has a constitutive consequence, in that what is described is informed by the manner in which components of the imagery report are assembled.

Perceptual markers can also be used to depict the participants' agency in the experimental procedure. This is apparent from extracts 4.5 to 4.8: in three of these, the production of 'I see' formulations or variants depict the participants' passive recipiency of imagery, whereas 'I'm looking' markers constitute an activity. This activity may either be a formulation of how the participant is attending to the imagery, or is indeed a component of the imagery itself. But there are other ways visual perceptual markers may be employed by participants to address issues of agency. In extract 4.9 below, following the report of the imagery of an eye opening, a subsequent item is reported as being 'in the centre of my vision', a formulation which is very similar to one which is produced in the last line of the extract. We can also see, in the arrowed line, a change in the way the participant marks the imagery as a 'live' experience.

(4.9)(01-41: E1/F)

((Mentation starts))

```
1     P:   hhh (0.4) I see:: an ey::e (0.2) open↑ing (1.5) °'s° ye:llo:w (2.7) it's
2          fl̲i̲ckeri:ng (3.8) >the:re's a< l̲a̲:rge: oval sh↑ape (1.3) in the ce̲ntre >of my
3          visio:n< (9.1) ˙hh (0.3) >in the< ce:ntre: >there's a< sma̲ller obje:ct
4          (12)
5     →    >I do:n't< see anything right ↑now
6          (22)
7          ˙hh >I can see< various obje:cts (0.5) moving acro:ss my visions
8          more li::nes I guess
```

An interesting aspect of this change in format when reporting the various mentation images is the way in which the invocation of 'my vision', as well as the objects that are described as passing in front of it, implies a different type of first person. Here the visual perceptual markers work to position the participant as being akin to an audience relative to the mentation imagery. The purely subjective cognitive experience of describing whatever imagery comes to mind can be set against the lack of agency in terms of how, and indeed what, is being experienced.

The way in which reports of imagery address participant agency evidences an orientation to the institutional properties of the context in which the mentation narrative is produced. All participants were briefed before the experiment as to the design and objectives of the procedure. All were aware, then, that there might have been someone actively projecting thoughts into their minds. For any imagery experienced during the mentation period then, its provenance was potentially at issue, because it could either have been generated by their own minds, or by someone else's. It is therefore unsurprising that issues of agency, ownership and the origin of experiences are matters bubbling close to the surface in numerous mentation narratives. (And in relation to this, it is interesting to note that the use of turn components which draw attention to the sudden or immediate appearance of imagery in consciousness, as illustrated in extracts 4.3 and 4.4, work, at last in part, to project a degree of surprise, or at least unanticipated recipiency, in the participants' 'coming to awareness' of their experiences.)

This sense of the participant being a passive non-agentic recipient of ever changing images is further underlined by the statement '>I do:n't< see anything right ↑now', the added temporal element of which ('right now') implies that the participant is orienting towards the mentation section of the ganzfeld procedure as — potentially — a sequence of externally generated, intermittent serial events.

There is further evidence that an orientation to the institutional context of the mentation narrative informs the participant's report of his experience. The disclosure that, at that moment, he sees nothing, exhibits an understanding that the role of a 'good' participant is to monitor for conscious imagery, and to report even if there is nothing to report. But it also exhibits the assumption that the absence of imagery may itself be of parapsychological significance, and therefore be interesting to the experimenter. Recall that the participants in the ganzfeld are aware that during their mentation, there is elsewhere in the building a target video clip, playing repeatedly, and that the idea is that they may be able to use extrasensory perception to 'tune in', or 'detect' or 'receive' or somehow gain knowledge of the content of this clip. So they know that the stimulus materials are concurrent and recurrent, and not intermittent. For participants who believe in the existence of ESP, or who are even open to the idea that it may exist, the absence of imagery would be a noticeable and potentially accountable matter. So if ESP is working to produce some forms of imagery at some points of the mentation period, periods when imagery is absent may reveal something about how (and when) the mechanisms that underpin anomalous information transfer work (or don't work). The claim not to 'see anything right ↑now' thereby evidences a relatively sophisticated appreciation of the design and purpose of the experimental context. This will be explored further in the next chapter.

Cognitive markers

References to 'thought' and 'thinking' occur regularly in the way that participants frame how they come to awareness of imagery. Invariably, in the mentation data, these kinds of cognitive markers perform the function of exhibiting doubt or circumspection in the participant's confidence in their imagery. For example:

(4.10) (01-18: E1/M)

```
1          (16.2)
2     P:   hh >some bit a trumpet music< I think it's louis armstrong
3          (4.9)
```

(4.11) (01-69: E2/M)

```
1          (6.8)
2     P:   train °agai:n° (2.7) >I think it's< (.) tha- japane:se (0.7) bulle:t- (0.2) °trai:n°
3          (8.6)
```

In these cases, the initial components of the imagery reports offer unmarked or un-modulated descriptions of, respectively, trumpet music and the re-appearance of imagery relating to a train. In the subsequent expansion of these images, both participants try to flesh out their sensation by offering specification of its character. The use of 'I think' formulations as prefaces to these specifications displays a degree of circumspection about their confidence in the accuracy or adequacy of these explanatory components.

Cognitive markers may also be used in turns that are designed to invite caution about the imagery. In extract 4.12, the initial component of the descriptive unit is 'I thought', thus framing what follows in such a way as to invite circumspection about its reliability or usefulness to the experiment, a quality which is underlined by the rising and 'self-questioning' intonation on the word 'face'.

(4.12) (01-42: E3/M)

```
1        (4.1)
2    P:  >I thou:ght- I sa:w a< face?
3        (24.9)
```

Furthermore, 'thinking' formulations often occur when participants report mentation imagery that is highly unlikely to be related to any stimulus materials they are meant to be parapsychologically sensing. For example, the first imagery in extract 4.13 concerns gaseous and changing imagery. This report is unmarked, in that there is no perceptual marker in their production. There is a silence of 17.2 seconds and then the participant speaks again.

(4.13) (01-91: E2/F)

```
1         (16.7)
2    P:   it's like lo:t's of smoke (1.4) °like a cross between° SMOke and CLOUds
3         (1.2) >kind've< continually changing shape
4         (17.2)
5    →    I'm thi:nking >that I< don't feel as relaxed as I ought t- be
6         (13.7)
7    →    thinking about my degree resu:lt (0.7) >whether I get- a< two=one or a
8         two=two:
9         (25.1)
10        (>ma:king of<) my ha:nds feel like I ca:n't mo:ve them
```

The two arrowed lines identify discrete imagery reports in the narrative. In the first, the participant refers to her bodily sensations at the time. This seems to be straightforward report of her ongoing experience or state of mind, as opposed to parapsychologically derived information about the target video clip. In the second, the participant (clearly a student volunteer) reports that she is contemplating her likely final degree result, and then elaborates this to reveal that she considers it likely that she will achieve one of two possible degree classifications (the 'two-one' and the 'two-two'). Again, it is highly improbable that any of the video clips in the database would refer to such a specifically individual and immediately relevant issue. Both these issues, then, seem to be personal matters, and likely to have a mundane and non-parapsychological provenance: how she feels right now given that she is meant to be in a relaxed state, everyday concerns and preoccupations of an undergraduate, and so on. These reports are framed by 'I'm thinking' formulations. (Relatedly: the partici-

pant's next utterance reports a feature of her current physical state, which
again is unlikely to reflect events in the target video clip. The initial component of this report is ambiguous, and the transcriber's best guess is
'making of'. But 'making of my hands' makes no sense; moreover, 'making' is similar to 'thinking, in that it shares the same number of syllables,
and the final syllable. It is at least possible, then, that this is a mispronunci-
ation – and mishearing – of 'thinking of'.)

Similar issue are at play in the following extract. Throughout the earlier
part of this mentation, prior to this sequence, the participant reports a
number of discrete images connected to vehicles that fly, specifically,
kites, hang gliders, and aeroplanes.

(4.14) (01-69: E2/M)

1		(7.5)
2	P:	m::: (0.5) m: dark (.) flickerin- li:ght in the ba:ck (2) candle
3		(19.9)
4	→	uh::::: thinking- I feel high as a ki:te- (1.7) very- relaxed
5		(9.5)
6		clou::ds (2.1) in a: (0.2) a re:d sky?

In the arrowed turn, the participant reports that he feels 'high as a kite'.
Given the predominance in his earlier mentation of objects which fly and
sensations of flight, this could be taken as more of that imagery. However,
he does two things to mark this as a report of his bodily and/or psychological state at the time. First, is in the previous extract, the participant frames
this experience by reporting it as something he is thinking. Subsequently
he adds that he is very relaxed, which explicitly indexes a current psychological state, and which thereby clearly disambiguates this reference to
'kite' from the other (more literal) uses throughout the mentation to refer
to sensations of flight.

A final use of 'thinking' formulations: in the next extract, the participant
is describing imagery connected to the work of a blacksmith, which then
develops to the activity of shoeing a horse. These images are unmarked.
But then the participant identifies a book she has read which was about
someone who was a blacksmith. Consequently, the content of the book –
and not the content of the target clip – could be the source of the imagery
she has been reporting.

(4.15) (01-52: E1/F)

1		(2.1)
2	P:	an a::: an a hammer? (0.8) and an anvil? (2.3) ((tutting sound)) (0.2) someone
3		beating a hamme:r (1.1) an- shoe:ing a ho:rse (4.4) same sort've thi:ng (0.8)
4		thinking of (1) A BOOK that I read thass (.) that's an idea (.) °that I'm

5   thinking of° (0.8) about (.) someone who: (2.6) °was a bla::cksmi:th°
6   (1)

The report of the book is marked in two ways. The word 'book' is produced at a volume noticeably greater than surrounding talk. In addition,
the participant states twice that he is thinking of this book. Participants can
thus use cognitive formulations as explicit doubt implicative markers, or
more subtly, to frame and imply the non-parapsychological origin of a
particular experience.

    In many cases, though, 'thinking' is generally positioned as an activity
in its own right, and participants can draw a distinction between cognitive
and perceptual markers.

(4.16) (01-91: E2/F)

((Mentation starts))
1   P: I:'m just seeing like a ball of fire in front of me >I'm not really thinking<
2   anything (0.3) ʰhhh
3   (9)
4   i*t looks like whe:n (1.3) the bomb went off at hiroshima (1.7) °like°
5   all of th- (0.9) a:ll the smoke going in the ai:r all the fire in the air

Here, the participant first reports seeing imagery and then immediately
after claims to be 'not thinking anything'. This degree of distinction
between 'seeing' and 'thinking' may occur even when the participant's
account implies a blurring of these two modalities. In the following
extract, for example, the participant initiates an imagery report with an
explicit claim that she is unable to see anything, but then goes on to formulate a report of imagery framed in terms of 'thinking'. This 'thinking' prefaced report has a vivid visual component.

(4.17) (01-52: E1/F)

1   (14.8)
2   P: ca:n't really see anythi:n- I'm (.) >s'rt've< (0.5) ʰhh I'm thinki::n- (.) about
3   viki:ngs (1.2) an- uh:: (0.2) battles? (1) people cha:rging at each othe:r
4   (1.1) on horse:s? (.) a:n- ah::: (1.1) a black ho:rse (1.3) with lots and lots
5   of hai:r (1.2) charging across the field (2.1) AN- um:: hhhh lots of tree:s
6   (.) gree:n tree:s (1.3) an- fie:lds (1.9) >s'rt've with< cloudy sky:
7   (2.1)

So while the report of 'thinki::n- (.) about viki:ngs (1.2) an- uh:: (.2) battles?'
(lines 2 and 3) represents generic categories of people and activities, as the
imagery report is developed, it contains stronger and stronger visual components, culminating in a report of the qualities of a specific horse and a
description of a setting which clearly presuppose perceptual acuity. This is

further illustrated by the longer sequence of mentation narrative from which the imagery report in extract 4.12 is drawn.

(4.18) (01-42: E3/M)

```
1         (7)
2    P:   I see: (1) loo:ks like si- ah:: STArs >or separate< do:ts
3         (2.9)
4         ((gulping sound))
5         (4.7)
6         (('lip smacking' sound, as in preparation about to speak))
7         (1)
8         everythi:ng's:: (.7) too va:gue
9         (3.4)
10        t'blAck: (5) >it's a< big ↑bla:ck obje:ct (3.3) i's:: s:: s:: su: filling out the
11        ↑red (3.2) >see:ms to be a: bi:g< black ma:ss
12        (6.6)
13        I do:n't seem to ha:ve any particula:r (0.2) thoughts or feelings? (3.6)
14        nothing that I: can pick up o:n
15        (11.4)
16        there's something at the left hand s↑ide (2.1) mo:ving a↑long (5.9) u-
17        hAhU (.) u- HHH (0.3) just an amorphou:s (1.5) °mass of sha:pes°
18        (4.1)
19        I thou:ght- I sa:w a face?
20        (24.9)
21        still no parti:cula:r thou:ghts
22        (4.8)
```

At line 2, the participant frames the mentation imagery purely in terms of visual perceptual markers, stating that he can 'see: (1) loo:ks like si- ah:: STArs >or separate< do:ts'. Whilst the next few items across lines 8 to 11 are also framed in terms of visually experienced imagery, despite the lack of any direct perceptual markers indicating sight, at lines 13 to 14 the participant delineates a different level of perceptual experience. In noting the absence of any cognitive and indeed, emotional experience ('I do:n't seem to ha:ve any particula:r (0.2) thoughts or feelings? (3.6) nothing that I: can pick up o:n') he indicates how he is categorising these varied perceptual experiences in different ways. Indeed, he specifically locates them as separate elements in his overall emotional experiences, since he subsequently goes on to imply visual movement across lines 16 to 17, explicit visual imagery at 12 (albeit qualified by the use of 'thought' in its function as a doubt implicative marker), before finally stating again that he is experiencing an absence of any specific cognitive imagery.

A sensitivity to the institutional context of the introspective report surfaces in a number of places in this extract. In lines 13 and 21 there are reports that the participant is experiencing no imagery (or no imagery striking enough to report at that moment). As we argued with respect to extract 4.9, reporting 'nothing to report' indexes its producer's understanding as to what counts as 'participating appropriately' in this kind of experiment. The claim in line 8 that 'everythi:ng's:: (0.7) too >va:gue<' offers an account for the absence of firm or detailed imagery; and as accounts occur when there is a departure from expected or projected actions, further supports the argument that the participant is operating with a normative understanding of his role in the experiment. There is a related, albeit more speculative point, in that the design of the talk across lines 13 and 14 may also display the participant's orientation to the wider context of his introspective account. A culturally available and 'common sense' account of the operation of psychic or parapsychological communication is that it is like a signal which the brain can detect in certain circumstances. Indeed, the development of the ganzfeld methodology, with its emphasis on mild sensory deprivation, was informed by anecdotal and experimental evidence that when brain activity is quietened, weak and otherwise unnoticeable psychic transmissions can be detected. This understanding of how parapsychological communication might work is enshrined in the title of one of the key early texts in parapsychology, Upton Sinclair's *Mental Radio* (1930). The participant's use of the metaphorical phrase 'nothing that I: can pick up o:n' depicts himself as a potential receiver of signals and thereby seems exquisitely designed to invoke wider publicly available assumptions about the likely mechanisms that underpin extransensorimotor information transfer (should it exist). Moreover, by identifying his failure to 'pick up on' signals, the participant provides an implicit account should he fail to identify the target video clip from the three decoys in the subsequent judging phase: his difficulty in identifying parapsychologically generated imagery is a consequence of *his* inability to detect it, and not because it does not exist. His imagery report thereby preserves the in-principle possibility of parapsychological communication, irrespective of the outcome of his specific experimental trial.

Visual and cognitive perceptual markers, then, do not merely capture the phenomenology of consciousness as it is experienced by the participant; they can be used to exhibit a stance towards, or particular appreciation of, the imagery or sensations being described. Moreover, it is clear that the stance or appreciation so exhibited may be informed by the participants' understanding of the broader goals of the experimental context in which the mentations are produced. We explore this further in the next section, in which we examine how participants display a stance towards the content of the consciousness in the way that their imagery reports are produced.

Resources in managing epistemic uncertainty

In extract 4.19, the subject describes imagery concerning a drill. During this report, he produces an exclamation, 'oh', with a marked rising or 'questioning' intonation (indicated by the use of a question mark).

(4.19) (01-18: E1/M)

```
1          (15.5)
2    P:    ˙hh it's in slow motion like a::, (0.6) ˙hh oh? i's: like a drill like a:, (1.4) ˙h I
3          see the threads of a drill spinning roun:d.
4          (5.0)
```

The question marked 'oh' occurs in a report with three discrete components. The initial component is a report of movement, 'it's in slow motion', which presumes an as-yet unstated object. There is an attempt to convey what the imagery is like, 'like a drill', which is prefaced by the question-marked 'oh'. Finally, there is a report of how this imagery appeared in consciousness: 'I see the threads of a drill spinning roun:d'. Three-partedness is a culturally available and normatively expected feature of listing and descriptive practices in a range of discursive contexts, such as conversational interaction (Jefferson, 1990), political rhetoric (Atkinson, 1984) and advertising materials (Drew, 2006). There are two features of three-parted organisations that are relevant here. Lists composed of three parts intuitively feel complete, almost satisfyingly so. (In this paragraph there is part of a sentence that illustrates the contexts in which three part lists have been found to operate, which, as it cites 'conversation', 'rhetoric' and 'advertising', is itself a three part list. Two examples would feel incomplete; additional examples would be redundant and render the sentence increasingly inelegant.) Related to this, studies have shown that three-part lists can be used to indicate a general quality common to the items in the list. It is a way of marking some commonality between the objects or events so described, (Jefferson, 1990). With respect to the section from extract 4.19, the three parted construction works to establish that the discrete items — 'movement', 'drill', and 'a drill spinning' are references to the same event in consciousness.

The question-marked 'oh' makes a particular contribution to the sense that there is a single phenomenological entity occupying conscious awareness. Heritage (1984b) has analysed the use of 'oh' in conversational materials and found that it is a 'change of state' news receipt token on the part of the speaker. However, this is not a claim that this particle is a public display of some real change at a cognitive or mental level. As Heritage observes, there are occasions when news is reported, or informings occur, but which are not marked with 'oh' receipts. For example, in medical consultations and news interviews, one participant will inform another on some matter, but these kinds of interaction are distinctive because of the *absence* of 'oh' particles (Heritage, 1984b: 336; see also Heritage, 2005). This strongly suggests that the use of 'oh' is informed by interactional contingencies of relevance to particular social contexts. In extract 4.19, the three part construction of the descriptive cluster incrementally establishes the sense that there is one determinate image or sensation manifesting in the participant's consciousness. In this context, the question-marked 'oh' change of state token does particular work, as it acts as a public display of 'coming to realize'; in this case, 'coming to realize what something was all along'.

Question-marked intonation is routinely used to register participant doubt or caution about the parapsychological relevance of their imagery or sensations. In the following extract, question-marked intonation occurs with respect to a longer segment of talk.

(4.20) (01-18. E1/M)

```
1           (11.0)
2    P:   >feel like< I'm much bigger:, (.) feel like °I'm:° (0.3) ˙h >hundred foot<
3           tall >u- feel< °u:::° (0.2) ˙hh my hands feel so light that they're very
4           heavy (6.7) >feel like there's uh< like I'm inflated from::. eh ˙hh
5           I'm:: >s't've< one big balloo::n
6           (21.5)
7           ˙hhh feel a bit of a pain in my lower stoma:ch, (.) like >my
8           lower gut< (5.6) °u: yu-° feel like I'm:, ˙hhh e:r:::
9    →    >could be something< like aeroplane:? t- uh,
10          (58.8)
11          now I manage to- (1.4) l- leave my body a bit (2.3) uh bu- I feel
12   →    less:, (.) u- inside my head (5.3) begin to feel s'r'ta higher?
13          (35.8)
14          I'm going upwards
15          (13.0)
```

There are two (arrowed) cases in these descriptive clusters: 'could be something like aeroplane:? and 'begin to feel s'r'ta higher?'. These components of the imagery description share some common properties, and perform similar tasks.

They are, first, in what may termed terminal position, in that they are the last component of the descriptive cluster. There is no further talk on that imagery; there follows a lengthy period of silence, and when the participant speaks again, they begin to report a different set of experiences. They are, then, devices by which description of a discrete imagery may be concluded. Second, both question-marked components seem to be touched off by some difficulty or dysfluency in the prior stretch of talk. So, in the first case, the talk prior to the question marked component is abandoned in mid-production, and the utterance 'could be something like aeroplane:?' is introduced with a speeded up delivery. In the second case, the report of the imagery is marked by perturbations and dysfluency; there are words cut off, attempts to describe the experience are launched but then abandoned mid-production, and there is notable fluctuation in the tempo of the delivery. It is in the context of this what may be termed a troubled report that the question-marked component is produced. In conversation analytic terms, the question-marked components are self-repairs (Schegloff *et al.*, 1977) on ongoing utterances. Finally, in both cases, self-referential pronouns ('I' and 'me') are absent. We may note that they may be *designedly* absent, insofar as there are personal references in the immediately preceding stretches of talk. So, for example, in the first case, the participant reports a pain in 'my lower gut'; and in the second case, there are several uses of the pronoun 'I'. The talk prior to the question-marked components then clearly exhibits the participant's perspective, or invokes his agency (for example, in trying to understand the experience being described). Yet this personal perspective is deleted in the question-marked components, and there is no reference to 'I' or 'me'. This absence is conspicuous in the second case, in that the clause 'begin to feel s'r'ta higher?' strongly implies the subject normally identified by a pronoun. The absence of a personal reference is in marked contrast to the last component of the prior cluster, in which the participant states declaratively the nature of his experience, and in which there is an explicit first person reference.

We propose that, in conjunction with a questioning intonation, deleting reference to personal agency is a discursive practice by which participants may establish a position of neutrality with respect to the content of a discrete report by which they attempt to clarify or convey the nature of their experience.

Why might a question-marked intonation be used for these particular descriptions? We offer some tentative observations. In the two cases from extract 4.20, the participant has been reporting on his experience of his own consciousness. In doing this, he is in a position of epistemic authority: we have rights to speak authoritatively on our inner experience. The talk in the question-marked components, however, constitutes a shift in focus. There is a move away from private experience ('what it is like in my mind at this moment'), and toward a characterisation of that imagery that draws from *everyday* or *publicly available* experiences (the bodily sensations encountered in aeroplane travel; the sense of elevation). This may be one basis for the subtle downgrading of epistemic certainty established by question-marked intonation.

Before we conclude this section, it is useful to demonstrate that these design features may be recurrent. The following cases come from later in the same mentation.

(4.21) (01-18: E1/M)

```
1            (9.8)
2     P:    I c'n see: a bal- it's like I'm flying over, (1.3) flying over a big canyon
3            no:w (0.6) ʰhh there:'s more like a valley I c'n see::, ʰh it's not a river
4            I can see s'rt've um::, (0.3) towns 'n (.) ʰh houses and a lot °of.° (1.1) by
5            flyin' above the:: uh:::: the level of the: (0.3) ʰhh hhh
6      →    it reminds me of u: miser verde?
7            (13.1)
8            mice:. >something< ʰhh (.) u-yes I >s'rt've<
9            can't've quite make it out
10     →    °u: u:° maybe 's that's why it makes you think of mice:?
11           (49.1)
12           a::nd >nicki< waiting ((continues))
```

Briefly: both (arrowed) question-marked components are in terminal position; they both occur in turns in which there is some expressed difficulty in describing the imagery, or a degree of dysfluency and perturbation in the prior speech stream; and in both, the agency of the subject is minimised, either via report of being (passively) reminded of something, or reporting that imagery makes 'you' think of mice; that is, it is a characterisation anyone might have arrived at given the nature of the imagery being reported.

Discussion

Introspective narratives have an unavoidably epistemic orientation, in that they report what is known to be occurring in consciousness (or what is claimed or thought to be happening), and how it is known. Ostensibly, they publicly exhibit private psychological phenomena and processes. Our analyses, however, suggest that epistemic talk may be used to address a range of pragmatic tasks relevant to the institutional setting of a parapsy-

chology experiment. For example, perceptual markers can be used to perform a range of activities: they exhibit a constructive property, in that they
are constitutive of the nature of the experience for which they stand as
(ostensibly neutral) reports. They can be used to depict the ongoing, live
nature of the imagery reported during the mentation narrative, or to
amend descriptions so that new information is made available. They are
vehicles via which participants can display or disavow personal agency in
relation to the appearance of the imagery; and they can be used to mark
circumspection about the participants' confidence in the imagery, or
indeed, its likely origin, which in turn bears on the parapsychological significance of the imagery being reported. Furthermore, perceptual markers
can be mobilised to allow participants to display their understanding of
the requirements of 'appropriate' or 'helpful' behaviour in this kind of setting. Thus reports of 'not seeing anything' are not mere reports of the
absence of imagery: they index awareness that, for example, participants
should continuously attend to their consciousness, as required by the protocol of the experiment. They can also be used to point to a sophisticated
awareness of the broader concerns of the ganzfeld methodology, in that
they exhibit sensitivity to the potential parapsychological significance of
the absence of imagery. In various ways then, the production of the
mentation narrative can exhibit the participants' tacit appreciation of the
institutional or work-related goals of the setting, common sense or culturally available understandings of the way that parapsychological cognition
may work, and the behavioural expectations incumbent upon volunteers
in (para)psychological experiments.

While these observations raise issues that will be revisited in subsequent empirical chapters, we conclude this discussion by sketching one
key issue: the implications of these findings for our understanding of
demand characteristics.

The concept of demand characteristics illuminates the ways in which the
research participant may try to infer the experimenter's reasons for asking
them to perform certain tasks, and will therefore consciously or uncon-
sciously amend their behaviour accordingly, thus producing potentially
robust experimental artefacts unconnected to the variables the experiment
was designed to study (Orne, 1962). The implications of the effects of
demand characteristics have not been fully explored or embraced in experimental psychology. This is perhaps because their consequences are
potentially far reaching and may radically change how we view experimental procedures. They arise from the participant's interactions with
parameters of the context of the experiment: their interpretation of experimenter's instructions, their understanding of the role of the experimental
participant, and so on. And all experiments will take place in some form of
context. Every experimental procedure, then, provides the seeds for the

emergence of robust artefacts that are independent of the variables and hypotheses the experiment was designed to explore. Taking account of the omnipresence of demand characteristics may significantly challenge accepted interpretations of evidence from experimental research, as well forcing a wholesale re-evaluation of the value of the experiment as a research tool in psychological investigations. Orne's work on demand characteristics focused on the impact of role expectations and subtle cues in experimental procedures. But the analyses presented here point to an extension of the concept to include the discursive and interactional procedures that underpin any social setting, including the formal institutional setting of the experimental laboratory. We propose that the discursive constitution of conscious imagery is a demand characteristic of the setting, in that the design of participants' reports is tacitly informed by their understanding of the requirements and expectations associated with the context in and for which they are produced. This, in turn, has implications for our understanding of the concept of demand characteristics, which we explore further in the final chapter.

Chapter Five

Silence and its management

As we have noted, a routine feature of the mentation narratives is that participants will leave sometimes lengthy periods of silence between discrete imagery reports. This is a puzzle, for two reasons.

As we outlined in chapter three, the mentation narrative is a very important part of the ganzfeld procedure. Therefore, during the pre-experiment briefing, the participants are explicitly encouraged to report out loud any images, sensations, feelings and thoughts that come to conscious attention during the sending period. We can find empirical evidence for this encouragement. On two occasions in the present corpus, the experimenter activates the intercom to speak directly to the participant. In both cases, the experimenter clearly reiterates previous encouragement to report comprehensively on conscious sensations and mental imagery. In extract 5.1, the participant's first recorded contribution directly solicits the experimenter's help; in the second case, the experimenter intervenes when it becomes apparent that the participant may be unclear about what is required of him.

(5.1) (01-46: E3/M)

```
1    P:   doctor wilson do I gi- you my impressions now?
2         (1.6)
3    E:   eh yes >yeah< just say whatever's coming to mind and that'll
4         be fi:ne (0.4) [ (please)
5    P:                  [ pardon?
6         (0.6)
7    E:   'h yes now now's the time to do it just say whatever's coming to mind
8    P:   okay
9    E:   okay?
```

(5.2) (01-31:E3/F)

```
1    P:   ((gulping sound)) (3.7) m:: (11.7) ↑hm (6.3) ((gulping sound))
2         (20.6)
```

3   P: ((*gulping sound*))
4   (3.3)
5   P: can't-=really see=a:nythi:n-
((*Some lines omitted – no descriptions offered*))
9   P: ʰh I'm- still not getting' any fixed image:s
10   (6.2)
((*Electronic clicking sound and experimenter comes on the line*))
11   E: ʰhhhh (0.6) Tre:vor >just to no:te< tha:t's oh: ka:y you don't ha:ve to
12   get anything that's li:ke a a full blown imag:e: uh: j'st go ahead er
13   just comment on er ʰhhh any kind've impressions that're coming
14   t- mi:nd even if they're they're really very ↑vague and there's no,
15   specific ima:ge to it: or even anythi:ng that ↑you ↓know kind've: y-
16   you find yourself: er:: thinking abou:t (.) that's all fair game it doesn't
17   have to be er >any- any< kind've really (.) specific uh visual °image?°

In extract 5.1, in response to the participant's query as to when to start describing his impressions, the experimenter states that he should report 'whatever comes to mind'. And in extract 5.22, in a rather lengthier set of instructions as to what is required of the participant, the experimenter stresses that every kind of imagery or impression merits description. The experimental procedure, then, explicitly encourages participants to report *any* conscious experience – imagery, thoughts, impressions – during the sending period.

Explicit instructions and invitations to report fully their experiences should encourage extensive participant description. But reflections on *what* is being reported should give us even greater confidence that participants would provide a flowing, continuous account of their experiences. This is because they are describing their consciousness and its contents.

Writing in 1890, William James captured the essential phenomenal reality of human existence: that consciousness of some sort goes on; and that what he called states of mind succeed each other, that is, each personal consciousness is continuous, and, crucially for our purposes, that consciousness is *attentional*: it is interested in some parts of the world to the exclusion of others (James, 1890). These intuitively self-evident observations hold true today, as contemporary philosophical investigations recognise that even transitory states of consciousness hold some attentional focus (Bailey, 2000). Being conscious, then, is to be conscious *of* something.

So, in an environment in which participants are explicitly encouraged to report on their ongoing and continuous phenomenal reality (and, indeed, in which other sensory distractions are minimised), we might expect an ongoing and continuous report. It is for this reason that periods of silence are unexpected and, therefore, analytically interesting.

Our analysis reflects the study of pragmatic and context-sensitive functions served by silence in linguistics, sociolinguistics and the ethnography of communcation (Basso, 1972; Bruneau, 2008; Jaworski, 1993; Jaworski and Stephens, 1998; Jensen, 1973; Johannesen, 1974; Maltz, 1985; Nakane, 2008; Poland and Pederson, 1998). Specifically, though, we adopt the position from conversation analytic research, in which absences of talk are understood in relation to the sequential context in which they occur, and also in relation to the jointly produced courses of interpersonal actions of which they are a part (for example, Drew 1989; Fox, Hayashi and Jasperson, 1996; Heritage, 1984a: 275-282; Jefferson, 1989; Sacks *et al.*, 1974; Schegloff, Koshik, Jacoby and Olsber, 2002; Sorjonen, 1996). The focus on the situated orientation of silence derives from some of Harvey Sacks' observations on pauses (Sacks, 1992). He explicitly identifies the importance of discourse structures and normative patterns in examining pauses. So, when considering pauses when people are spelling out the letters of a person's name, he argues that 'how what a pause does is a function of what sort of structure is being produced or intended' (Sacks, 1992, Vol. I: 784); and further, 'in order to know what a pause is doing, one is attentive to the structure within which the pause is being produced' Sacks, 1992, Vol. I: 785). Moreover, he observes that pacing in conversational activity such as story telling — and the momentary pauses that may subsequently arise — may be bound by norms and expectations; and that 'pacing rules might constitute quite powerful normative techniques on their own' (Sacks, 1992, Vol. I: 722). Our analyses of the function of silences in these introspective reports draw from Sacks' observations, and focus on robust structural discursive practices, and the normative frameworks they exhibit.

We begin by developing further an observation from an earlier chapter: that the periods of silence between discrete reports are routine, regardless of the detail or extensiveness of the participants' imagery reports. Second, we argue that continuations of discrete imagery after a lengthy pause are extremely rare; and that when they do occur, participants do particular kinds of work to establish that continuation is occurring, thereby displaying a normative assumption that further talk after a lengthy silence is likely to be heard as a report of new imagery. Third, we consider evidence that the inter cluster gaps may be organised to a weakly patterned personal metric for the duration of silences; in particular, we consider cases where participants report that 'there is nothing to report', and examine whether these utterances may be ways of marking the tolerance limit (Jefferson, 1989) for periods of appropriate or normatively acceptable silence in this context.

The routine character of inter utterance silence

Short descriptions of imagery are common in the data, as illustrated by extracts 5.3 and 5.4, which are taken from different participants' narratives. (Extract 5.3 comes from the start of the respective narrative; the sequence in extract 5.4 comes towards the end.)

(5.3) (01-09: E3/M)

```
1     P:    heat (1.7) melting
2           (26.0)
3           deep and distant
4           (7.7)
5           uniform
6           (34.5)
7           da::rk shadow.
8           (38.7)
9           wa:ves
10          (69.0)
11          deep (.) dark (0.5) tunnel
12          (41.8)
13          s:pots of light,
14          (69.4)
15          ho:le.
16          (102.0)
17          ever decreasing circles
18          (36.8)
19          (tk) °s:pace°
20          (58.9)
21          stroking, (7.1) soft
22          (77.1)
23          bubble, (.) clo:ud
24          (19.8)
25          diffuse
26          (40.5)
27          shadows an eclipse °scene.°
28          (76.6)
            ((continues))
```

Some silences are similar to those found in everyday interaction. For example, the report of 'deep (.) dark (0.5) tunnel (line 11) is punctuated by pauses of the kind that can intersperse clausal, phrasal or sentential turn construction units (Sacks *et al.*, 1974). Similarly, participants may report a series of images that are developed from or touched off by an initial image or sensation. In these cases, gaps between items may not be excessive, as in the first imagery reported, '<u>heat</u> (1.7) melting'. What is clear, though, is that silences between discrete reports are routinely considerably longer than periods of silence in conversational discourse. Moreover, they are routinely longer than intra utterance periods of verbal inactivity.

Reports of conscious experience in this fragment are produced after some considerable periods of silence, some of which last over a minute. This is a general characteristic of this participant's mentation. However, despite these lengthy periods of verbal inactivity, the overhearing experimenter does not initiate communication with the participant to assist, offer encouragement, or inquire as to the participant's well being, actions which would demonstrate the experimenter's understanding that the silences reflect some difficulty on the part of the participant, and which thereby constitute some problem to the procedure. The absence of trouble oriented experimenter intervention implicitly recognises that the distinctive temporal attenuation of the participant's reports is unaccountable.

Inter utterance silences are not always so extended.

(5.4)(01-69: E2/M)

```
1         (33.2)
2    P    a black (.4) cloa:k (1.8) blowing in the wi:nd (1.8) s'rt've o:ld
3         (2.8) hhh hangman's tree:: °s'rt've thi:ng° (1) cloak's hanging from it
4         (14.8)
5         °train agai::n°
6         (8.6)
7         people in hard ha::ts (4.2) writing °on the ha:ts°
8         (19.2)
9         big lo:bster
10        (13.6)
11        °a:nd a::° (1) >a man and woman again walking in a pa:rk (3) °I:'ve
12        seen this before° (0.8) punt- in the backgrou:nd<
13        (8.6)
14        ah::::: (2.1) an art gallery: (0.2) >I visited on my honeymoon<
15        (3.8)
16        °a:::° lassie >looks just like a picture in the gallery:< (5.2) °uh: lookin' out°
17        (7)
18        uh looking up at the sta:rs
```

19   (15.7)
20   planets:::
21   (13.5)
22   °tram ca:r°
23   (23.5)
24   u:::m (1.5) wondering when this'll e:nd (1.6) I see: (1) °uh° doctor
25   battersby in the roo:m (7.1) °uh° (.) see lots of her equipmen:- (0.3)
26   ha:nd reaching for i:-
27   (14.4)
28   hh hot- air balloo:n (6.1) re::d (0.4) an- yello:w
29   (18)
30   f::ootstep::ps (2.5) °on a::° (.) a roa:d (2.6) °can hear them clicki:ng °
31   (22.5)
32   s::: (.) °stimpy: from (.) ren and stimpy:°
          ((continues))

Silences throughout the mentation from which this extract is taken are
considerably shorter than those illustrated in extract 5.3. This is tentative
evidence that, while participants recognise that it is appropriate to leave
sustained periods of verbal inactivity between reports of discrete experiences, the length of these periods of silence may vary between participants. There may be, then, idiosyncratic realizations of what counts as
appropriate participation in the production of the introspective narrative.

So far we have examined extracts from mentations in which participants
produce relatively short descriptions of discrete experiences. But even in
mentations composed of more extensive reports, it is routine to observe
lengthy silences between discrete imagery. Consider extracts 5.5 and 5.6,
the first of which comes from the start of the mentation period.

(5.5) (01-82:E1/M)

((Mentation starts))
1   P: the first thing I notice is- (0.3) um:: (0.6) for a start that my body doesn't (.)
2   feel (1.3) quite as though I'm sitting in a chai::r it- (1) it's as though
3   my ar:ms feel thi:s (0.4) u h::: they were :: (0.7) the other way up (0.2)
4   than they we:re (0.4) to start off wi:th (.) >and bu- I'm I'm< not
5   >sort've< sitting in the same positio:n (1.5) that (.) almost as though it e:
6   (0.5) the feeling that you might get if you're sort've (0.5) drifting in space
7   (20.3)
8   there seems to be some sort've:: (.) i:mpression of:: (0.3) um:: (1.3)
9   I mean maybe it's the >it's the< noi:se >that's reminding me of the
10   sea: but s'rt've (0.8) sitting on a :: a- a- a- cliff on on on the top of a
11   hi:ll an- (1.3) not so much (.4) hearing the sea as >j'st s'rt've< (0.4) staring
12   out at a big expanse of of of sea

13   (70.2)
14   someho:w I get the jdea of a lot've (0.5) uh: colours (0.2) °uh I
15   don't kno:w° (2.3) u::::: I don't know what colours or anything but
16   s'rt've<u::: >or whatever the other they're reasonably< (.) bri:ght (0.3)
17   >they're not< um::: (3) s-s- s'rt've u m::: (1.5) °u:::° (.)
18   psychedelic >they're not u m::: (.5) >°they're not°< natural (1.4)
19   °° u:::°° (.) something like on a:::: (.)° a::° (.)° a::° (0.4) ° a::° (.)
20   >s'rt've< (0.3) ° a::° (0.7) ˙hhh unreal like a gamesho:w or something
21   or: or: °um:::° (2) o :n the:se (.) these adverts (0.3) ° u::°
22   (45.6)
23   >I: also: get the impression of< (.7) feeli:ng (.6) um:: (.3) qui:te-
24   o:pposi:te s'rt've (0.2) ˙hhh (feeluh) isolated a::as th ou:gh (0.3) u::m
25   (2.7) >I dunno< u::::: (.) very diffcre:nt as as though you:: you're in a
26   a (0.6) yu:: u:: (0.2) big long tunnel o:r:: (0.2) ˙hhh (0.2) in an ice cave or
27   something like that where where:: (0.4) n: n-n-not- that- (0.4) you:'re the
28   only one that- (0.7) just that there's< ˙hhhh (0.7) ° u::° (0.2) you're
29   surrounded by: (0.2) by: (1.6) ° u::m° (0.7) ° u::° (0.2) somethi:ng
30   something very big (.) u::m (0.5)˙° u:m° (0.8) something tha- you
31   can't tou:ch (.) °maybe :: (.) that sort've thing°
32   (20.7)
33   I'm also: getti:ng
          ((continues))

This illustrates common feature of the more extended reports. The first
component of the utterance establishes a topic that is then developed;
either the participant offers sustained reflection on that imagery (such as
in the report over lines 14 to 21), or describes changes to their imagery,
such that they act as a 'ring side' reporter documenting the ongoing
changes in their consciousness. This latter form of imagery development is
illustrated in lines 10 onwards of the following extract, in which an initial
report of abstract shapes ends with a report of a washing line via successive reports of a doorway, a tunnel, travelling through the tunnel, being in
a room, seeing a mask in the room on which there is a tick, and then a grid
such as those found in mathematics exercise books.

(5.6) (01-52: E1/F)

1   (14.4)
2   P: an- (0.2) ((sound of mouth opening)) (0.7) fingernai:ls (0.8) bi:g (0.3)
3   fingernails holdi:n- (3) holding a metal rod °of some sort° (.) but it was a
4   co:ffee bean a minute ago (.) an- it turned into a red fingernai:l (3.1)
5   we:ll (0.5) °uh-u° (0.7) I think tha- (0.5) °that's the° thing I ma:de (0.2) i:s
6   (0.5) °is° (0.2) fingers (1) brown finge:rs (2.1) °↑stu-a-↑stuck in the::
7   (1.5) °in a:° (0.6) in the cla:y (4.8) li:ke (0.6) rollin' round (.) round on their

8   finge:rs
9   (21.1)
10   j'st seein' uh:::: (0.2) abstact sha:pes (2.3) and a doorway (0.5) ˙hhhh UH
11   (.) ri:gh- (0.7) °it's° throu:gh a big tunnel (0.7) an- I'm::: going past
12   someo:ne (0.9) and it's really dark but it's sunny at either end (0.5) °a::n-
13   I've just° >come outta tunnel and I'm coming up to some really big
14   doors< (1.1) a:n- °uh-° (1) right (0.4) the:y're (.) they're >opening and
15   I'm goin- i:n< ˙hhh (0.3) a:nd (0.2) I'm in a big roo:m (0.3) a:nd (.) there is
16   this like circular (1.6) a:nd (0.8) 'n the:re's a ma:sk (1.7) AN a big tick (.)
17   on the mask (1.5) like (.) correc- tick (1.5) ˙hh (0.5) hhh an- a grid (.) lik-
18   like in a maths boo:k (4.2) and a washing line (1.1) heh hhh ˙hh hhh
19   (h)hm:: (1.8) hhhh ach: I dunno
20   (36.2)
21   hhhh I keep getting- this pictu:re (1.4) like an i- (2.4) it FLAshes alo:ng
         ((continues))

Participants may thus extend an initial report in such a way as to embellish the topic in turn initial position so that the terminal stages of the report seem to be describing new imagery. Participants may note the degree of topic shift. For example, in lines 18 and 19, the short spate of laughter seems to acknowledge the incongruity of the eventual imagery of the washing line.

While the ostensible topic of a report may shift in extended descriptions, it is, though, extremely unusual to find topically discrete imagery reported contiguously within an utterance.

In this experimental setting, participants are asked to provide a full report on ongoing imagery and sensations to which only they have access. Despite the institutional license to provide extended — or, indeed, continuous — accounts of conscious experience, there are extended periods of silence. Moreover, these periods of verbal inactivity are massively present in the majority of mentation narratives; moreover, experimenters do not intervene and topicalise silences as problems, either for the participant or the experiment. There is, then, in this institutional context, a social organisation for the production of introspective data that is largely independent of the inner mental experiences the experiment is designed to capture. We may speculate as to the origins of this organisation, given that a key feature — saying nothing — is precisely what is *not* required by the experiment.

The mentation narrative is produced under unusual circumstances. Setting aside the pre-experimental induction of a relaxed state of mind, and the mild sensory deprivation, there is a non-participating but overhearing experimenter. So, although the design of the mentation can not be said to be fully interactional, in that turns are not designed to be responsive to a co-interactant's prior turns, the mere presence of an (albeit) inactive co-participant means that, as Schegloff has described it, an interactional *dimension* is 'inescapable' (Schegloff, 2002:152).

This interactional dimension may be relevant in two ways. During the mentation narrative the overhearing experimenter is taking a hand written record of what the participant says. The participants are told that this will be happening in the pre-experiment briefing. It is possible that the periods of silence arise as a consequence of the participants withholding further talk to allow the experimenter to complete his or her record of the immediately prior report, and may, therefore, display their understanding of the institutional role of the experimenter. Relatedly, the extended periods of silence may work pragmatically to demonstrate 'proper' or appropriate participation. Periods of silence clearly demarcate the cessation of one set of images and the onset of others. They manage the mentation narrative so that its products are recognisable as discrete phenomenal events. This displays an orientation to one of the key design features of the experiment: participants know that, in another room, another experimenter is mentally projecting *specific* images from a video clip (as opposed to the *entire* clip), and in the later phase of the experiment the participant attempts to identify the clip based on his or her imagery. The absence of continuous description thereby ensures that what is reported may more closely match the way in which the participants understand how the target video materials might impinge in their consciousness if extra sensory processes are in fact occurring. In this, orientation to the broader institutional arrangements of the context in which the mentation is produced is constitutive of precisely the experiences those arrangements were designed to facilitate or elicit.

Establishing continuation of imagery reports post-silence

Just as there are few cases of topically discrete reports produced contiguously within an utterance, so too are there few cases where the participant returns to prior imagery after a period of silence. When this does happen, the post silence turn in which an earlier topic is continued is designed in such a way as to suggest that participants are sensitive to some minor normative breach constituted by that turn. In extract 5.7, the participant reports hearing a piece of music which is (tentatively) identified (line 2). There is then a silence of nearly ten seconds, which is commensurate with silences in this narrative that mark topically discrete imagery reports.

When the participant speaks again, he revisits the topic of the piece of music.

(5.7) (01-18: E1/M)

```
1        (13.0)
2    P:  °m-° (.) piece of tchaikovsky's fifth symphony:: (1.7) ·h I think, (2.0) yeah?
3        (9.7)
4        >another °piece of the° same symphony:< °hh roof (0.6) BEAMS (.)
5        >GIRders a< roof:: (0.9) ·hh um, seeing it from underneath:: the white roof
6        with black (.) black bea:ms: (0.2) like top've a::: (.) barn (2.6) a horse:
7        (59.5)
8        >°uh something° >I can't quite make out< °uh° like a u:- u:- u::
9        °>th- th- th's a<° tee shape
         ((continues))
```

Immediately after reporting that he can hear another section of the music identified in the pre silence utterance, there is a short intake of breath and then a new topic of a 'roof' is introduced. This topic is developed throughout this utterance as the participant reports various aspects of, or associations with the roof, eventually culminating in a report of a barn and then a horse. What is happening here, then, is that the revisiting of a prior topic intrudes into the report of new imagery. It is noticeable that the turn initial item in this utterance, the reference to the music reported previously, is rushed relative to the immediately prior talk, and the subsequent imagery report. The hasty manner in which this business is done displays the participant's awareness of the inauspiciousness of its placement in turn space in which new imagery should be reported. The pronunciation of the two words that articulate the new 'roof' related imagery might also display the participant's sensitivity to the departure from normal proceedings. The first word, 'roof' is emphasized, and then the words 'beam' and 'girders' are entirely or partially vocalised louder than surrounding talk (this participant speaks more loudly on only one other occasion in a full mentation narrative, the transcript of which extends to five single spaced pages). In these turn design features, then, we see evidence of the participant's orientation to a form of procedural requirement underpinning the temporal placement of reports of new imagery.

In the previous extract, an old topic intruded into a post silence utterance in which, overwhelmingly, new topics are reported. In the following case, the post silence utterance is entirely addressed to the topic of the prior utterance. There is, then, no intrusion of one topic into the report of the next. Yet even here, the post silence turn displays design features that orient to and address the minor normative breach of procedure in resuming reports of imagery after a topic terminal period of silence. In extract 5.8

the participant progresses through various images and sensations: a kitchen, birds, and trees. Between the reports of the first two items, and the first report of tree related imagery, he leaves silences of 67.3, 64 and 15.2 seconds.

(5.8)(01-25: E1/M)

```
1           (68.5)
2     P:    °(tk) m:° kitchen:
3           (67.3)
4           °hh° mo:(h)re:, (.) vague impressions of birds
5           (64.0)
6           tree::s °an-° (8.7) °(h)u:m:° (1.5) tree::s a:nd a kind've: (.) palm tree:
7           (0.6) °° ˙hh°° °h(h)um(hhh)::° (4.1) or:: (.) f-firs °mebbe:,°
8           (15.2)
9     →     ((swallows)) °yea(h)m hh° ˙hh pine, (.) pine tree::s or °>something<°
10          (2.4) u:rm, °m::::° (1.0) looking up to the ↑sk(hh)y:
11          (19.8)
```

Although shorter than the preceding two silences, the silence of 15.2 seconds in line 8 is in the range of inter utterance silences in this participant's mentation narrative (for example, the next seven inter utterances gaps after the one shown in line 10 last 15.3, 49.5, 10, 18.2, 7.0 and 8.9 seconds). After this silence, however, he returns to the topic of trees, and reflects further on the kind of tree in his imagery. However, his resumption of this topic is marked. After an audible gulping (arrowed, line 9, which is common throughout this narrative), the subsequent turn initial component is a very softly spoken articulation of 'yeah', followed by the naming of the kind of tree. The 'yeah' here has a responsive quality, and given that there is no interlocutor, the verbalised response can be heard as being directed to some internal sensation or imagery. It is epistemically loaded, in that it claims a change in the state of knowledge (Heritage, 1984b), in this case, an emergent certainty, a 'coming to realise what something was all along', or 'achieving clearer perception or understanding'. This epistemic function of 'yeah' is particularly clear in the following extract in which the participant is reporting the imagery of geometric shapes.

(5.9)(01-18: E1/M)

```
1           (8.2)
2     P:    °u- u-° (.) angles: now u::::: th'r s'rt've (2.5) yeah triangles (.) ˙hhh little
3           triangles a bit like I'm flying through:: (.) triangles (6.6) °u-° very close
4           together °bu- th:°
5           (21.2)
```

In extract 5.9, the internally directed, self-responsive 'yeah' portrays the participant as 'coming to realise' the precise nature of his imagery. This display of 'coming to realise' stands as a change of state marker with respect to the prior topic of the mentation, and as such, warrants its resumption.

To return to the mentation narrative featured in extract 5.8. In this narrative there is only one other instance of the use of 'yeah' or 'yes' in turn initial position in this narrative, and it exhibits very similar properties to this instance. (At this stage in the mentation, the inter utterance pauses are relatively short, approaching on the length of silences routinely found in conversational interaction.)

(5.10) (01-25:E1/M)

```
1          (2.9)
2     P:   shells (0.5) shell tunnels
3          (2.0)
4          a(u)m:, °m:::° ((swallows)) person: face:: (.) (h)um:, °.hh° r:elation (.)
5          friend?
6          (1.4)
7          °m::° um::::, °h ˙h° (0.4) sun ha:ze: (0.3) °m::: on° (.) on fi:lm
8          (3.1)
9          °m:: s'rt've° a(u)m: (0.5) reflecsh- (.) reflective °sort've° spectrum
10         thing
11         (3.4)
12         °m:° u(h)m::,
13         (4.3)
14         ye:ah (.) looking into the sun (1.8) um::? >quite a< sma:ll sun?
15         (1.4) >but< a::, °m:::::° s:plit out >by a< (1.6) by a le:ns
16         (12.1)
```

In line 7 the participant reports visual imagery of a sun haze in film. In line 9 this is continued as he tries to clarify his imagery; there is a further resumption in lines 14 and 15, in which he explicitly refers to the sun again. This resumption is again marked by the production of a 'coming to realise' display via the use of 'yeah'. It is interesting to note that the resumption of the topic in line 9 is also marked. There is a short hesitation and then the turn initial component is a contraction of 'sort of' followed by a longer hesitation marker, thereby projecting that the topic of the prior utterance was not concluded.

The data we have examined so far suggest that participants orient to the topic terminal character of their silences; such that, specific practical work is required to warrant the resumption of that topic after such a silence.

This would suggest that there is an inferential sensitivity to the pacing and placement of imagery reports in these experimental conditions.

'Nothing to report' reports and evidence of personal metrics

In the previous chapter we noted that, on occasions, participants will report that they are experiencing no imagery and, therefore, at that moment there is nothing to report. In the following two cases, participants report no visual imagery. For example:

(5.11)(01-28: E2/F)

P: I can't see anything.

(5.12)(01-41: E1/F)

P: >I do:n't< see anything right ↑now

There is something analytically interesting about 'nothing to report' (here-after, NTR) reports. Participants routinely exhibit that they have nothing to report by reporting nothing, and remaining silent over sometimes very long periods of time. In which case, why do participants occasionally ver-balise that which is overwhelmingly implied — and indeed established — by their silence?

   If we extend extracts 5.11 and 5.12 to include the prior and subsequent mentation imagery, it becomes apparent that NTR reports tend to occur after periods of silence that are characteristic for each participant of silences between substantive reports.

(5.11 Extended)

1		(10.3)
2	P:	my feet are beginning to feel very very heavy
3		(34.2)
4		°(another thing is that-)°
5		(7.9)
6		I feel like the <u>pressure</u> in my <u>ea:rs</u> is in<u>credi</u>ble (1.6) °>it's<° building up
7		building °up° hh
8		(45.0)
9		I can't see anything.
10		(17.4)
11		°I can° see myself getting frustrated with things that I °haven't° done,

12   (1.7) °I should° be doing? (6.3) °>attempting<° to do things and I j'st
13   can't put down things °that I want to do°

(5.12 Extended)

((Mentation starts))

1   P: hhh (.4) I see:: an ey::e (0.2) <u>open</u>↑ing (1.5) °'s° ye:llo:w (2.7) it's
2   fl<u>i</u>ckeri:ng (3.8) >the:re's a< <u>la:</u>rge oval sh↑ape (1.3) in the <u>centre</u> >of
3   my visio:n< (9.1) ˙hh (0.3) >in the< ce:ntre: >there's a< <u>small</u>er obje:ct
4   (12)
5   I do:n't see anything right ↑now
6   (22)
7   ˙hh >I- can see< various <u>obje:</u>cts (0.5) moving a<u>cro:</u>ss my visions more
8   li::nes °I guess°
9   (4.8)
10   lo:ts o:f::: (2.8) <u>circle:</u>s <u>fla:</u>t <u>ci:</u>rcle:s
11   (2) ˙hhh (0.4)
12   u:m:: (0.3) I se:e: a fai:nt- ima:ge <u>o:</u>f: (0.3) <u>tee::</u>th: (0.8) >in the<
13   ba::ckgrou::nd

In extract 5.11, the participant reports on sensations concerning his feet; there is softly spoken utterance that sounds like the start of an aborted report; and then there is a report of pressure in the ears. After a 45 second silence she then reports that she can't see anything, and there is then a 17.4 second silence before the report of the next imagery. In 5.12, the NTR report occurs after period of 12 seconds and precedes a silence of 22 seconds.

Inspection of the temporal distribution of imagery reports for these participants reveals a curious observation: if the NTR reports had not been offered—that is, had the participants actually said nothing when they report they have nothing to say—then the resulting periods of silence between the prior and next substantive reports would have exceeded the normal period of silence that is characteristic of these participants. In the mentation of the participant from which extract 5.11 is taken (experiment number 01-28) there is only one other period of silence that exceeds 40 seconds (see the discussion of extract 5.14, below); there are a few silences that exceed 30 seconds, but the majority are considerably shorter. To illustrate: the inter-utterance silences that appear on a randomly selected single page of transcribed mentation from experiment 01-28 are: 3, 6, 9, 4.1, 19.2, 5.1, 6.7, 12.2, 9.5, 5.3, 11.2, 17.9, 5, 10.9, 12.2, 5.5, 9.5, 12.1, and 22.3 seconds. If we perform the same exercise on the corresponding page of transcript for the participant in experiment number 01-41 (from extract 5.12), we find that substantive reports are distributed between silences of 2.8, 7.6, 5.4, 26.5, 9.9, 5.9, 3.1, 6.6, 5.3, 6, 27.4, 2.3, 6 and 8.2 seconds. Had the

NTR reports not been uttered, then the resulting periods of silence would have been 62.4 and 34 seconds, both of which substantially exceed the normal period of silence of the respective participants.

There are two implications of this observation. First, it may be the case that there is some form of 'personal metric' by which participants temporally organise their reports of conscious imagery in this experimental setting. (The design of the participant's report in extract 5.12 may provide a degree of support for this, in that the claim that she can not see anything 'right now' points to her understanding that at *that* specific moment a report of imagery would have been appropriate or expectable.) There are of course parallels in the organisation and normative significance of silence in conversational interaction. Jefferson's (1989) study of silence in conversational interaction identified a *standard* metric of approximately one second. Her analysis of instances of silences falling within a 0.8 to 1.2 second boundary demonstrates that speakers orient to this critical period as a 'tolerance interval' (Jefferson, 1989: 170) which marks the normatively acceptable length of absence of talk in conversational interaction. Second, it may be that NTR reports can be used as a vehicle to preserve this personal metric when, in the absence of a report, the resulting silence would exceed the normal period of silence of that participant. Here again, Jefferson's study is relevant in that she describes how utterance production may in part be informed by underlying expectations of what period of silence is normatively appropriate. She describes how, after silences of approximately 0.8 to 1.2 seconds, speakers can be observed to begin talking so as to terminate the silence, evidence that silences that reach beyond approximately 1.2 seconds are being treated as signs of trouble in the conversation.

There are other kinds of report that may index the operation of a personal metric. In extract 5.13, after a succession of reports of images and sensations, there is a lengthy period of silence at which point the participant observes that previously reported sensations are still ongoing (line 18).

(5.13)(01-46: E3/M)

```
1          (34.5)
2    P:    cars
3          (13.8)
4          trees
5          (29.7)
6          ˙hhh
7          (21.4)
8          ˙hh le:aves:: (0.8) s: sh:ape
9          (15.2)
```

```
10        °s'rt've° (0.4) fa:lli:ng (0.8) spinning (0.2) sensati:on
11        (12.1)
12        hhhh
13        (5.4)
14        hhhhh ˙hhhh
15        (10.3)
16        ˙hh
17        (33.5)
18        ˙hh j's keep on (0.3) spinning (0.3) round
19        (16.9)
```

The utterance 'j's keep on (0.3) spinning (0.3) round' may be termed a
'steady state' report, in that it offers no new imagery, but merely reinstates
the ongoing relevance of imagery or sensations described in an earlier
report. It is noticeable that this steady state report terminates a period of
silence (broken only by audible breathing) of over one minute, which is
one of the longest silences in this participant's mentation.

   In the following extract there is in line 3 a silence of 45 seconds that is
conspicuously long compared to other silences in this mentation (this is
the only other silence of over 40 seconds in the mentation narrative from
experiment 01-28).

(5.14) (01-28:E2/F)

```
1         (21.3)
2    P:   got this s:trange feeling of fear it's unreal:?
3         (45.0)
4         going back to the thoughts:, (.) >of< earlier on::, (.) before I left (1.6)
5         °on° my way he:re (1.2) feeling the same kind've °↑fear° (1.3) anxious:
6         (1.9) (a)sh::: (p)hhh
7         (13.1)
8         s:till got this wa:ter: running (4.8) 's:: just gu:shing wa:ter.
9         (6.7)
10        ((swallows)) this, (0.7) ˙hhhh °thi:s hhh°
11        (31.0)
```

In line 2, the participant reports a sensation of fear, there is a longer than
normal silence, and then she begins a report of earlier contempla-
tions — anxieties about taking part in the experiment — which is the vehicle
to refer again to the fear/anxiety she is currently experiencing, and which
was reported in the prior utterance. The turn component 'going back to the
thoughts:, (.) >of< earlier on::, (.) >°be°fore< I left (1.6) °on° my way he:re'
does not only link pre experiment concerns to currently experienced sensation; the phrase 'going back to' invokes a common topical history: something the participant and the non-participating-but overhearing

experimenter have discussed previously. However, the participant is not invoking something said previously in the mentation. At no point earlier in this narrative does she raise any issue related to her concerns. Consequently we can assume that she is referring here to discussion of these anxieties in conversations with the experimenter before the start of the experiment. As such, it is unlikely to be relevant to any scenes from the target video clip, images of which are at that moment being mentally projected, and the later identification of which is the key task of the experiment. This is evidence, then, that in the absence of relevant imagery, participants may even resort to reporting experiences prior to the experiment to ensure that periods of silence do not exceed their idiosyncratic upper limit.

However, there are instances of participants terminating silences by reporting that steady state or ongoing sensations have ended.

(5.15) (01-69: E2/M)

1		(16)
2	P:	s:till (.) feel as if I'm movi:n-
3		(18.7)
4		I:: can see <u>steve</u> in a <u>roo</u>:m (.) scratching his hea::d
5		(8)
6		thermomete:r (6) docto:r (2.3) m::::y::: (0.5) <u>father</u> in a wheelchair?
7		(20.2)
8		an o:ld s<u>choo</u>l trip to see a boa:t-
9		(24.8)
10		flight simulator on my computer at h<u>o</u>:me
11		(13)
12		my wife sitting at the compu'e:r (2.5) clu:msily trying to get the hang
13		of the mouse (6.5) she never holds it ri:gh-
14		(22.8)
15		I d<u>o</u>:n't- fee:l any moveme:n- (0.2) <u>any</u> mo:re
16		(30.7)
17		°li:ghtni:ng°
18		(10.3)
19		eh::::: (0.5) °u:° the pretenders on top of the po::ps

Here there is a steady state report (line 2) that establishes the continuing experience of a sensation reported earlier (not shown in this transcript). It is noticeable that this report occurs after a 16 second silence, which is commensurate with other inter utterance reports in this participant's narrative. However, in line 15 the participant reports that the sensation of movement has ended. This too terminates a silence typical of the participant's inter utterance reports.

Inspection of the transcripts examined so far reveals that within a single mentation narrative there will be clear variation in periods of silence between imagery reports. Notwithstanding that, though, it is possible to discern some clear differences in the timing of reports between different participants. The timing of production of NTR reports, and reports of the continuation or cessation of sensations, does seem to provide some evidence of the operation of personal metrics that exert a (relatively weak) organisational principle for the temporal placement of imagery reports that is relevant to the institutional requirements of the experiment.

To conclude the analysis we will examine one more pragmatic feature of NTR reports that displays a much clearer orientation to procedural requirements of participation in the ganzfeld experiment. In line 14 of the following extract, the participant reports '°can't°see anythi- hh'.

(5.16) (01-28: E2/F)

```
1     P:   it's going back to re:d ˙hhh seems to be gettin' light seems to be
2          going li:ghter,
3          (5.3)
4          now all I seem to think about is war- water seems to be rush, ˙hhh
5          (11.2)
6          feels like I'm just constantly: floating from place to pla-, ˙hh
7          (17.9)
8          s'like I'm getting further and further away from everythi(hh)ng
9          (23.2)
10         seems incredibly darker agai(h)n?
11         (5.0)
12         body's feeling heavier,
13         (10.9)
14         °can't° see anythi- hh
15         (12.2)
16         >'s< going blue:? (3.5) ˙hh sh(h)it °ẏhh hhh° (5.5) >it feels< like blue
17         wa:ves::: going over my eyes:? (.) I don't understa- ˙hh
```

This NTR report comes after a series of utterances that focus on sensations, thoughts and feelings. In lines 1 to 12 she describes colours; what she is thinking about; a floating sensation; a sense of distance and removal; darkness, and the weight of her body. In this sequence there is no report of a clear visual image. (It may be objected that the reports of colours and relative degrees of light index sight. However, these reports point to experience of the degree of light the participant can perceive, and do not convey specific visual *imagery*. See the discussion of extract 5.17, below.) Participants have been briefed prior to the experiment that *any* imagery or sensation is to be reported; and there is explicit evidence of this licence from the experimenter's interjections reproduced in extracts 5.1 and 5.2.

The NTR report focuses upon the absence of visual imagery: the participant can't *see* anything. This may exhibit sensitivity to the local history of the mentation. In the context of a recent succession of reports focusing on sensations, feeling and thoughts, this utterance demonstrates that the participant is also attending to visual imagery, and therefore diligent in her conduct as a participant required to report all events in her consciousness. Moreover, it establishes that the absence of any visual imagery is not due to a failing on her part as a participant, but simply reflects the absence of visual imagery in her conscious experience. The report of nothing to see evidences an understanding of the obligations relevant to participation in the experiment.

This phenomenon is also evident in the following extract.

(5.17) (01-28: E2/F)

```
1    P:   I feel kind've a: tingling sensation ˙hhh (0.5) >around my body< I
2         don- hh (1.0) ˙hhh (1.2) °j'st then hhh°
3         (3.0)
4         's(hh):: (spea::r? hiss)
5         (6.0)
6         >all I can think of< is::, (0.1) tra:ins >↑huh< hhhHH ((coughs))
7         (9.0)
8         °'s: nothing° (1.2) ˙hh feel heavy:? (.) feel like I'm °si(h)n-° (2.2) °like
9         I'm fallin'(a) throu:gh something.°
10        (4.1)
11        as though I'm falling through the sky: but I'm not t-, (0.8) °'s(h)::°
12        (19.2)
13        °noise seems to be calming, down°
14        (5.1)
15        >can't< see anything, (2.0) all I can see is j'st red forever, (1.2) an-
16        (6.7)
17        physically my knee:s, (.) feel ˙hh (.) °legs° I feel like I can't move my
18        le:gs
19        (12.2)
20        °still feel like I'm? f::° (0.6) ˙hhh can't stop thinking about, °u-° (.) uh::,
21        this sounds me-, °uh° hhh (>me °over°<) ˙hhh (1.0) keep thinking of the
22        people back in my fla:t
```

In line 15 the participant claims the absence of visual mental stimuli, but then reports that she can see unending red. By this the participant distinguishes two separate sensations indexed by the word 'see': the first refers to imagery in the 'mind's eye'; the second refers to her awareness of the

conditions of the experimental room, in which there is a red light, the illu-
mination from which is dispersed evenly over the retinal field by masking
taped over the participant's eyes.

By contrast, in extract 5.18, we see an NTR report that suggests the participant here is sensitive to the absence of reports of *thoughts* in the context
of a series of descriptions of largely *visual* mental phenomena.

(5.18) (01-42: E3/M)

```
1      P:  I j'st reali:sed wha:t I:'m seei:ng (2.6) >it's the sha:pe of the:se< goggles?
2          (3.7) terrifi:c
3          (19.3) ˙HH (10.9) ((gulping sound)) (1.6) ((vocalized clicking sound))
4          (0.9)
5          do:ts (2.6) ↑white (2.4) °do:ts (.) in the centre:°
6          (3.7)
7          car (4.8) a road?
8          (6.4) ((gulping sound)) (7.7)
9          so:mething flying?
10         (3.5)
11         a horse
12         (1.3)
13         do:g
14         (20)
15         ˙hh (0.3) sti:ll no: parti- ticula:r thou:ghts or feeli:ngs
16         (3.1) ((gulping sound)) (6.8)
17         a tunne:l (2.3) or li:ke (0.6) °like° a jetstrea:m (.) from an aeropla:ne
18         or (.) inside an aeropla:ne
19         (4.5)
20         a wate:rfa:ll (1.7) >it's mebbe just the white noi:se again?<
```

In line 15 the participant reports an ongoing absence of thoughts. This
utterance comes after a sequence of descriptions of unambiguously visual
imagery (he describes seeing shapes related to the masking around his
eyes, referred to here as 'goggles'; and he reports dots, which presumes
some visual apprehension). But he also reports imagery which is ambiguous: 'car', 'a road', 'something flying', 'a horse' and 'dog' could be reports
of visually apprehended images or concepts which come to mind non
visually. In this context, the report of 'no particular thoughts or feelings'
achieves two things: it terminates a silence of 20 seconds, which is considerably longer than other inter utterance silences in this mentation narrative, and it has a disambiguating function, in that the explicit claim of the
absence of thoughts invites an interpretation of the prior reports as being
visually apprehended objects in the mind's eye, rather than concepts of
which the participant has become consciously aware.

Discussion

In this corpus of introspective reports, participants' silences are routine and unaccountable: participants offer neither apologies nor excuses for them; and, once the mentation has commenced, there is no remedial intervention by the experimenters to suggest that they regard the silences as a reflection of procedural or personal difficulties. The only exceptions are 'nothing to report' reports that seem designed to terminate silences that exceed or are likely to exceed the outer limits for periods of silence in the individual participant's mentation; but even these kinds of turns point to the broader normative framework underpinning the participant's conduct.

In the previous chapter we argued that the design of imagery reports are informed by the participants' understanding of the overarching purpose of the experiment and the conditions under which the narrative is produced. The same argument applies to the absence of talk in the mentation narratives: periods of silence manage the participants' contributions such that their reports of inner experience are recognisably descriptions of discrete images or sensations, which thereby reflecting a 'common sense' or lay assumption as to how the parapsychological processes under investigation may actually impinge on their conscious awareness. In this, their contributions to the mentation — and, for all practical purposes, their inner phenomenal realities — are designed with respect to the wider institutional or task related goals of the setting (Boden and Zimmerman, 1991; Drew and Heritage, 1992; Heritage, 1997; Heritage and Clayman, 2010; Heritage and Greatbatch, 1991). Furthermore, 'nothing to report' reports not only display participants' understanding of the normative framework underpinning the production of this kind of introspective report, but are a vehicle for pragmatic work. They allow disambiguation of the nature of the experiences described in immediately prior reports, and they provide a resource by which the participant can exhibit the appropriateness of their conduct: there is, then, identity work here, in that participants pragmatically claim to be diligent, judicious or careful observers of the phenomenological events on which they are required to report.

In summary, the management of silences in the mentation introspective reports exhibits the participants' tacit understanding of the task-related or institutional requirements of the setting, their awareness of lay or 'common sense' accounts of the way parapsychological cognition may work, and their appreciation of the normative behavioural expectations incumbent upon volunteers in (para)psychological experiments. As such, silences in the mentation narratives might be said to constitute part of the 'fingerprint' (Heritage and Greatbatch 1991: 95–6) of talk in this institutional setting. They are not merely an absence of talk relevant to the experiment's overarching concerns: they are a normative and organised mechanism by which what talk there is comes to be hearably produced as appropriate for and fitted to this context.

These periods of silence are rarely noted in the parapsychological literature on performance in ganzfeld experiments (for example, Carpenter, 2004; Wackermann, Putz and Allefeld, 2008). Indeed, research laboratories' own transcripts of these tapes routinely edit out the silences, thereby portraying the mentation narrative as a continuous report. This would suggest that parapsychologists treat the silences in mentation reports as unimportant because they regard them as semantically vacuous. Indeed, informal ethnographic observation of the parapsychological community would suggest that it is assumed that during the periods of silence participants are simply deciding what to say. They are regarded as relatively insignificant events that simply reflect the operation of inner psychological processes: categorisation and ordering of imagery, inner observation with the 'mind's eye', and so on. However, parapsychologists – and consciousness researchers – should be wary of disregarding these periods of silence: there are not simply moments when the participant is taking 'time out' from the real business of the experiment. They are fundamentally implicated in the achievement of that which the experiment is designed to elicit: reports of conscious experience.

The implications of this are not confined to parapsychological investigations of how mental imagery may reflect extra sensory processes, if they exist. They are relevant to the wider study of consciousness more generally, and the renewed interest in introspection in mainstream psychology and cognate disciplines. It is increasingly argued that it is important that we pay attention to self reports of the lived experience of a mental life (Hektner, Schmidt and Csikszentmihalyi, 2006; Hurlburt and Heavey, 2006).

Discussions of the methodology of research on introspective reports tend to focus on techniques of data collection, and the well-known difficulties of reliance on human testimony. But there is practically no discussion of the way in which introspective reports are designed to address the contingencies of the setting in which they are produced, nor of the normative frameworks relevant to participation in formal or laboratory contexts. It is as if introspective reports are produced in an interactional vacuum: merely neutral verbal expressions of inner mental phenomena that more or less capture conscious experience in flight. But any and every kind of introspective data will be elicited in some actual setting, with its attendant constraints and requirements, organised and mediated by specific others (even ostensibly non-participating others), to meet particular kinds of work related requirements.

In this chapter we have examined how periods of silence may be managed by experimental participants to address institutional and interpersonal matters relevant to the context in which they produce introspective reports. But this range of pragmatic concerns has to be negotiated by any person producing a report of their inner mental life for the purposes of research on consciousness and lived experience. As such, empirical projects we may undertake to understand conscious experience should foreground the discursive conditions and their attendant pragmatic requirements under which introspective descriptions of consciousness are produced.

Chapter Six

'And the smell of death and the sound of silence'

Poetics and reports of subjective experience

In this chapter we examine how mentation narratives display a range of poetical structures and organisations. Our interest in the poetics of introspection stems from the recognition that, on occasions, imagery reports exhibit clearly poetical qualities. For example, the quote in the title of this chapter comes from the following section of a mentation.

(6.1)(01-50: E2/M)

```
1          (6.9)
2    P:    >thinkin- about< (0.3) human skeleto:n (3.2) th-
3          shape of the ri:bs (2.7) an- how heavy a person is:
4          (4.1)
5          'n- the smell of death:
6          (4.9)
7          'n the sound of si::le:nce
8          (4.5)
```

If this were to be reformatted as:

> Thinking about [the] human skeleton
> The shape of the ribs
> And how heavy a person is
> And the smell of death
> And the sound of silence

…then it could easily be a section of a poem of solemn reflection on corporeality and human mortality.

Although the mentation narratives provide examples of these conventional poetic forms (and, as we shall argue later, some unconventional forms as well), our interest is mainly in how *conversational* or everyday poetics inform descriptions of conscious imagery. The poetics of everyday discourse refers to a range of phenomena, such as repetitions, puns and other figures of speech (Johnstone, 1987; Lloyd, 2007; Norrik, 2000/2001; Tannen, 1987, 1998; Wales, 2009). In this chapter, though, we are primarily concerned with the range of poetic phenomena first identified by Harvey Sacks in his studies of mundane conversation.

In his published lectures on the organisation of conversational interaction, Sacks examined various data extracts that suggest the operation of turn design procedures that establish poetical relationships. We will discuss three to illustrate the kinds of phenomena he was beginning to notice in his research. Poetic relationships can built from the repetition of particular sounds. For example, Sacks discussed a section of naturally occurring talk in which someone says 'Oh God! Christmas has gotten so damn painful…no one likes what they're getting' (Sacks, 1992, vol. II: 306). He argued that the repetition of the hard 'g' sound in 'God', 'gotten' and 'getting' may not be accidental, but the outcome of tacit word selection procedures that display a historical sensitivity to what has come before, or indeed, what might be coming up next. He also discussed data extracts in which word selection may be informed by categorical relationships. For example, in examining a sequence in which a woman remarks on a visit to an empty bar, he focused on her claim 'God there wasn't a soul in we were the only ones at the bar'. Sacks noted that the phrase 'wasn't a soul' not only established the emptiness of the bar, but is fitted categorically with the word 'God' (and the pun facilitated by the homonymous relationship between 'soul' and 'sole') (vol. II: 291). Sacks also identified sequences he called reversals, in which particular sound or word sequences seem to be conspicuously inverted to achieve a form of acoustic mirroring. From his data, he showed how the phrase 'get things for' is followed soon after by 'let's forget it'; here, 'get… for' is reversed in 'forget'. Sacks noted other examples in his corpora of inverted sound patterns in close proximity, such as 'that's just…' and 'just that…', and 'how, now', and 'now, how' (vol. II: 308). Many of these kinds of everyday poetic phenomena were further explored by Jefferson (1996) who provided a more formal and expanded account of the catalogue of poetic phenomenon Sacks (and subsequently, his colleagues) had been collecting: sound associations, categorical relationships, poetical connections formed from names, numbers, colours, and fractured idioms (in which a spate of talk seems to echo or reflect well known phrases, such as the titles of television programmes).

The poetic forms in the introspective reports mirror the phenomena identified by Sacks and Jefferson in conversational interaction: sound runs achieved by alliteration or assonance, reversals, in which a constellation of sounds is then reversed in subsequent talk, puns and pun-like categorical relationships, and so on. It is important to stress, however, that we are not claiming that the poetic forms we identify in the constrained environment of the laboratory setting are the same as instances identified in conversational data from naturally occurring interaction. Our point is simply that everyday poetics of the kind found in mundane interaction can also be found in this institutional setting, and are used to allow the participants to address particular requirements or contingencies of the setting, a point to which we return in the conclusion. In this, our analyses this extends the range of discourse contexts in which poetic phenomena have been studied. Later in this chapter we show that some poetic phenomena in our data resemble well-established figures of speech common to poetry and other literary and religious texts, suggesting a link between formal poetics and everyday discourse practices. But we begin with some observations on sound runs in the ganzfeld introspections.

Sound runs within and between imagery reports

Sound runs can occur within a discrete report of conscious experience. Extract 6.2 is the first imagery report from the start of the period of introspection.

(6.2) (01-05: E3/F)

((Mentation starts))

```
1     P:   u:m: (2.4) something: about (0.3) ˙h butterflies (3.8) ˙h and there's
2          somebody swimming
3          (27)
```

Here, there is alliteration in repeat of the 's' sound in 'something', 'somebody' and 'swimming'. In addition, there is a run of an 'm' sound in these words (and perhaps, in the initial turn component, in the selection of 'um' as opposed to 'err'), as well as repetition of 'b' in 'about', 'butterflies' and 'somebody'.

   In extract 6.3 the sound run is achieved through selection of words in which a particular 'i' sound is prominent: 'bicycle', 'child's', 'bike', 'wide', 'white' and 'tyres'.

(6.3) (01-88: E1/F)

```
1         (9.8)
2    P:   a: red bicycle: (1.5) child's bi:ke (0.5) very sma:ll (1.4) with
3         wide white tyre:s
4         (65)
```

The last phrase 'with wide white tyres' combines assonance and alliteration, and has an overtly poetic, almost musical quality.

Although sound runs can be extended across discrete imagery reports, they tend to be localised within spates of talk. Routinely they can be observed to cluster within discrete imagery reports. Extract 6.4 contains the end components of an imagery report about hands/fingers (lines 1 to 6) and one further complete report about windows (lines 8 to 10).

(6.4) (01-52: E1/F)

```
1    P:   ... got gloves on (1.1) and they're pointing up to the sky (1.4) but
2         there's nothing else but the ha:nds there's nothing tha- (0.3) at the
3         e:nd of the ha:nds (3.7) an:d >and a fi:st< (0.4) an- (1.5) a scraped ou-
4         (1.6) bits that fi:ngers have ma:de (0.3) in in the mu:d (2.8) an s'rt've
5         bits've (.7) LIttle bits (0.3) little lumps've mud (0.7) piled up in a
6         triangle
7         (12.9)
8         lots of windo:ws (0.3) like gothic (1) ˙hhhh (0.4) like u:m big
9         archway windo:ws (2.7) ((dental click)) (0.5) in in a (.) in a ro:w (0.3) like
10        hundreds and hundreds >of them in a row on a wa:ll<
11        (47.5)
```

There is no evidence of any poetic repetitions within the report of imagery about hands prior to the section that begins on line 3 with 'an:d >and a fi:st<', at which point five intersecting sound runs emerge. There is a run of hard 'i' sounds in the words 'fist', 'fingers', 'in' 'bits' and 'little', which is continued in the repetition of the latter two words. To a lesser degree, there is a run of 'm' sounds in 'mud' (repeated), 'made' and 'lumps', and a run of 'l' sounds in 'LIttle bits (0.3) °little lumps'. There are two cases of the 'eye' pronunciation of 'i' in 'piled' and 'triangle' (which also extends the immediately prior run of 'l' sounds'). Finally, there is a brief run of 'v' sounds in the truncated articulation of 'of' in 's'rt've', 'bits've' and 'lumps've'. The imagery report that begins in line 8 has a more simple sound run: a series of (sometimes repeated) words beginning with or containing 'w': 'windows', 'archway', and 'wall'. (The repeated 'row' could also be included, here, although the 'w' sound is not as unambiguously prominent as it is in the other words in this series.)

This short extract illustrates two important points. First, the specific sounds out of which repetitions are composed may change, which in turn suggests that the conspicuous reoccurrence of any particular sound is not merely the expression of an idiosyncratic tendency towards that sound on the part of a specific individual. Second, it is not the case that participants whose introspection narratives at *some* points exhibit poetic features exhibit those features at *all* points. That is, there is evidence of a degree of selection of poetic forms — or at least, evidence of their distribution throughout an introspective report.

Sound runs may be short lived, exhibiting a highly localised relevance. In the following there is a run of 'p' sounds over three (arrowed) discrete reports. The preceding and subsequent reports do not contain this sound run.

(6.5) (01-88: E1/F)

```
1           (39.1)
2    P:     °there's a very° bright white light (.) in the top of my view (7.5) hh
3           °seems to be° >moving< it's got a jagged edge
4           (7.4)
5    →      c'n see the profile of a person >I'm not sure who it i:s<
6           (14.5)
7    →      (n)hh hh ˙hh it's a picture of gi:les working a- his desk HH (2.9) makes me
8           laugh cos he's probably not at a:ll HH
9           (4.2)
10   →      °↑u° I've got a view of pollock (.) I can hear the noi:ses there (.8)
11          °there's° people walking around
12          (5.8)
13          hh °uh° victoria fa:lls (1.7) that's the noi:se the water falli:ng (1.3) 'ow
14          it's getting more dista:nt- (3.7) or >NIAgra< fa:lls
```

Each of the reports contains two words beginning with 'p': 'profile' and 'person'; 'picture' and 'probably', and 'Pollock' and 'people' (Pollock Halls are student residences at the University of Edinburgh).

In some cases, though, sound runs can extend over long periods of a mentation. This runs counter to research suggesting that creative language, such as the use of metaphor, clusters at particular discursive moments in which key emotional or interpersonal matters are being addressed (Cameron, 2007; Carter and McCarthy, 2004; Tannen, 1998). In the following extract, for example, there is a sustained run of words beginning with 'p', and numerous other words in which a 'p' sound figures prominently, that extends across several imagery reports.

(6.6) (01-46: E3/M)

1   (33.5)
2   P: ˙hh j's keep on (0.3) spinning (0.3) round
3   (16.9)
4 →   's::pe:ckle:d (figh-) (0.7) sort've (1) dalma:tion type (.) pattern
5   (43.8)
6 →   ˙hh (1.3) dark: (0.3) pipes: (2.2) wit wa:ter (1) >undergro:und pipes<
7   (12.3)
8   °(och um)° (0.4) corner of a (0.2) a white room
9   (14)
10   corrugated (.) surface
11   (6.1)
12 →   ˙hh (0.5) like the face of (.) pla:ying cards (.) like th- (.) ace of spa:des?
13   (10.6)
14   ˙hhh (ts) (0.2) 's like a (1.1) a mohican hairstyle? (0.4) 'gainst a (1) °s'rt've°
15 →   (1.6) (t:) (0.4) pinkish (.) ba:ckgrou:nd
16   (9.2) ((creaking noise)) (60)
17   (wheels)
18   (14.5)
19 →   ˙hh (0.5) 's like an ear sha:pe
20   (32.5)
21   ˙hhh
22   (6)
23 →   pa:rro:t
24   (14.7)
25 →   ˙hh (0.4) 's: like a (.) a ro:bo:co:p (0.4) type (0.2) fi:gu:re
26   (10.7)
27 →   ˙h (0.4) pro:fi:le of a fa:ce
28   (24)
29   ˙h (1.8) ˙hh (0.3) got a (0.2) image of like- (0.3) the insi:de of a roo:m
30   (16.2)
31 →   ˙h s'like an ol:d (0.2) <u>bi plane</u>

Words beginning with 'p' in this sequence: 'pattern, 'pipes', 'playing', 'pinkish', 'parrot' and 'profile'. The sound also figures in 'spades', 'speck-led', 'Robocop' and 'bi plane'. The constellation of 'p' sounds seems quite dense. There is a similar phenomena in the next extract, in which words beginning or featuring 'f' seem to occur with conspicuous frequency.

(6.7) (01-85: E2/M)

1 → P: °it's s'rt've° VAgue sh- >outline< of: the:: (.) ˙hhh a to:wer in flore:nce (.)
2   that I <u>drew</u> e:ndlessly: (1.2) °thi:s su:mme:r° (0.5) ˙hh at f:: obscure

3   a:ngle
4   (16.8)
5   →   >FLOre:nce< ˙hhh (0.3) the city bei::ng (0.5) diss↑o::lve:d (1) fro:m above (.)
6   →   ˙>a:nd it's:< featu:res wi::ndi:ng: >e- le-< to the left (.) °into the sky:° (2)
7   >now=the=whole image is mo:ving off to the left<
8   (8.7)
9   points:: (0.3) °u:: th::° lo::ng narrow >poi:nts< like stee:ple:s
10   (40.4)
11   →   m::↓ stra:nge: (1.3) °oo::::=uf:° (.) F:Urrowi:ng °u- uhm::::° (0.6)
12   →   Caterpillar like effect (.) °but-° when you: (.) s:: flick a ca:rpe:t- °an- it
13   u:° (0.2) ˙hh the loo:p trave:ls like tha:t >except it's a kind of< maggot
14   →   (2) °u° from its hea:d to its tai:l it (.) >fl↑icks< (5) uh:: as if it's
15   →   ↑ski↓ing (5) >°it's got little°< fly: like features at the front
16   (5.1)
17   →   a footpri:nt (2) a::: v- a fa:ke footpri:nt (4) somethi:ng's (0.5)
18   got a ho::ld of it (2.3) a lo:ng ha::nd o:r (.) >s'rt've< a wi:nding crea:ture
19   →   ty:pe thi:ng:: ho:lding thi:s (0.3) ˙hh (.3) FRAme of a footpri:nt (1.8)
20   °playing >with it<° (0.8) TAPPing it with lo:::::ng nai::ls (1.2) black (.) sharp
21   nai:ls
22   (5.7)
23   →   °u::° an archwa:::y (0.6) >I see a kind've< ar:chwa:y with finger
24   shapes poin- reaching the top (0.4) ˙hh (0.2) uh tha:'s also a- a:: an obscu:re
25   angle:
26   (8.2)
27   °a- b-° hhhh
28   (15.8)
29   →   I see a- °f:: u-° ˙hhh (0.2) °u:° ma↓donna: (1) ˙hhh (0.2) bu:t
30   >as if she's been badly dr↑awn:< (1.5) ˙hhh (0.3) an- her head's the shape
31   of a ke::yho:le (4.5) >or a< pawn
32   (20.6)
33   →   people sliding do:wn >a kind've< flu::me water shoot °into water° (2.2)
34   again a >kind've< ↑really j's::: sh::eer perspective of somethi:ng (0.2) ˙hh
35   →   (0.6) >feeling of being really high u:p and they're all kind of< winding
36   →   do:wn (1.7) fa:cele:ss
37   (18.1)

The run of 'f' sounds consists of (and ignoring the use of the word 'feeling'
to introduce sensations): 'Florence' (repeated), 'from', 'features', 'furrow-
ing', 'flick', 'flicks', 'fly', 'features', 'front', 'footprint' (repeated), 'fake',
'frame', 'finger', 'flume' and 'faceless'. The sound is also present in words
such as 'left', 'off' and 'effect'. But there are other ways in which the run of
'f' sounds is continued. There are some unusual phrases that seem
designed to concentrate the appearance of 'f' sounds: 'fly: like features at

the front' (line 15); 'a f<u>oo</u>tpri:nt (2) a::: v- a fa:ke footpri:nt' (line 17), and 'FRAme of a footpri:nt' (line 19). There is redundancy that extends the 'f' run: the participant reports 'people sliding down a flume water shoot'; but by definition a flume is a form of water shoot. On two occasions the participant appears to begin to say something beginning with 'f' but then self repairs, abandons the projected word and then produces an alternative word: 'at f:: obscure a:ngle (line 3) and 'I- see a-< °f:: u-° ˙hhh (0.2) °u: ° ma↓donna: (line 29). In both cases the subsequently-to-be-abandoned 'f' sound is stretched and thereby momentarily extended in the sound stream of the utterance. It would seem that the participant is using various speech mechanisms to continue and extend the sound run, an observation that is developed in the next chapter.

Poetic and rhetorical organisations

The ganzfeld introspective narratives exhibit a common pattern: a report of an imagery or set of related images, then a period of silence, and then a report of new imagery, then silence, and so on. This distinctive robust description — silence — description — silence structure facilitates a range of poetic phenomena and rhetorical figures more commonly associated with formal poetry and literary and religious texts, such as ploce, epanalepsis, anaphora, anadiplosis and chiasmus (see also Hopper, 1992, and Hymes, 1977, on the way that components of a verbal play activity may be retranscribed to highlight resemblances to verses or stanzas in conventional poetry).

In poetry, *ploce* is the repetition of words interspersed with intervening words, for example, the use of 'some' in the following line from Donne's 'Upon the translation of the Psalmes': 'So though some have, some may some Psalmes translate' (Magnusson, 2006: 191). Ploce is common in the imagery reports, and although it does not have the stylised or crafted feel of the poet's words, there are poetical echoes in the concatenation of sounds thereby generated.

(6.8) (01-52: E1/F)

```
1            (3.7)
2     P:     an:d and a fi:st (0.4) an- (1.5) a scraped ou- (1.6) bits that fi:ngers have
3            ma:de (0.3) in in the mu:d (2.8) an s'rt've bits've (0.7) LIttle bits (.3) little
4            lumps've mud (0.7) piled up in a triangle:
5            (12.9)
```

(6.9)(01-85: E2/M)

```
1          (8.5)
2    P    hhh kind of shuttered images shutterin- acro:s (.) not movi:ng (0.2) hhh (1.4)
3          smoo:thly (0.5) mo:ving in t- (.) shu:tters like a:: (.) s:: (0.2) hh animated
4          (6.9)
```

In extracts 6.8 and 6.9, word repetition, in conjunction with consonance, works to establish a musical quality. In extract 6.8, this is achieved by the repetition of 'bits' and 'little' (and the two different rhyming 'i' sounds echoed in 'fist' and 'fingers', and in 'piled' and 'triangle'); and in extract 6.9, it comes from variations on the word 'shutter' (and the rhyming 'moo' sounds in 'moving' and 'smoothly moving').

   Word repetition may occur as participants expand upon an initial report of their imagery. So, in extract 6.10, there is the following description.

(6.10) (01-80: E1/M)

((Mentation starts))
```
1    P:   I see a bridge (7.5) I'm looking down on a bri:dge (5) large (6) silver (5.4)
2          bri:dge
3          (35.4)
```

Here the participant incrementally reveals more information about his imagery: he sees a bridge, he then reports the perspective from which he perceives it in his mind's eye, he notes its size and then reports its colour. In these subsequent references to the bridge, the participant does not use pronouns or other elliptical references, but repeats the word 'bridge' twice, thereby establishing a poetic repetition. Repetition of words that capture core components of imagery is a routine feature of descriptions that subsequently provide more detail.

(6.11)(01-05: E3/F)

```
1          (17.6)
2    P:   h(h)uh, hh a t- (.) a foot (0.3) can see the toe::s (1.4) 's a big foot (2.2) got
3          white toenail:s (3.3) I'm looking down on it like it was my foot hh but it's
4          no::t (0.4) 's too b(h)ig
5          (9.0)
```

(6.12) (01-29: E2/M)

```
1          (17.5)
2    P:   woman carryin- shoppin- (2.1) an' droppin- the shoppin-
3          (20)
```

(6.13) (01-41: E1/F)

```
1          (8.2)
2    P:   and I: just thou:ght of a bir:d soari:ng like a big- (0.4) 's big bat wi:ngs (1.4)
3          'n poi:nt triangular wi:ngs (1.5) and 's looking fr'm the bird's eye view agai:n
4          (1.9) fr'm the back of the bi:rd (1.3) and the bird's bea:k hhh (.) agai:n hh
5          (15.7)
```

In these reports, 'foot', 'shoppin-' and 'bird' are repeated. In some cases the repetition seems conspicuously produced: for example in 6.12, to say 'woman carrying shopping and dropping it' would convey the same sense (and be more elegant); and there are numerous ways to avoid the repetition of 'bird' in extract 6.13. The rejection of available pronouns in these cases suggests that participants' descriptions may be designed to achieve a poetic character.

Epanalepsis refers to the repeat of a word or clause at the beginning and the end of a line. We can illustrate this figure of speech by reference to Donne's poetry. From his poem 'The Dreame', the word 'when' occurs at the start and end of the line 17: 'When thou knew'st what I dreamt, when though knew'st when' (Magnusson, 2006: 191). There are some cases in the introspective data of participants saying the same word at the start and end of a discrete report of imagery.

(6.14) (01-80: E1/M)

```
1    P:    pebbles (4.8) pebbles on a beach (4.8) a lo:ng bea:ch
2          (12.2)
3    →     sea: (5.8) doesn't ↑move (3) no wa:ves (5.9) static sea:
4          (30.4)
5    →     a face: (19.7) no li:nes (.) ju:st a- (4.2) a hint (0.4) of eye: (2.4) and
6          no:se (6.6) ° but I- feel a face° (4) sense a face
7          (36.3)
8          a ↑cat (5.5) a ca:t (5.3) bri:ght (0.7) pai:nted (9.2) empty (.) ca:t (1.7)
9          tipped (3.4) (no horse)
10         (117.5)
11   →     ro:cks (6.1) ro:cks (1) fla:t (3.1) no:t a cliff (4.7) hhh (5.6) like (1.7) >a
12         ↑fist< (3.5) fist of ro:cks
```

In this short section there are three instances of imagery reports that begin and end with the same word or phrase: 'sea' (line 3), 'a face' (lines 5 and 6) and 'rocks' (lines 11 and 12). This is not an idiosyncrasy of this participant.

(6.15) (01-52: E1/F)

```
1          (1.7) ((coughs)) (1.2) ((swallows)) hhhh ˙hhhh hhhh
2    P:    bla:ck ho:rse (.) °uh° just this really bla- >I dunno if I've just< got it
```

3   (.) stuck in my hea::d (0.7) about a <u>bla</u>ck ho:rse
4   (4.3)

(6.16) (01-69: E2/M)

1   (8)
2   P: sta::mps (7) ora:nge (.) °book abou- sta::mps°
3   (3.5)

More common, however, are instances of an *acoustic* form of epanalepsis, in which the first and last words begin with the same sound.

(6.17) (01-69: E2/M)

1   (25.5)
2   P: co:rk bobbing around in a: (.) a bucke:t- (6) pin through 'em (2.5) 's a
3   compa:ss
4   (20.4)

Acoustic, alliterative forms of epanalepsis can provide more evidence of the designed character of poetic forms in the participants' descriptions. In extract 6.17, there is no epanaleptic relationship in the original imagery report (although there is an alliterative one in 'bobbing' and 'bucket'). The epanalepsis occurs only when the original imagery is expanded to include a reference to a compass. The additional description not only provides more information about conscious experiences — the core requirement of this part of the experiment — but acts as vehicle for the accomplishment of an epanaleptic relationship. Extract 6.18 provide even stronger evidence of the designed character of epanalepsis.

(6.18) (01-05: E3/F)

1   (24.0)
2   P: 'n a< moun:tai:n
3   (27.1)
4   well there's a load've windo:ws, (0.8) in a wa::ll
5   (35.1)

The epanalepsis occurs in line 4. The first word is 'well', which is an unusual lexical choice in this turn, in that it does not seem to do the kind of work it might be used to perform in conversational interaction. It does not mark a disaffiliative response, because there is no prior turn offering an assessment to which the participant has to respond; it does not preface a turn in which the participant changes her mind about, extends or amends a prior description, because the turn it prefaces is topically disjunctive to the prior turn (the topic of which was 'on [or in, or and] a mountain'); it is not an idiosyncratic speech habit of this participant, as no other imagery reports in this introspective monologue begin with 'well'; and, finally, it is unlikely to mark the participant's surprise at the imagery, as, 'a load of windows' is not particularly striking, and it is in keeping with the imagery she has reported previously. There is no reason for it to be used; but it does establish an alliterative relationship with the key word in the subsequent imagery report.

Alternative forms of epanalepsis are illustrated in the following extracts.

(6.19) (01-85: E2/M)

```
1        (26.9)
2    P:  >people:< (0.3) tramp? (.) u:- of (0.3) BO:y: with lo:ng hair ˙hhh (0.3)
3        BOUncing u:p (0.6) >into my vision and away again as if from a
4        trampo↑line< (2.9) loo:ks ha:ppy:
5        (5.5)
```

In this case, the poetic relationship is not established through the use of the same sound to start the first and last words, but through words in which the same sound is prominent: the 'p' sound in 'people' and 'happy'. And in extract 6.20, the epanalepsis is achieved via an adjective to describe an aspect of the imagery that echoes the first sound of the description.

(6.20) (01-95: E1/F)

```
1        (40.3)
2    P:  (.3) fly:ing on an aeropla:ne (.) an:- looking do:wn at- the clou::ds °fro:m
3        abo:ve°(1.5) a:ll fluffy: whi:te
4        (62.5)
```

Anaphora refers to the repeat of a word or phrase at the start of adjacent clauses or phrases within rhetoric or poetry. In the introspective reports, there is an acoustic parallel in which sounds, not words, may be repeated at the start of adjacent imagery reports. Acoustic anaphora is achieved through alliteration, or repeated assonance or consonance at the start of adjacent utterances reporting discrete unconnected imagery. Extract 6.21 provides a simple example.

(6.21) (01-46: E3/M)

```
1        (12.3)
2    P:  (och um) (0.4) corner of a (0.2) a white room
3        (14)
4        corrugated (.) surface
```

Here, the 'cor' sound of 'corner' is repeated in 'corrugated' (and is partially echoed in the traditionally Scottish expression 'och'). However, sound runs at the start of imagery descriptions may extend beyond two discrete reports. For example:

(6.22) (01-29: E2/M)

```
1          (16)
2    P:    a fi:re ba::ll (3.3) co:me:t: (6.2) hi:ttin- the gre:enho:use
3          (18.5)
4          fa:ces (2.8) 'n fre:d fli:ntsto::ne
5          (24.7)
6          (tt) ˙hh an' a fat man with ey::es comin- out:
```

(6.23) (01-83: E2/F)

```
1          (6.3)
2    P:    °u::m: ° a s:pider? ↑or something? or a flower?
3          (7.1)
4          °uh° (0.2) SPINni:ng (0.5) circular
5          (6.3)
6          u::h (.) speck >of< light (0.2) moving fr- to the bottom ri:ght- (3.1) diagonal
7          line top left to bottom ri:ght (0.9) moving do:wn towards the bottom ri:ght
8          (2.8)
9          RIpples in the wate:r
```

In these two extracts, three consecutive reports begin with the same sound: respectively 'f' ('fire', 'faces' and 'fat') and 'sp' ('spider', 'spinning' and 'speck'). There are other sound relationships hinted at in these data. In extract 6.22, there is a strong 'a' sound in 'fat' and 'faces', and the subsequent addition of the cartoon character 'Fred Flintstone' to an initial report establishes an epanaleptic relationship within that turn. In extract 6.23 it is noticeable that the last item begins with 'ripples', a word that strongly preserves the 'p' sound in the three prior turns.

Some participants provide very short, or even one word, descriptions of their imagery, and in these cases, the anaphoric relationship can be prominent over long stretches of turns.

(6.24) (01-46: E3/M)

```
1          (6.6)
2    P:    ˙hh (1.4) fi::li:ng (0.6) pa:pe:r
3          (10.2)
4          like a neon (0.6) sig:n
5          (17.4)
6          foo:tprints
7          (35.2) ((clicking sound)) (0.8)
```

8	's like a (.) a wrought ir:on ga:te
9	(13.1)
10	fer:ns:
11	(42.1)
12	for:k:
13	(15.5)
14	sunse:t
15	(32.8)
16	sta:rs
17	(32)
18	s:nowfla:kes
19	(9.6)
20	(fie:lds)
21	(92.2)

In this extract, there seems to be a broad clustering of two sounds: 'f' in 'filing', 'footprints', 'ferns', 'fork' (and in what sounds like 'fields'), and 's' in 'sign', 'sunset' and 'stars' (and is given prominence in ''s' like a' by the elision of the 'i' sound in 'it's'). These sounds can be said to exhibit such a strong anaphoric presence that they might be considered to be locally relevant sounds to this period of the introspective report. One word, 'snowflakes', rather nicely captures both locally prominent sounds (as well as the 'n' sound found in 'neon', 'footprint', 'iron' and 'sunset').

Anadiplosis is the repetition of a word ending one clause and the start of the next. The acoustic variant sees assonance, consonance or alliterative relationships between the last utterance of an imagery report, and the turn initial components of a subsequent report. In extract 6.25 this is established by the 'l' and 'n' sounds in 'lens' and 'lion'. In extract 6.26, there are two consecutive cases: the 's' in 'swollen' and 'smoke', and the 'ka' sound in 'castle' and 'candle'.

(6.25) (01-25: E1/M)

1		(3.4)
2	P:	°m:° u(h)m::, (4.3) ye:ah (.) looking into the sun (1.8) um:: >quite a<
3		sma:ll sun? (1.4) >but< a::,m::::: s:plit out >by a< (1.6) by a le:ns
4		(12.1)
5		hh l:ion (2.7) °m:::° hhh ˙hh (0.7) m:::::::: hhh ẏhh (2.4) m::: hhh
6		>lion?< ˙h um: (.) chinese dragon hhh (1.9) m(hh): s:- (.) >pseudo< lion
7		(13.2)

(6.26) (01-29: E2/M)

1		(11)
2	P:	ey::es:: s:wollen

```
3        (3.5)
4        smoke an- mist round a ca:stle?
5        (13)
6        candle holders (.) on a wall (1.5) wooden
7        (4.2)
```

As we noted earlier, it is possible to discern other sound relationships in the vicinity of more formal structures such as anadiplosis. For example, in extract 6.25 there is a concentration of words beginning with an 's' sound ('sun', 'small', 'split' and 'pseudo'). It also contains an instance of epanalepsis, in that the word 'lion' begins and ends a discrete imagery report. And in extract 6.26, 'castle' and 'candle' are both two syllable words that both begin with a hard 'c' and end with an 'l' sound; and there is a recurrent 'n' sound in the words 'swollen', 'round' 'candle' and wooden'. (With respect to which, the curtailed 'and' in 'smoke an- mist' ensures that there is another 'n' sound given prominence in this run.)

Acoustic anadiplosis can be achieved by words with similar sounds, even if they are structurally very different.

(6.27) (01-18: E1/M)

```
1        (33.5)
2   P:   ʰhh feel like I'm >wobbling< from side to si::de
3        (4.4)
4        cycling (0.5) >cycling< down north bridge
5        (6.1)
6        the big issue.
```

Here there is alliteration and assonance in the 's' and 'i' sounds of 'side' and 'cycling'. (And there is a further echoic relationship established by the repeat of the word 'cycling', thus mirroring the lexical repeat in the phrase 'side to side'.) Although it is not so clear-cut, there may also be anadiplosis in the relationship between the 'b' and 'i' sounds of 'bridge' and 'big'.

In the following extract, anadiplosis is achieved by words that stem from different languages.

(6.28) (01-18: E1/M)

```
1        (9.8)
2   P:   I c'n see: a bal- it's like I'm flying over, (1.3) flying over a big canyon
3        no:w (0.6) ʰhh there:'s more like a valley I c'n see::, ʰh it's not a river I can
4        see s'rt've um::, (0.3) towns 'n (.) ʰh houses and a lot of (1.1) by flyin' above
5        the:: u::::: >the level< of the: (0.3) ʰhh hhh it reminds me of u: mesa verde?
6        (13.1)
7        mice:. something ʰhh (.) u- yes I >s'rt've< can't've quite make it out °u: u:°
8        maybe 's that's why it makes you think of mice:?
```

9   (49.1)

In the first extensive report, the participant is describing the things he can see during a sensation of being in flight. This concludes when he reports imagery of housing that brings to mind a specific place, Mesa Verde, which he pronounces with a strong Spanish accent. (He is presumably referring here to famous cliff dwellings in Mesa Verde National Park in Colorado, US, an area that was named by Spanish explorers in the 1760s.) The next imagery report is 'mice', which echoes key sounds in 'mesa' (and continues a sound run of words beginning with words containing 'm': 're-mind', 'something', 'make', 'maybe' and 'makes').

Anadiplosis may be delayed by the insertion of words or phrases prior to the key word in an imagery report. For example, they can be delayed by turn components that announce that imagery is available, or that describes how it is apprehended (such as 'there's a' or 'I can see'). In its simplest form, anadiplosis can be delayed by an indefinite article. There are two cases in the following extract: 'dot' and '*a* doorway' and 'past' and '*a* picture'.

(6.29)(01-05: E3/F)

1   (25.5)
2   P: (hh)wa:y:, in the horizon >far away< (1.3) °j'st a° dot
3   (19.4)
4   ʰh a:: doorwa:y h (0.7) ʰh made of stone,
5   (15.4)
6   hhh things seem to be- (.) um:, (0.9) pa:ssing (2.4) going pa:st.
7   (28)
8   hh ʰh u- a picture (0.4) in a fra:me
9   (11.3)

In the introspective data, there are descriptive sequences in which sounds seemed to be repeated, but in reverse. For example, in extract 6.30, the 's' of 'spider' and the word 'like' are echoed in the repeat of 'like' followed by 'star'.

(6.30)(01-83: E2/F)

1   (8.5)
2   P: sp̲ider like (0.2) l̲ines converging agai̲:n (0.2) °like a star°
3   (34.8)

As we noted in the introduction, Sacks had observed this phenomenon in conversational data, and called it reversal. This kind of reversal may be a form of *chiasmus*, a rhetorical figure in which sounds, letters, words, phrases or ideas are reversed to make a broader point. (The term chiasmus derives from a Greek word *chiazein*, meaning 'to mark with or in the shape of a cross'. It is related to antimetabole, which has similar properties; however, for the purpose of exposition, and following other scholars, we shall adopt the term 'chiasmus' to refer to both rhetorical forms). Chaismus appears in Greek and Latin writing from the time of Homer to the later Roman authors (Welch, 1981a). It is most commonly associated with the analysis of religious texts but occurs in a range of textual forms such as everyday maxims (Grothe, 1999), nursery rhymes (Welch, 1981b), in the discourse of advertising (McQuarrie and Mick, 1996), and in the plays of Shakespeare (Davis, 2003). Chiasmus can also be formed around the reversal of sounds, and instances have been examined in plays such as *Romeo and Juliet*, and in poetry, such as Milton's *Paradise Lost* (Nanny, 1994). On his website, Grothe offers an example from the first lines of Coleridge's poem *Xanadu*, here represented schematically and then phonetically:

in *Xan*-a-*du*

X

did *Ku*-bla-*Khan*

In *Zann*-uh-*doo*

X

did *Koo*-bluh-*Kann*

(From www.drmardy.com, accessed 15-8-2009)

The phonetic reversals are apparent: the 'an' and 'oo' sounds are reversed in the second clause of the line. It also occurs in the introspective data. Represented phonetically, the relevant sounds from extract 6.29 looks like:

sp̲id*uh like*

X

like uh s*tar*

Here there is clear repetition of the word 'like', and its inversion in the two phrases; there is also repetition of the 's' in 'spider' and 'star'; but there is also repetition of the 'uh' sound of 'a' and the last syllable of spider. The following two extracts show further instances within discrete descriptive turns.

(6.31) (01-18: E1/M)

```
1        (6.6)
2    P:  °>I c'n<° see things (.) pa:ssing >sort've< (2.4) patterns in the dogs 'n
3        co:nes,
4        (33.0)
```

*c'n ... pa*ssing

X

*pa*tterns *co*nes

Here, the c/n sound in the truncated 'can' and the 'pa' sound in 'passing' are repeated and reversed in the words 'patterns' and 'cones'.

(6.32) (01-85: E2/M)

```
1        (26.9)
2    P:  >people:< (0.3) tramp? (.) u:- of (0.3) BO:y: with lo:ng hair ˙hhh (0.3)
3        BOUncing u:p (0.6) >into my vision and away again as if from a
4        trampo↑line< (2.9) loo:ks ha:ppy:
5        (5.5)
```

*people... **tramp**... boy*

X

*bouncing... **tramp**oline...ha**pp**y*

In this case, there is a clear reversal in the sequence tramp/boy and bouncing/trampoline, an echoic relationship that is further established in the way that the first sounds of 'boy' and 'bouncing' are spoken at a louder volume than surrounding talk. And although not displaying the same neat symmetry within the structure of the report, the 'p' in the first word, 'people', is echoed in the last word, 'happy'.

There are, then, a number of poetic forms in the introspective reports produced by participants in this experiment: repetition of words, sound repetition at the start and end of turns, echoic patterns in sounds across discrete descriptions, and repetition and reversal of sounds that strongly resemble chiasmus identified in a range of classical texts.

Chiasmus can also occur across adjacent reports. In the following case, chiasmus and anadiplosis combine.

(6.33) (01-94: E2/F)

```
1        (6)
2    P:  and aga:in a fa::ce in the middle: (1.1) it ↑seems li:ke (.) stylistic (2) pi:ctures
3        (20.3)
4        a perso:n::? (0.2) °u-° sitting? an:- watching
```

***st**ylistic...**pi:**ctures*

X

*per**so:**n::...**sit**ting*

(6.34) (01-18: E1/M)

```
1          (14)
2    P:    balloon >I fel' like< (.) hh (2.5) 'h feel like I'm inside a big balloo:n
3          (33.5)
4          'hh feel like I'm >wobbling< from side to si::de
5          (4.4)
```

inside a big balloon
X
wobbling...side to side

Here sounds of the last words of one discrete imagery report are reproduced in reverse order, over thirty seconds later, in initial components of
the subsequent report.

Studies of chiasmus in classical literary and religious texts tend to focus
on the ways in which ideas or themes may be reversed, often in complex
forms, to achieve rhetorical ends. The following example is taken from
Welch's study of chiasmus in the Book of Mormon, and illustrates a conventional way in which complex forms of chiasmus can be represented as
a series of repeated and inverted themes. It is found in a speech by
Benjamin in which he tells the nation that they will be lost until:

[a] They *humble* themselves
   [b] and become as little *children*
      [c] believing that salvation is in the *atoning blood of Christ*
         [d] for the *natural man*
            [e] is an enemy to *God*
               [f] and *has been* from the fall of Adam
               [f] and *will be* forever and ever
            [e] unless he yieldeth to the *Holy Spirit*
         [d] and putteth off the *natural man*
      [c] and become a saint through the *atonement of Christ*
   [b] and becometh as a *child*
[a] submissive, meek and *humble*

(Welch, 1981d: 203)

This illustrates some of the ways in which echoic relationships may be
established: by the repeat of specific words ('humble'), phrases ('natural
man'), alternative references to the same thing ('God'/'Holy Spirit') and
alternative or contrastive formulations of the properties of a state of affairs
(the description of temporality in 'has been' and 'will be').

In studies of longer texts it is common for authors to identify the key
themes that arc inverted to achieve chiasmus. Following this step, we can

see that in their introspective reports, participants in the experiments do occasionally order their descriptions to display broadly charismatic structures. In the following extract, the participant is reporting imagery of animals.

(6.35) (01-52: E1/F)

```
1          (3.1)
2     P:   an- a dog with floppy ea:rs (0.8) >but it's not a real dog it's< (.) it's like uh::
3          (0.9) °an anima:ted dog° (2.2) uh (0.4) uh::: (0.3) dunno it's like it (looks like
4          a monkey)
5          (14.4)
```

The chiasmic form of this report is:

[a] an- a *dog* with floppy ea:rs	Report of animal
[b] but it's *not a real dog*	Unreal status
[b] like uh:: (0.9) °*an anima:ted dog*°	Unreal status
[a] dunno it's like it (looks like a *monkey*)	Report of animal

Here the first and last turn components report an animal, in this case, a dog and what seems to be a monkey; and the two intervening turn components both address the fact that the dog is not real.

There are clear methodological difficulties in attempting to identify chiasmus over longer stretches of talk. The key issue is grounding the analytic description of a turn or section of talk as a particular kind of turn. For example, with respect to the case in extract 6.35, it might be objected that the first and last turns are not chiasmic because one is about a dog and the other is about a monkey, and that the achievement of a chiasmal relationship — the commonality or connection between turn components — is simply achieved by noting that both are animals. The concern, then, is that the chiasmal relationship is not intrinsic to the organisation of the talk, but is imposed by analytic fiat. This is a reasonable objection, and one that is recognised to be relevant to all scholarship on chiasmus in literary and religious texts. As Welch has said, 'Evidence of chiasmus is not entirely objective and quantifiable', and that it is necessary to adopt broad or loose definitions of what chiasmus is (Welch, 1981b: 13), and, by implication, the criteria by which it can be identified. Any empirical claim, then, must be treated with caution. Our interest in looking for complex chiasmus organizations in the introspective data is supported by three observations. Notwithstanding the recognized methodological difficulties in warranting empirical claims, there is still a substantial body of scholarship on chiasmus, suggesting that there is a real set of phenomena to be addressed.

Second, the data from the introspective reports are at least indicative of chiasmus: it seems hard to reject the examples of acoustic chiasmus described earlier, and candidate instances of more complex forms we present here seem at least plausible candidates. Finally, we are emboldened by the position adopted by Sacks and Jefferson when they first began to collect and examine instances of conversational poetics: that, when first noticing a possible phenomenon, it was worthwhile to develop exploratory lines of analysis as far as they might be taken. In this spirit, we turn to the following extract, in which we argue that there is complex chiasmus that extends over several discrete imagery reports.

(6.36) (01-95: E1/F)

```
1         (26.3)
2    P:   remembered I left my bedroom window open?                              [1]
3         (14.3)
4         ((quiet click of mouth opening)) (1) gree::n jagua:r                   [2]
5         on a motorwa:y
6         (21.1)
7         iMAgini:ng I:'m flYi:ng in a spa:ce ro:cke:t                           [3]
8         (21.8)
9         ˙hh (.) ca:n see: a li:ttle:? (.) ˙hh (0.4) s::TRE:a:m (.) runni:ng    [4]
10        throu:gh (1.5) cracks ln a mountai:n? (1.3)
11        ANd- a rainbow? (0.4) fro:m one si:de to the: othe:r?
12        (29)
13        r'ME:mberi:ng I- have to pay the telepho:ne bill (6.3) And             [5]
14        the electricity: bi:ll
15        (14.3)
```

In this section of section of the participant's report there are five discrete imagery reports (numbered in square brackets in the extract) over which there are several recurrent and inverted themes. In the first discrete report, she recalls leaving her bedroom window open; and in the last discrete report she remembers that she has to pay telephone and electricity bills. There is one unambiguous form of inverted repetition here, in that both discrete reports are recollections, and begin with 'remembered'/'remembering'. However, both turns also refer to her concerns with domestic matters to do with *home*. (There is also a sense in which these turns are concerned with the participant's *responsibilities* toward the home: to keep it secure, and to pay service charges.) In the second discrete report, she reports imagery of a *green* jaguar car; the theme of colour is taken up in the last turn component of the penultimate imagery report, in which she refers not to a specific colour, but a *rainbow*, a natural phenomenon strongly associated with colours. The third discrete report and the first part of the penultimate report both address movement, and are introduced by reference to the manner by which imagery is apprehended in the 'mind's eye': so she says first, she is *imagining* that she is *flying* in a space rocket; she then says that she can *see* a stream *running*. Consequently, this sequence displays the following chiastic form:

[a] remembered I left my bedroom <u>win</u>do:w ope:n?

   [b] <u>gree</u>::n <u>jagua</u>:r on a <u>motorwa</u>:y

      [c] i<u>MA</u>gini:ng I:'m <u>flY</u>i:ng in a spa:ce ro:cke:t

      [c] ˙hh (.) ca:n se<u>e</u>: a li:ttle:? (.) ˙hh (0.4) s::<u>TRE</u>:a:m (.) runni:ng throu:gh (1.5) <u>cracks</u> <u>in</u> a <u>mountai</u>:n? (1.3)

   [b] ANd- a <u>rainbow</u>? (0.4) fro:m <u>one</u> si:de to the: <u>othe</u>:r?

[a] r'<u>ME</u>:mberi:ng I- have to <u>pay</u> the <u>telepho</u>:ne bi:ll (6.3) <u>And</u> the electricity: bill

Given the difficulty of making firm empirical claims about chiasmus, these analyses must be regarded as tentative evidence of the operation of a form of chiasmic organisation in the participants' descriptions of their mental imagery. But they are, at least, suggestive.

Discussion

Conversational poetics are common in everyday interaction. Many of these kinds of phenomena are also massively present in popular culture (in addition to literature and poetry): for example, what Jefferson called sound runs are found in the kind of alliteration that occurs in song lyrics, in advertising, and, in the UK, in the headlines of 'red top' tabloid newspapers. We are immersed in examples of this verbal playfulness, and therefore we might expect that everyday conversational practices such as poetics would be found in language in more unusual settings, such as the psychology laboratory. What is striking, though, is that in these data, it is clear that the participants do not merely use alliteration; there are some quite complex sound patterns that resemble figures of speech found in poetry, rhetoric and even classical texts. It seems unlikely that there was anything common to the participants' background to explain this. They were not recruited from a population known to have interest in rhetoric or the study of classical texts. Moreover, there was nothing in the experimental instructions that would lead the participants to aspire to poetic ornamentation in their reports. They had received no special training or instruction in how to describe during the experiment. So, whereas it seems easy to understand how participants in this experiment may be (tacitly) familiar with simple forms of poetics, such as sound runs, it is less easy to understand how they may be able to reproduce patterns that resemble complex forms such as anadiplosis and chiasmus.

Perhaps there is a simple explanation. Playfulness with vocalised sounds may be a feature of discourse and interaction from the moment humans evolved language. The pioneering studies of Sacks and Jefferson provide strong evidence that it is routine in everyday communication. And students of classical texts have argued that some rhetorical forms pre-date written language, and emerged initially in early oral traditions of poetry and story telling (Watson, W.G.E., 1981). If this is the case, and the sound patterns pre-date the written instantiations of those patterns, then what subsequently became known as anadiplosis, chiasmus and so on, are simply formalised expressions of everyday communicative competences. It is not that we have to explain how participants in the experiment produced complex sound organisations that resemble rhetorical figures of speech; what we have to explain is why they are not found more often.

This raises the question: what is it about *this* context that does facilitate poetic practices?

The conditions under which people took part may hold clues. There is anecdotal and experimental evidence that ostensible parapsychological phenomena are more likely to occur when people are in altered states of consciousness, such as those associated with deep relaxation and sensory deprivation. Consequently, the participants in this experiment were required to listen to a relaxation tape before the experiment began. During the experiment they were seated comfortably, by themselves, in a sound proofed room. They wore headphones that played white noise. Artificial lighting was switched off, except for a solitary lamp in the room that issued a soft red light, and their eyes were masked in such a way as to ensure an even light distribution over the retinal field. These conditions were designed to induce a mild form of sensory deprivation. Although participants knew that an experimenter was listening to their reports, they were informed that there would be no communication from the experimenter until this part of the procedure was complete. So: participants were asked to report out loud their imagery, while alone in a room, in a state of sensory deprivation, during a period in which their attention was focused entirely on their inner mental state, without any kind of feedback from the experimenter. Essentially, then, they were participating in an artificially engineered and interactionally constrained environment. Their attention was focused on their inner mental imagery, not on their external social and interactional context; their utterances constituted a monologue; there were no verbal responses to their reports; and there was no way visually to monitor any non-verbal reactions to what they were saying.

In the light of these considerations, there is a telling remark in Jefferson's (1996) paper on poetics. Her paper was based on a talk she had given and included transcription of a question and answer session at the end. In response to one question she remarked:

> there is a disproportionate amount of this stuff occurring in things like interviews or sportscasts, things where people are forced back into their own resources to talk, and keep re-using their own materials. I get the feeling that if they are kept out for long of this ongoing instant-by-instant monitoring of each other, they're almost in a state of sensory deprivation. (Jefferson, 1996: 48)

Jefferson's point was that, deprived of the 'ongoing instant-by-instant monitoring of each other' that occurs in everyday interaction, people's attentional states change, and therefore they become predisposed to draw upon poetic forms and practices. Some of her most compelling examples of conversational poetics were collected from radio sports commentaries, in which the commentator's job is to describe ongoing, live events to an overhearing audience that is denied visual access to the events being described. The parallels to the task of the participants in these experiments are striking: they, too, have to describe (in this case, *wholly* private) experiences for a non-interacting, overhearing audience. Perhaps, then, we should not be surprised to see conversational poetics emerging in these introspective reports, as the experimental procedures under which they were generated also happen to be highly conducive to the use of poetic forms.

Chapter Seven

Poetics as achievement

In the previous chapter we observed that some imagery reports seemed conspicuously designed to initiate or extend poetic forms, such as runs of a particular sound. In this chapter we consider four kinds of evidence that suggests participants may tacitly seek to realize poetics via pragmatic descriptive work: puns, and pun like relationships; extensions to imagery reports; conspicuous word selection, and speech errors. Our argument is that poetic phenomena are not accidental or happenstance, but that the poetic quality of introspective reports is an achievement. This has an important methodological implication for researchers using verbal introspective data to study consciousness and subjective experience, as it illustrates how the content of a report may be constituted through, and contingent upon, broader practices of description.

Puns, and pun-like relationships

The following extract contains a simple example of a pun.

(7.1) (01-05: E3/F)

```
1          (7.7)
2     P:   a book (.) open (5.4) big book
3          (31.0)
4          ˙hhh hh a ca(h)ke (1.0) with lots of tiers
5          (3.7)
6          tearful.
7          (4.8)
8          an' a ray of sun (0.8) ˙h going in a window or: >something<
```

In this extract there are four discrete imagery reports concerning a book, a cake, (being) tearful and a ray of sunlight. The pun concerns 'tiers' and 'tearful', and has two dimensions. Acoustically, it revolves around the repeat in 'tearful' of the root sound in the word 'tiers'. Semantically, it trades on an understanding that 'tiers', as in layers of a cake, is an homonym of the word 'tears', as in crying. The homonymous quality of 'tiers' and 'tears' highlights the work the participant has done to establish that a pun is being produced. So, had she simply said 'tears' then, as that has exactly the same pronunciation as 'tiers', she might have been heard as merely repeating the final word of the prior report. The adjectival form of the word establishes that it is not a mere repeat, and thereby makes the pun explicit. The pun-like character of the reports in the following extract also derives from recognition of alternative hearings of words.

(7.2) (01-25: E1/M)

```
1    P:   °m: um::° water °sorta:° ripply (0.2) pattern
2         (7.0)
3         u::m:, °m::::: hhh `hh° (.) stone:, ground? °uh: earth:: so,°
4         (8.9)
5         sun::?
6         (8.2)
7         u:m:, °m::.° parents
8         (13.0)
9         °m::° faces (.) °n'° `hhhhhh (.) people sitting:: (n)hhhhhhh
```

There are two puns here, each of which rests on the way that words in a prior report can be heard as relating to alternative sets of category relationships. In line 3 the participant reports imagery relating to land and rocks: 'stone', 'ground' and 'earth'. But 'earth' is also the name of the planet, and the next report, 'sun', also a celestial body, trades on this hearing. And then he reports 'parent', which puns on the alternative hearing of 'sun' as 'son'. Interestingly the report of 'parents' not only establishes a pun, also continues a run of 'p' sounds that is common in this stretch of the participant's mentation, as evidenced by 'ripply', 'pattern' and 'people' that also feature in this short section.

The cases we have examined so far seen to have their roots in the exploitation of immediately prior sounds. As such their provenance is identifiable in the surface of the narrative. But other puns have roots that are deeper in the participant's immediate experience. Extract 7.3 comes from the mentation of participant who regularly remarked upon his physical sensations.

(7.3) (01-79: E2/M)

```
1    P:   pressu:re bui:lding in ↑legs (2.1) che:st getting- warm: (4.8) pressu:re
2         >in the ear:s< (4.2) ˙hh (0.2) fo:rehea:d wa:rm (1.7) f:o:rea:rms wa:rm (2.4)
3         ↑BRIghtne:ss
4         (11.6)
5         a ↑WA::ve (3.4) body: fee:li:ng bouya:nt as if a wave:'s (2.5)
6         coming over?
7         (15.2)
8         blue:
9         (21.5)
10        full body: no:w ge:tting wa:rm (9.8) °clou:d° (0.7) ↓coo:l
11        (8.3) ˙hhh (0.8)
12        WAve: of pressu:re i:s (1.5) wAvi:ng ˙hhhhh ove:r my ↑body
13        (18.2) ˙hhhhh hh (0.6)
14        'n-↑sigh hhhhhhhhh
15        (2.7) ((gulping sound)) (5.2)
16        lig:ht blu:e (0.2) fla:sh
17        (10.8)
18        ↓warmth a↑gain
19        (14.8)
20        ˙hhh (0.4) warmth over:- (0.2) ↑whole body: (0.8) forehca::d (2) arm:s leg:s
21        (20.6)
22        >bird<
23        (8.4)
24        blue:: sky?
25        (9.3)
26        ↑SEA
27        (14.8)
28        s:ma::ll shi:p (1.2) sail
29        (13.3)
30        I- ˙hhh (6) ˙hhhh (2.5)
31        naval ho::t
32        ((Inaudible whispering)) (0.6) peach
```

Not only does the participant report the general sensation of warmth (line 18), he identifies which parts of his body feel warm at particular moments: his chest (line 1), his forehead (lines 2 and 20), his forearms (line 2), his arms (line 20) his legs (line 20) and his full body (lines 10 and 20). He then produces a series of reports which seem to display a topical coherence, in that discrete images relate to the category of the sea or seaside: so, the 'sea' (line 26), 'small ship' (28) and 'sail' are all objects that might be associated with a seafront vista (as might 'blue sky' and 'bird', in lines 22 and 24, and the repeat of 'wave' earlier in the extract). At this point he returns to the theme of warmth, and identifies another part of his body that feels hot, his navel (line 31). In the transcript, this is written as 'naval', but the addition of 'hot' strongly suggests that this is a further report of the sensation of heat. This is markedly different to other reports of bodily sensations, in that it identifies a specific and intimate part of the body. The word 'navel', however, seems particularly fitted to the prior theme of the sea in that it is acoustically identical to the word 'naval', which refers to the navy or warships. With respect to this, it is notable that the transcriber wrote 'naval', not 'navel', thus suggesting that she too heard the word as relating to its association with the sea, and not the body.

Routinely, puns, or pun-like relationships, seem to be built around categories of objects, activities, people and so on. The first extract of the previous chapter, for example, the participant invokes the senses, referring to how *heavy* a body is, the *smell* of death and the *sound* of silence. And in extract 7.2 a pun is built from the category 'family'. These category related puns are very numerous in the corpus. Here is another example of a family related sequence.

(7.4) (01-95: E1/F)

```
1          (21.3)
2     P:  ↑I ha:ve t' go shopping: befo:re the sho:p shu:ts (1) ge:t my da:d a
3          FAthe:r's da:y ca:rd
4          (31.4)
5          fee:ling a bit apprehensive about meeting bernard's mu:m again (6.8)
6          hoping we get along better this time?
```

The reference to 'dad', 'father' and 'mother' is also the vehicle of a contrast between the positive implications of celebrating one's father, against the implied frostiness of a meeting with another's mother. The following extract illustrates how a pun-like relationship can be built from a very specific category, in this case, the mouth.

(7.5) (01-85: E2/M)

```
1     P:  °u h::::° like >going into a< whi:rpoo:l
2          (6.3)
3          >lot:s've< °u:::° shu:dden light ↑image:s descending into it- (0.3)
4          ˙hh (0.2) be:ing sucked awa:y fro:m me
5          (4.2)
6          sudden:: (0.4) two: lines of ligh- like ↑teeth (0.3) °sha:rp° inciso:rs >°or
7          something°< ˙hhhh cutti:ng do:w:n (0.5) °throu:gh° (0.2) °°a:::°° (0.2)
8          >how I see:<
```

As part of his whirlpool imagery, the participant reports seeing light 'sucked away' (line 4). His next imagery report concerns sharp teeth. Both teeth and sucking are objects or activities associated with mouths.

As these kinds of pun-like relationships are so common, we will only examine cases that seem to suggest that the underlying organising principles can work at very subtle levels.

In extract 7.6, the participant is first describing imagery relating to the actor, Cary Grant.

(7.6)(01-69: E2/M)

```
1        (15.4)
2    P:  cary grant? (0.8) bla:ck and white fi::lm (5) °sta:ndi:ng° (0.2) >walking
3        down< towa:rds someo:ne
4        (22)
5        compass needle agai::n
```

After the initial report of the actor's name, the participant reports a black and white film, and then generic actions that might be seen in a film. There is a 22 second silence, and then the next discrete imagery report is 'compass needle again'. Initially, there seems to be little connection between the two reports. However, one of Cary Grant's most famous films is *North by North West*, directed by Alfred Hitchcock, the title of which is taken from points on a compass face. Is it possible that a chain of associations from 'Cary Grant' to the film, 'North by North West' to the concept of 'points on a compass' surface in a veiled form in a subsequent report of a compass needle? It seems unlikely; but there is another feature of this report that has a bearing on this issue. The participant reports that he is experiencing the imagery of the compass needle *again*. Reference to a compass occurs only once earlier in the mentation.

(7.7) (01-69: E2/M)

```
1    P:  a strong sensation of movement-
2        (25.5)
3        co:rk bobbing around in a: (.) >a bucke:t-< (6) pin through 'em (2.5) °'s
3        a° compass
5        (20.4)
6        °an::::° w:onderin- if you understand my voice? (.) is it? (0.4) seems a bit
7        slurred I'm so rela:xed
```

Two observations. Contrary to the participant's report in extract 7.6 that he is seeing the compass needle again, in this earlier reference to a compass there is no explicit mention of a needle (although it may be implied by reference to a pin). This is not a repeat of earlier imagery, then, but a reformulation of earlier imagery to which reference to a needle is an explicit addition. Furthermore, in the first reference to a compass (in which there is no report of a needle), the prior and subsequent reports are, respectively, about a sensation of movement, and reflections by the participant on his slurred speech—events and impressions wholly unconnected to specific compass points. The needle, though, is explicitly referenced immediately following a report that refers to Cary Grant, whose most famous film takes its title from a compass direction indicated by a needle. The modified repeat of the compass imagery, with the addition of reference to the needle, is further evidence of a pun like relationship between the two sets of images, a relationship that in turn points to the operation of a complex series of associations that inform the design of imagery reports.

Similarly complex associations may be implied by the imagery reports in the following extract.

(7.8) (01-18: E1/M)

```
1        (8.0)
2    P:  >and a< bob dylan song (0.8) I can't- >well I can-< don't know the na:me
3        (16.7)
4        someone's: (.) holding something up °I s-° I can't see but I know it's a fish:
5        ´hh s'rt've they've pulled the fish out've the water:,
         ((Continues))
```

Amongst his many achievements Dylan is credited with making one of the first video clips to accompany a pop song—the forerunner of the music promotional video. In 1965 Dylan released the song *Subterranean Homesick Blues*. In 1967 this song and the accompanying film were featured in a documentary about Dylan called *Don't Look Back*, directed by D.A. Pennebaker. The relevance of this to the two imagery reports is that Dylan's video famously depicts him standing in a street holding up and then discarding large pieces of card on which are written words and phrases from the lyrics, while the song is played on the film soundtrack. Dylan's video has been extraordinarily influential: the visual trope of a person holding up and then discarding cards on which were written song lyrics has been copied in numerous music videos (and in other media; there is, for example, a scene in the film *Love Actually* when a character surreptitiously woos another on her doorstep via the use of declarations written on large cards, which are subsequently discarded). In the light of this, it is at least intriguing, then, that the imagery following the report of an unnamed Bob Dylan song is 'someone's: (.) holding something up'—a description that captures the defining feature of a Dylan video that has attained iconic status in contemporary popular culture.

Poetic relationship by extensions to initial imagery

We have seen that participants can describe their conscious imagery via complex reports in which an initial description is subsequently expanded upon, extended or elaborated. This occurs even when there is no reason to suppose that the imagery being reported is changing or in flux, a circumstance that might necessitate ongoing and developing commentary. For example, in extract 7.9 the participant reports a sensation connected to a personal relationship (as opposed to an event or sensation being perceived in her 'mind's eye'); there is a 1.3 second gap and then she continues this imagery, offering further reflection on that relationship.

(7.9) (01-95: E1/F)

```
1          (65.6)
2    P:    not looking forward to kay coming ↑home (1.3) HOping we don't have
3          more argume:nts
4          (72)
```

Here the first word of the extension component, 'hoping' echoes the 'ho' sound of the last word of the initial report, 'home', an echoic relationship strengthened by the slight increase in volume on the production of the first, key syllable. Omission of 'I am' or 'I'm' prior to 'hoping' facilitates the adjacency of the echoic sounds, thereby making them more prominent, and provides further evidence of an orientation to achieve poetic relationships.

   Extensions to initial imagery reports are routinely used to establish a poetic relationship, or, if a sound run is always underway, to develop that further, as illustrated in extract 7.10.

(7.10) (01-85: E2/M)

```
1    P:    a dark shadow like a- 'at °of a cl- a° clou:d
2          (33.3)
3          °as° thou:gh (.) ˙hhh (0.3) things rushi:ng past >from the right to the le:ft<
4          (0.4) °all the ti:me° (1.9) >like ripple:s<
5          (15.7)
```

In line 3 the participant reports 'things rushing past'. This could be the end of the report in that it has reached the end of a turn construction unit (Sacks *et al.*, 1974). However, this potential terminal point is rejected and the subsequent rushed through component (Schegloff, 1982) contains the word 'right', echoing the prior 'r' sound in 'rushing'. After two further potential terminal points (after 'left' and 'time') there is a further extension containing the word 'ripples', thus consolidating the 'r' run emergent from the prior turn components.

Complex, multi-component imagery reports may be the vehicles for the development and consolidation of a number of related or intersecting sound runs. For example, in extract 7.11, there is an initial prominent sound run established by words containing a hard 'i' sound. (This is a reformatted version of extract 6.4)

(7.11) (01-52: E1/F)

```
1    P:   ... got gloves on (1.1) and they're pointing up to the sky (1.4) but
2         there's nothing else but the ha:nds there's nothing tha- (0.3) at the
3         e:nd of the ha:nds (3.7)
4         an:d >and a fi:st< (0.4)
5    1→   an- (1.5) a scraped ou- (1.6) bits that fi:ngers have ma:de (0.3) in in the
6         mu:d (2.8)
7    2→   an s'rt've bits've (0.7) LIttle bits (0.3) little lumps've mud (0.7)
8    3→   piled up in a triangle
```

The relevant sequence begins in line 4 with the description 'an:d >and a fi:st<'. This constitutes a potentially complete turn, terminated at the end of the word 'fist'. The report continues, though, and there are three subsequent extension sequences (arrowed and numbered in the transcript): the first beginning in line 5 ('scraped ou- (1.6) bits that fi:ngers have ma:de (0.3) in in the mu:d'), another in line 7 ('an s'rt've bits've (0.7) LIttle bits (0.3) little lumps've mud') and then finally at line 8 ('piled up in a triangle'). Each extension 'picks up' and develops a sound prominent in the prior TCU-bounded description. The 'f' sound in 'fingers' echoes 'fist'; the hard 'i' sound run is developed and consolidated through the first and second extension components; a sound run around 'm' is initiated in the first extension and developed in the second extension, and the third extension component develops the 'l' sound prominent in the second extension component. Extensions to initial imagery reports, then, can be exploited to establish or consolidate poetic sound runs.

It may be objected that participants are merely reporting the experiences and sensations of which they are introspectively aware, and not evidence of an orientation to a design procedure. There are two responses. First, there is a substantial empirical and philosophical literature (that need not be rehearsed here), that rejects the idea that words can simply correspond to events or states of affairs in the world, (be they 'objective' external events or ostensible 'inner' mental phenomena). But more prosaically (but perhaps just as compelling), there are instances in the data where evidence of turn design to achieve a poetic relationship seems utterly transparent.

(7.12) (01-85: E2/M)

```
1          (15.8)
2    P:    >I- see a-< °f:: u-° ˙hhh (0.2) °u: ° ma↓donna: (1) ˙hhh (0.2) bu:t
3          >as if she's been badly dr↑awn:< (1.5) ˙hhh (0.3) an- her head's the shape
4          of a ke::yho:le (4.5) >or a< pawn
5          (20.6)
```

If we exclude breathing, non lexical vocalizations, silences and projected but abandoned words, then this sequence can be rewritten to highlight its rhyming qualities.

I see a Madonna but as if she's been badly drawn
and her head's the shape of a keyhole or a pawn

It is the phrase 'like a pawn' which establishes the rhyming quality of the description, but this is added after a relatively long intra-report silence of 4.5 seconds. This is speculative, but it is at least possible that the participant tacitly recognised that, given the rhythm of 'I see a Madonna but as if she's been badly drawn', that 'and her head's the shape of a keyhole' seemed somehow incomplete; and that this recognition informed the production of a further extension component terminating with a word that rhymes with 'drawn'.

The following extract provides a clearer example of the way that introspective reports may be designed to achieve a poetic character.

(7.13) (01-95: E1/F. In this case, names have not been anonymised; this is because the poetic relationship is intimately tied to the sound components in the names used by the participant; see Jefferson, 1996.)

```
1          (16.6)
2    P:    remembering going to: (0.6) tatton PArk (1) with tracy an:- (0.2) ma:rk
3          (18.1)
```

In the initial component the participant reports her recollection of an event: a visit to a park. There is then a one second gap, and she extends the report to name others who were with her. Setting aside that the participant could have selected not to extend the report, consider her identification of the other people referred to in her subsequent talk. She names them, but did not have to: 'with others', or 'with friends' would have been logically as accurate; moreover, she could have described them as Mark and Tracy. But neither of these formulations would establish a poetic relationship with her prior talk. Her extension is designed exquisitely to stand as a rhyming and rhythmic couplet in which 'Tatton Park' is rhymed with 'Tracy and Mark',

Poetic associations via conspicuous word selections

In her examination of poetics in ordinary conversational interaction, Jefferson noted instances in which a particular poetic phenomenon, such as a sound run, may be constituted through a turn that exhibits a peculiar design, or which seems clumsy, or slightly forced, or ill fitted to the occasion in which it is produced (Jefferson, 1996). This is true also for the mentation narratives: there are numerous instances in the data where the participant's use of a word seems conspicuous, because its relationship to the ongoing talk seems strained. For example:

(7.14) (01-85: E2/M)

```
1        (7)
2    P:  a little yapping bit of light yapping >°like a little hyena:°<
3        (2)
```

There are three components to this imagery report: 'a little yapping ', 'bit of light yapping and '>°like a little hyena:°<', the last two of which repeats some aspect of the prior. The participant is describing his impression of a sound, 'yapping', which transpires to be a noise made by an animal (as opposed to a non-serious or exaggerated characterisation of talking). The first conspicuous feature of this report is the use of the adverbial use of 'little' and 'light' to describe the 'yapping', as both seem unfitted to the job of capturing a quality of a noise made by an animal. This is particularly evident if we substitute a synonym for 'yapping', such as 'barking', as 'light barking' is not a common phrase, and indeed, seems particularly unusual. But more conspicuous is the phrase '>°like a little hyena:°<'. First, the choice of 'hyena' is odd because it is wild animal that is not indigenous to Europe (let alone Scotland). But more significant, hyenas are known to make — and are conventionally associated with — a high pitched noise often said to resemble (cruel) laughter; they are not known for 'yapping'. An animal more conventionally associated with 'yapping' would be a (small) dog. Of course, though, 'hyena' preserves the run of 'y' sounds initiated via the repeat of 'yapping', whereas 'dog' does not. It seems that the historically sensitive word selection procedures hypothesised by Sacks (1992, vol. II: 342) have in this case delivered a word fitted to locally prominent or relevant sounds, even if that word is ill fitted to — and indeed, jars with — the conventional expectations implied by the prior talk.

Conspicuous word selections can be fitted to sound runs developed over multi-component imagery reports. In the following extract the participant's report of a series of geographical related images is built from numerous words beginning with 'p', or in which a 'p' sound is prominent: 'precipice', 'shape', 'point', 'peaks', 'perspective', and then 'pyramid', which is repeated. He then names a specific person.

(7.15) (01-25: E1/M)

```
1          (11.0)
2    P:    precipice: (2.0) um:::::: kinda shape, rising to a point, (3.6) concave sides
3          (5.1) hum peaks (4.8) peaks °m:::° UM::: °m° (.) peaks °uh° with a:
4          in perspective (4.8) (h)um:, °m:::° (4.2) ((swallows)) (0.9)
5          °m° sorta co:nes? °m::° (7.2) going off to a: °uh,° (0.4) ˙hh
6          a (.) horizon: (1.2) pyramid, (5.5) °°m::::°° pyramid: °um::°
7          anish kapoor::, (.) sculpture
8          (9.8)
```

Anish Kapoor is a well-known artist working in the UK. His surname sustains the 'p' sound run established in prior imagery reports. Stating his name also facilitates a further extension, in that it makes relevant and leads to a report of the category of art for which he is renowned, sculpture, which also contains the relevant sound (though less explicitly than previous word selections). But other than sustaining ongoing acoustic relationships, there seems little to warrant his name being mentioned: the prior description concerns geographical features, which then develops into a report on geometric shapes; it is not about explicitly aesthetic or artistic shapes, as might be associated with sculpture. As in the case with the previous extract, a conspicuous and unanticipated word selection (in the form of person identification), and (in this case) category selection, sustains an ongoing poetic relationship.

Conspicuous word selection can exhibit extraordinarily delicate properties. The next extract is taken from part of an introspective report in which there is a very strong run of words again starting with or containing the letter 'p'.

(7.16) (01-46: E3/M)

```
1    P:    pa:rro:t
2          (14.7)
3          ˙hh (0.4) 's: like a (.) a ro:bo:co:p (0.4) type (0.2) fi:gu:re
4          (10.7)
5          ˙h (0.4) pro:fi:le of a fa:ce
```

In the context of a run of 'p' sounds (as evidenced here by 'parrot' and 'profile') is the report of 'a ro:bo:co:p (0.4) type (0.2) fi:gu:re'. *Robocop* is the title of a very well known science fiction film about a half-human, half-robot police officer (Orion Pictures, 1987, directed by Paul Verhoeven), which went on to spawn two sequels, television series and computer games. The special effects design of the cyborg police officer is very distinctive, so much so that it could be said to have attained an iconic status to science fiction fans, and in movie lore more generally; it would certainly be known to someone who would refer to the film to clarify some aspect of their imagery. The participant does not say 'Robocop', however, but 'a Robocop type figure'. This is odd: had the participant wanted to convey general robotic aspects of his imagery — for example, staccato mechanical movement, or metallic humanoid shapes — then the word 'robot' would have sufficed, and citing a specific robotic character would have been unnecessary. Similarly, had the participant experienced an image of the visually distinctive Robocop character, he could have simply reported 'Robocop', and not that 'type [of] figure'. There is, though, a poetic logic to the design of this turn. 'Robot' would not sustain the ongoing 'p' run, whereas 'Robocop' does. And qualifying the imagery as a being of that *type* further continues the poetic form. The words 'robocop' and 'type' therefore extends the already established acoustic poetic.

Poetic relationship by speech errors

In her study of poetics in conversational interaction, Jefferson observed how poetic events may be constituted through, or reproduced in, the production of an incorrect or repaired word selection (Jefferson, 1996; see also, Hopper, 1992). This also occurs in mentation introspective reports.

(7.17) (01-52: E1/F)

```
1          (12.9)
2     P:   lots of windo:ws (0.3) like gothic (1) ˙hhhh (0.4) like u:m big
3          archway windo:ws (2.7) ((dental click)) (0.5) in in a (.) in a ro:w (0.3) like
4          hundreds and hundreds >of them in a row on a wa:ll<
5          (47.5)
```

In this imagery report there is a run of 'w' sounds ('windows' repeated, 'wall', and 'row' repeated). In line 3, the participant is trying to describe the kind of window being experienced in her 'mind's eye', and she says first, that they are gothic, and then, that they are *archway* windows. An archway is a passage or entrance, and is not a word conventionally associated with window shapes. However, an *arched* window is both a common phrase and a distinctive (and not uncommon) shape of window. There are grounds, then, to assume that she has made an error in her word selection, and that she was attempting to say 'arched' and said 'archway' by mistake. The error contributes towards and continues the sound run in progress, a continuation that would not have occurred had the participant selected the correct word, 'arched'.

Poetic phenomena arising from speech errors can display delicate relationships to ongoing and subsequent talk.

(7.18) (01-94: E2/F)

```
1          (17.6)
2    P:    looking fro::m? °ri:ght to le:ft° (.) like i:n? (0.6) profill profi:le
3          (12.7)
4          somethi:ng li:ke the- (0.5) pOI:nt of a finger? (6.2) °a graduating? poi:nt of
5          finger?° (1.4) it cha::nges: (1) mo:ves:
6          (76.3)
```

In this sequence, the participant makes an error in her pronunciation of the word 'profile', saying 'profill' instead, and then corrects herself. There follows a 12.7 silence before she begins the next discrete imagery report, which is an attempt to describe ambiguous imagery that involves shapes, perspective, change and movement. In this report she says 'point of a finger' and then later, 'point of finger'. What is interesting is that the earlier incorrect attempt at 'profile', 'profill', anticipates features of the subsequently repeated phrase: the last syllable of 'profill' pre-empts the 'fi' sound in finger, whereas the different 'i' sound in 'profile' does not. Perhaps even more subtle, the 'p' and 'o' sound of 'profill'/'profile' anticipates the key acoustic component of 'point'. (And it could be argued that 'point of a finger'/'point of finger' are further examples of conspicuous or odd turn design, in that there is ambiguity as to what they actually refer to or mean, and that they are not common phrases. But the alternatives — 'a finger pointing', or 'the end of a finger' — would not achieve the acoustic symmetry with the 'p' then 'o' then 'f' sound template established by 'profill'/'profile'.)

The final two cases present a methodological problem in that, although the analytic observations focus on observable and describable features of utterance design, the nature of the poetic relationships so implied invite a degree of speculation about unobservable or unconscious psychological phenomena. This interpretative step is unfamiliar and uncomfortable to many working in a broadly conversation analytic tradition, but we proceed, on three grounds. First, the demonstrable features of turn design seems strong enough to warrant a measure of speculation; second, in her extensive analysis of conversational poetics, Jefferson (1996) frequently made reference to psychological processes, especially in her discussion of speech errors; and finally, we believe this step is in the spirit of Sacks' exhortation to remain open to the possibility that poetic phenomena can exhibit complex forms of orderliness (Sacks, 1992).

(7.19)(01-95: E1/F)

1	P:	˙hh °ca-° see: the turre:ts o:f a ca:stle:?
2		(21.3)
3		wo:ndering if my boyfriend's got SA:fe ho:mely?
4		(26.3)
5		((*sound of mouth opening and closing*))
6		remembered I left my bedroom window open?

At the arrowed line the participant reports her preoccupations with her boyfriend and his well-being. She says 'safe homely', which is very likely to be an incorrect attempt at 'home safely' — she has simply inverted the order of words 'home' and 'safe' (with a slight increase in volume on the 'sa-' sound). This error is not repaired, so it can be assumed that she is unaware of the mistake. The report on her boyfriend's well-being is a discrete imagery report. There follows a silence of over 26 seconds, and then she reports that she has remembered that she left her bedroom window open (produced with a rising intonation, suggesting a measure of doubt as to whether she had left it open or not). An open window to an unoccupied room invites anxieties about intruders, burglary, theft and so on. The error in the prior imagery report is 'safe home' (modified to an adjectival form by the addition of 'ly' to 'home'), a phrase which poetically chimes with precisely the kinds of concerns about security that follow from realising that one's home may be vulnerable to criminal acts.

The inversion of the sounds in the phrase 'home safely' is a spoonerism. Jefferson argued that these kinds of errors can be viewed as a form of Freudian slip, where the errors point to something of psychological significance to the speaker. She discusses a case from a commentary on an American football match where the commentator is reporting action involving black players, and says 'Jones was not open on that pay — play, both backs in their blocking'. The error here is saying the word 'pay' instead of 'play'. She argues that the commentator was trying to avoid saying 'both blacks', which would pointedly focus on the racial characteristics of the players, and that in an attempt to ensure that the 'l' did not get misplaced from 'blocking' to 'backs', making 'blacks', he removed it unnecessarily from the word 'play', hence the incorrect word 'pay' (Jefferson, 1996: 8). The 'safe homely' error has similar properties, in that it registers matters of personal significance of which the speaker may have no conscious awareness. But there is something different about the 'safe homely' case.

In the kind of data Jefferson examined, the relevant psychological or personal issue is inferentially available at the time of the speech error. It manifests at the same moment in the talk in which it is repaired: in the case from the sports commentary, in an immediate self-repair within the turn construction unit containing the repairable item (Schegloff, *et al*, 1977). In the case from extract 7.19, the relevance of the error 'safe homely' does not become apparent until the next imagery report, nearly thirty seconds later. Perhaps this tells us something interesting about the way the mind works. If we assume the report on the window reflects unconscious concerns about personal security that were touched off by the error 'safe homely', then this fragment suggests that these kinds of unconscious concerns can resonate for some time after the error which is their trigger, or at least withheld until it is appropriate to offer another imagery report. There is another possibility, of course: it may be the case that the error represents a precognitive anticipation of a thought yet to come.

Discussion

There are a number of contemporary discussions of the methodological problems in the collection and evaluation of introspective data (Cardeña, 2004; Hurlburt and Schwitzgebel, 2007). Most critiques of the value of introspection revolve around problems that are well known in social sciences: in reporting their inner experience, people may exaggerate, confabulate or self-censor their experiences; they may provide the kind of responses they think the researcher is looking for; they may lack the linguistic skills accurately to capture their phenomenal experience, and so on. Underlying these kinds of critical observations is a 'common sense' view that consciousness or experience is an entity that, in principle, can yield to observation and description. But rarely is consideration given to the possibility that the descriptive resources by which inner experience is 'discovered' and made public for analysis may in significant ways *constitute* those experiential phenomena.

But that seems to be happening in the introspective narratives we have examined here. There is evidence that the range of poetic phenomena we have identified are not just a pleasing happenstance, but achieved outcomes of tacit, descriptive work: the extension of an initial report of imagery to include more locally prominent sounds, or the selection of words that initiate or sustain a run of a particular sound, even when the words selected may be conspicuously ill-fitted to their environment; or the production of speech errors the properties of which resonate with deeper psychological relevancies. The orientation to produce poetics shapes the very content of participants' descriptions: they report 'Tracy and Mark', and not 'other people'; they report a 'hyena', as opposed to a dog (or any other animal whose name does not include a 'y'); they report being aware of Anish Kapoor, or 'bits that fingers have made in the mud', or 'wide white tyres', or the sensation that a sensed movement is 'like ripples', and so on. In the context of the experimental setting in which they were produced, these verbal reports stand as records of inner conscious experience; yet it is highly likely that their appearance in the narratives, and their composition, reflects a broader orientation to poetic description, rather than a literal rendering of inner experience.

There is, then, another reason to be cautious about the use of introspective data to study consciousness and experience. Reports of inner experience are (usually) verbal discursive acts, and the socially organised practices of description unavoidably texture, shape and constrain what is described. In the attempt to grasp the phenomena of consciousness and experience, understanding the discursive practices through which introspective reports are produced may be just as important as cataloguing their ostensible content.

Chapter Eight

Retrospective interviews and introspection

Consciousness researchers (and researchers interested in other aspects of inner experience or cognitive operations) have tended to ask people to introspect about their ongoing phenomenal consciousness: for example, researchers may ask people to perform various tasks and ask them to report out loud what is in their minds at particular moments during their activities. The mentation narratives are an example of this kind of introspective report about concurrent experience. However, consciousness researchers have also used interviews to supplement these kinds of first person introspective data. The data collected through interviews are always retrospective, because they explore what a research participant had experienced at some occasion prior to the interview. Our first objective in this chapter is to outline the methodological rationale for the use of retrospective interview data, and to illustrate the way that researchers have used these kinds of interviews in their research. However, we also wish to strike a warning note: we argue that researchers in consciousness studies do not adequately take account of the situated and interactional features of the research interview (a criticism that applies equally to much interview based qualitative research in the social sciences). Drawing from conversation analytic studies of interview interaction, we identify a range of potential problems that arise if the interactional nature of the research interview is not thoroughly foregrounded in the subsequent analysis of the data it yields. In the following chapter, we examine data from the mentation review part of the ganzfeld experiments, which is a form of interview. We use these empirical materials to ground and extend our critique of the use of interviews in consciousness research, and also to sketch a range of interactional phenomena that need to be considered when inner experience is explored through interview data.

Interviews in the study of inner experience

Amongst the earliest introspection researchers there was scepticism about the value of asking research participants about their experiences, the concern being that any active intervention by the researcher might shape the content of the introspective report. This argument influenced (the few) researchers who subsequently used introspective data, and they would restrict their engagement with research participants, for example, speaking only to offer encouragement or provide instructions about the experimental procedure (Vermersch, 1999). Given the earlier caution about engaging with participants, why have contemporary researchers embraced interviews more enthusiastically?

A first obvious point is that the interview is a very common method for the collection of qualitative data about events and experiences to which the researcher does not have direct access. It would not be controversial to say that most contemporary qualitative research in the social sciences is based on the analysis of verbal data generated either from semi-structured interviews, in which the researcher follows a relatively structured interview guide, or informal or focused interviews, in which both interviewer and interviewee engage in more conversational interaction around a particular issue, and during which new topics or issues may emerge as the discussion develops. It would perhaps have been surprising had consciousness researchers not adopted interview methods to allow them to explore further peoples' subjectivity and inner experience.

The field of consciousness studies, and renewed interest in introspection, emerged in the 1990s, during which time there were growing arguments that psychological and related disciplines should pursue more ecologically valid research. So for example, Ulric Neisser and his colleagues conducted studies in which topics such as remembering, autobiographical memory and the self were explored in more naturalistic, everyday contexts, rather than through formal and highly controlled laboratory experiments (Neisser and Harsch, 1992; Neisser and Fivush, 1994; Neisser and Winograd, 1988; Pillemer, 1984, 1992). The argument for the use of ecologically valid and naturalistic data can be seen to have impacted on consciousnesses studies, particularly in development of methodologies to capture inner experience in everyday life, away from the psychology laboratory. For example, descriptive experience sampling (Hurlburt, 1990; Hurlburt and Heavey, 2006, 2008) and experience sampling methodology

(Hektner, Schmidt and Csikszentmihalyi, 2006) both seek to capture regularities in and dynamic fluctuations of the phenomenological content of everyday life, through reports that are assumed to reveal 'online conscious experience'. Both methods involve the collection of reported experiences that are embedded in natural environments; consequently experience is reported in response to triggers *in vivo*, in interaction with meaningful life events rather than in constructed laboratory scenarios or in response to hypothetical questions. As we described in chapter two, research participants are provided with technologies, such as an ear piece, that will randomly beep, at which point the participant is required to describe the details of their inner experience at that very moment via a notepad or voice recording device. Participants respond to random beeps over a period of days, and at the end of each day they are interviewed, during which the inner experience associated with each beep is examined and clarified. In these ecologically oriented approaches, then, the interview plays an important role.

Interviews have also been adopted because researchers argue that particular aspects of conscious experience can only be accessed via interviews. For example Hurlburt (2009) argues that only through a sustained period of interviewing can the researcher gain access to what he calls pristine experience: the play of consciousness on the world prior to its mediation through interpretation and reflections. To identify pristine awareness, Hurlburt advocates an iterative interview procedure in which particular moments of experience are repeatedly probed and re-examined. Through this iterative process, he argues that the researcher can identify and set to one side mediating processes and variables, such as the intrusion of tacit presuppositions and difficulties in articulating inner experience, thereby refining the participant's introspection on to their pristine experience.

Other researchers have also developed interview techniques because they argue that people are not naturally able to articulate the essence or core features of their conscious experiences without the careful intercession of a skilled interviewer. One kind of retrospective interview is called the explicitation interview (Vermersch, 1999), the core assumption of which is that

> The descriptive expertise which is the heart of introspection is not innate in any way, it is provided by the interviewer in the form of non-inductive guidance of the formulation of the experience. (Vermersch, 2009: 23)

So, Petitmengin uses the explicitation interview method to enable research participants to overcome obstacles that stand in the way of them gaining awareness of their pre-reflective subjective experience, such as a tendency for their attention to drift, and the conflation of experience and its subsequent representation. Her interview method emphasises the importance of the 're-enactment' of a moment of consciousness, and then further subsequent re-enactments to provide more and more detailed accounts of the operations of consciousness on that occasion (Petitmengin, 2006; Petitmengin-Peugot, 1999). This procedure echoes the iterative approach developed by Hurlburt as part of his descriptive experience sampling method. Similarly, Maurel (2009) adopts an explicitation interview technique that is designed to place interviewees into a 'special relationship with the past' (p. 60) in which she can probe for pre-reflective accounts of inner experience. In the explicitation interview, then, the interviewer's role is crucial because they do not merely facilitate the interviewees' accounts, but seek to establish in the participant an attentional focus that permits the investigation of hitherto un-noticed aspects of inner experience.

Finally, it may be the case that interviews are being used more frequently in introspection research because interview techniques have improved, making them a more accurate and sensitive data gathering tool. For example, Vermersch observes that 'some progress has been made in interviewing techniques since the 1990s' (1999: 36), noting that there is greater awareness of the way in which prompts can be used and questions designed and ordered so as to assist the interviewee to reflect more accurately on the phenomena of their subjectivity and inner experience.

To illustrate the iterative and explicitation interview, here are two extracts from interview transcripts. The first is a section of a transcript in Hurlburt and Heavey's (2006) overview of descriptive experience sampling; the second is a section of a transcript in Petitmengin's (2006) account of her interview method in a science of consciousness.

(8.1) (From Hurlburt and Heavey, 2006: 93-95. To make the text more readable, we have deleted text boxes, interspersed through the transcript in the original, in which Hurlburt and Heavey make analytic comments about the interview. R[uss] is the interviewer, Russell Hurlburt, and S[andy] is the research participant and interviewee. The numbering of each participant's turn is from the original, but line numbering has been added.)

1   R 1:   Then let's go on to [sample] number 15
2   S 1:   (Looks at sampling notebook) At 8.25 [yesterday evening] — this is
3   going back to all the other samples. I was reading — I was staring at
4   the word "life" in the book — in the Primus book — and I had an
5   image in my head — it was a black and white image, by the way — of
6   …OK, I was staring at the word "life" and I had said "life" to myself
7   in my own tone of voice, so…
8   R 2:   (Interrupts) and that was just before the beep at the beep also?
9   S 2:   At the beep…

10 R 3:   OK.

11 S 3:   ...and immediately an im...a black and white image came in my
12   head and it was like the word "life" because it was...the background
13   was black and the word "life" was white and it was right here (ges-
14   tures with left thumb and forefinger about a foot in front of her eyes
15   and perhaps 8 inches to the left) and then I had...uh... I don't
16   know whether it was my hand or somebody else's hand but it was
17   a hand like this (gestures with right hand, palm directly up about a
18   foot to the right of where she had indicated the word "life") with the
19   brown soft sand right there (uses fingers of left hand as if touching
20   something on the right palm) and then it was tricking down like
21   somebody was pouring it.

22 R 4:   OK. So the, so there's like a black background...

23 S 4:   (Interrupts) Yes.

24 R 5:   ...and the word "life" is printed somehow sort of on the left side of
25   this image, and...

26 S 5:   (Interrupts) Yes...yes (gestures again with left thumb and forefinger
27   "C" just as before)

28 R 6:   ...and, and, and is it possible to answer the question what kind of
29   letters are these printed in? Is it like written-out letters or printed
30   letters or typewritten letters...

31 S 6:   (Interrupts) Lower case...lower case typed letters, but the were
32   big, pretty big for...(trails off but has quizzical look apparently at
33   the incongruity of the typewritten nature and the size of the letters)

34 R 7:   And by "typed" do you mean like a sort of an old fashioned
35   typewriter...

36 S 7:   (Interrupts) Yes, yes.
              ((Continues))

(8.2)(From Petitmengin, 2006: 261-2. 'J' is the interviewer, 'C' is the interviewee.)

1 J So Chantal, I spoke to you earlier about an object, in fact I lied to you
2   slightly. It's not an object that I'm going to ask you to think of. I'm going
3   to ask you, right now, to think of an elephant.

4 C Silence (5 s), then nods her head smiling.

5 J OK. So what we're going to do now is.... how can I say this to you? It's as
6   though we had a video recorder: we're going to go backwards, and then
7   we're going to replay the sequence, and then we'll see what you did to
8   think of this elephant. OK? So it's very easy, as you've done it, so we're
9   going to rewind, and to do that I'm going to ask you to immerse yourself
10   again in this experience. Remember, I started out by saying that I had lied
11   to you: I would like you to hear again my voice telling you: "I lied to

12   you. It's not an object that I'm going to ask you to think of. I'm going to
13   ask you to think of an elephant." So you did something, something
14   happened. At the moment I said to you "Think of an elephant", what did
15   you do, what happened?
16 C The first thing that happened is blackness, that is the screen was not lit. Or
17   rather it had reset itself, it had been erased, as in fact I was not prepared
18   for evoking an elephant.
19 J I'm often going to repeat what you say to me, which will enable me first
20   to make sure that I have understood you correctly, and then as the
21   information comes, it will help me to memorise. Don't hesitate to tell me if
22   I am wrong, for that can happen, if what I repeat does not exactly
23   correspond to what you did, to what you experienced. OK? In fact.
24   according to what I understand that you experienced, there was me saying
25   "Think of an elephant", and what you tell me is that first there was
26   blackness, or more precisely there was the screen, and the screen reset
27   itself, because were not ready to evoke an elephant. Can you describe
28   this screen to me? Let's go back in time. You were saying to me: "There is
29   this screen, there is blackness." How does it reset itself, this screen?
30 C (…) I think…gradually.
31 J Gradually…
32 C The images fade away to leave something new behind.
33 J Gradually, the images fade away to leave something new behind. What
34   you are going to do now Chantal, is that you are going to return into this
35   experience, hear my voice again. I said to you, remember I said to you:
36   "Chantal, I lied to your earlier. It's not an object that I'm going to ask you
37   to think of. I'm going to ask you to think of an elephant". And then there is
38   this screen, and you tell me there are images on the screen. What kind of
39   images are there on the screen?
40 C (…) When you told me it was not objects, that is some objects of which I
41   had vaguely thought, well they had to be erased.
42 J They had to be erased.
43 C That's why I pulled across a screen.
44 J You pulled across a screen so as to be able to erase them?
45 C (…) To push them away. They were quite blurred but they moved away
46   gradually as the screen opened.
47 J All right. A screen that came out and put itself in front?
48 C In front. Very…very clearly. From the left to the right.
49 J Very clearly, from the left to the right.
50 C In front of me, I could see it left to right
51 J You saw it coming from left to right, and it came right in front of you.
52 C That's right
53 J What size was it, the screen?

54 C. ...

55 J Find it again, start again. Now you can do that very well. Go back in time,

56   find my voice again: "You know Chantal, I lied to you. It's not an object

57   I'm going to ask you to think of....

       ((Continues))

These extracts illustrate several key features of the respective interviewing methods. In both there is clear evidence of the way in which the interviewer keeps returning to a particular cognitive moment to elicit a clearer account of its properties or qualities, or to grasp some deeper experience, untainted by mediating and distorting factors. So, in extract 8.1, the interviewee describes what she was doing at the time of one of the beeps. The interviewer seeks clarification about the chronology of her imagery with respect to the stimulus sound (line 8), summarises her prior turn, (lines 23 and 24), and then seeks further detail about a particular aspect of her imagery (lines 28 to 30 and 34 and 35). In extract 8.2 the iterative approach is evident in the way that the interviewer frames her turns in relation to the organisation and underlying goals of the interview. The interviewer begins by asking the participant to think of an elephant, and not, as she had earlier suggested, an object (lines 1 to 3), and the rest of the interview is an attempt to specify in detail what was the nature of the interviewee's inner experience at precisely that moment. So, after the instruction, the interviewer first reports that she will be repeating the interviewee's words as a technique to clarify what had been experienced. She then uses reported speech to re-introduce parts of her own prior turn, thereby refocusing the interviewee's attention on a particular moment and, presumably, the imagery and sensation associated with it (lines 5 to 15). This technique is repeated after the interviewee's first account of what happened when asked to think of an elephant (lines 16 to 18). In her subsequent turn the interviewer incorporates parts of the interviewee's prior turn, but at the same time re-directs her attention back to the moment at which she was instructed to think of an elephant.

Both extracts exhibit features common to research interviews in general. They are interactional: participants take turns to speak, turns are responsive to prior turns in real time, and on a moment-by-moment and turn-by-turn basis, interviewer and interviewee collaboratively fashion an intelligible encounter. These are, however, unlike ordinary conversational interaction. They are led by one participant, rather than being jointly produced. Neither participant seeks to introduce topics that are not relevant to the concerns of the interview (there are no jokes, personal questions, intimate disclosures, remarks about local politics, sport, or the weather, for example). And both participants perform a limited range of discursive activities; broadly (although not exclusively), the interviewer asks questions, and the interviewee does answering. But although it is clear that in important respects these interview exchanges depart from ordinary conversational *interaction*, it is also apparent that the participants are drawing on everyday conversational *competences* to manage and produce the interview: they take turns, apparently without overlap or (most of the time) excessive periods of silence; they design utterances that are recognisable as questions, answers, and clarifications; they engage in self-correction or repair; interviewers summarise or formulate interviewees' prior turns, and so on. These routine conversational skills and practices are being drawn upon in this setting in such a way that the exchange is recognisable as semi-formal interview interaction.

There is another sense in which these encounters are wholly unlike everyday interaction: they are research interviews convened in the service of, and conducted for, a specific work related task: scientific research on inner experience. As such, these interviews will be informed by a broader *institutional* set of goals and requirements (Drew and Heritage, 1992b). The broader institutional orientation of the interview can be discerned in the way that particular vocabulary is used (Heritage, 1997); for example, the reference to 'the beep' in 8.1 indexes the function of specialised equipment in the service of scientific research. Also, in this extract the interviewer's turns are often prefaced with 'and' (lines 8, 24, 28 and 34). 'And-prefaced' questions regularly occur in interaction that occurs in institutional contexts, such as courtoom cross-examinations and doctor-patient consultations (Sorjonen and Heritage, 1991). The basic organisation of the interaction as a series of question-answer sequences also embodies an understanding that there is an institutional requirement to manage the encounter so as to achieve goals related to the broader research project to which these interviews contribute.

The interview techniques developed by researchers such as Hurlburt, Vermersch and Petitmengin are intended to generate a specific kind of data — verbal accounts — that allow the researcher to perform a specific analytic task — to identify core aspects of subjective experience, unfettered by mediating and distorting variables. However, these interviews are periods of *social interaction*, in the context of a *research interview*, which reflect specific *institutional* or work related requirements. Although consciousness researchers discuss a range of psychological or interpersonal issues that might impact on the retrospective interview (for example, Hurlburt and Schwitzgebel, 2007; Vermersch, 1999), the interactional and institutional features of interviews are not given prominence in methodological discussions. In this and the next chapter we draw from conversation analytic research on talk in interviews and institutional settings to illustrate some of the problems that arise if the interactional nature of retrospective interviews are not taken into consideration. We begin with a general methodological issue: transcription.

Orthographic transcription and the missing detail of interaction

Hurlburt and Petitmengin use their retrospective interviews to collect accounts of inner experience; in this they are primarily focused on the content of the interviewees' talk. Their transcriptions reflect this emphasis, and capture what was said, rather than how it was said. This is not unusual — it is standard practice in the vast majority of social science research based on data collected in informal or semi-formal interviews. However, this means considerable detail of the participants' conduct through which they produce their introspective narratives is lost, and therefore unavailable for analytic inspection.

To illustrate why a detailed transcript is so important, it is useful to compare two different transcriptions of the same data fragment. Consider the two following extracts, which are alternative transcriptions of the same section of a mentation review session, which is a form of retrospective interview about inner experience (the idea for which we are indebted to Ian Hutchby). The first comes for the KPU's transcript; the second comes from a retranscription by the first author using conversation analytic conventions. It is important to stress that the comparison between the two transcripts should not be taken to imply inefficiency on the part of the original transcriber. The comparison is designed to highlight the level of detailed information, and features of possible analytic interest, lost in conventional transcription practices.

(8.3) (01-47: E1/F)

1 E: Something red, looks like it might be a porcupine with lots of spines standing
2   up. And then a frog, a frog's face peering over something. A ghost coming
3   out of a door or a chair like a mirror in a funny house. Shapes in this funny
4   house and shapes look like bunny rabbits with weird ears. Then you said
5   sheep lots of sheep.
6 P: Loads of sheep — I didn't know what it was
7 E: Okay. Something in the ceiling

(8.3 retranscribed)

1   E: ˙hh something re:d. ehrm:: i- looks like it might be a porcupine with
2   lots of spines standing hhh standing up

3   P: yeah hh
4   E: and then a frog=a frog's face peering over something (0.8) ˙hh a ghost?
5   coming out of a door: or a chai:r (0.5) like a mirror. (.) in a funny house,
6   P: yeah=
7   E: =˙hh shapes (0.3) ahr:: are in this funny house and shapes
8   look like ehm ↑bunny rabbits with weird ears
9   P: yeah (ch)hhuh huh ˙hhhh
10   E: then you said sheep lots of sheep
11   P: ˙hhhh (g)oads of sheep (pf)ah didn't know what
12   it was (hi-) ˙h [hhh (k)huh uh ((smiley voice))
13   E: [ok(h)a(h)y (0.5) ˙huh ((smiley voice))
14   (3.5)
15   E: okay ˙hh something in the ceiling

Consider the features of the interaction made visible in the CA transcript.
First, there are ostensibly 'minor' contributions and non-lexical items. So,
The participant's turns in lines 3, 6 and 9 are included. These might be minimal contribution to the interaction, but even minimal turns consisting
only of one word may display the speaker's sense of 'what is going on
right now', and thus may be consequential for subsequent turns. The transcript also includes audible breathing. Again, it might be objected that this
is an unnecessary detail to include, but audible or emphasised inbreaths
are a way of marking a launch into a turn and thus can display an
interactional orientation: to obtain the floor before someone else begins to
speak, for example. The transcript also records non-lexical items such as
'er', 'erm' and their variations. Again, research has shown that these items,
rather than filling empty space or representing 'thinking time' on the part
of the speaker, serve delicate interactional functions: for example, they
display that the current turn might be ongoing, thus establishing continued speakership rights (Jefferson, 1984; Schegloff, 1982). Transcription
also attempts to capture laughter and words that are produced in conjunction with breathy bubbles of laughter. It also seeks to identify those words
that sound like they have been delivered through a mouth forming a smile
(as indicated by the 'smiley voice' characterisation). This is an arduous
task: transcribing laughter, and words which are punctuated by breathy
plosives, is extremely difficult; but there are analytic dividends. First, we
can begin to see how the recipient matches a current speaker's laughter in
their subsequent turn. So in lines 11 to 12, the participant expresses puz-
zlement about an image from her mentation and produces a short bout of
breathy laughter. Note that in her subsequent turn, the experimenter
matches this by pronouncing the word 'okay' with a slight roll of breathy
plosives. Research on interaction has shown that the next positioned production of 'matching' laughter is a delicate matter, and a key method for
displaying alignment and affiliation with the speaker's ongoing talk (Jef-

ferson, Sacks and Schegloff, 1987). Moreover, the careful recording of the onset of affiliative laughter indicates that its production is timed with respect to the ongoing turn. The experimenter's 'ok(h)a(h)y' in line 13 begins just after the first contracted bubble of laughter in the participant's ongoing turn. It is not only that the experimenter's turn is affiliative: it is delivered almost at the same time as the turn to which it is affiliative. Finally, the CA transcript captures the way in which words are delivered. This has clear interactional consequences. For example, consider how the experimenter says '↑bunny rabbits'. The first part of 'bunny' is emphasised and the onset of the word is marked by a clear rising or 'punched up' intonation. Its unusual delivery marks it as something for the recipient's attention, and it seems to elicit a brief confirmatory turn by the participant.

This exercise has simply tried to identify the kinds of interpersonal events that are exposed in close attention to the detail of what actually happens in interaction. In the retranscribed version of this exchange we can now see how the participants' turns are oriented to a range of interactional matters, such as intention to speak, alignment and affiliation. It is widely recognised in the methodological literature that these kinds of interpersonal matters may have a bearing on the outcome of the interview (and certainly the participants' experience of it), and they are negotiated in the detail of the participants' conduct — detail that is obscured by more conventional orthographic transcriptions.

Standard transcription techniques may be intuitively sensible — often reflecting literary conventions — but in practice they can be obstacles to research because they obscure important details. For example, the following sequence comes from the Hurlburt transcript. Note the use of a row of dots, which is often used in fictional writing to indicate some pause or disruption in talk.

```
4   S 1:    I had an
5           image in my head — it was a black and white image, by the way — of
6           …OK, I was staring at the word 'life' and I had said 'life' to myself
7           in my own tone of voice, so…
8   R 2:    (Interrupts) and that was just before the beep at the beep also?
9   S 2:    At the beep…
10  R 3:    OK.
11  S 3:    …and immediately an im…a black and white image came in my
12          head and it was like the word 'life' because it was…the background
13          was black
```

It seems unlikely that the events captured by the use of three dots are the same. There is a clear self-repair in lines 6 to 7: the turn continued with 'of' is abandoned, and the participant then embarks on a different kind of turn.

The dots are used to indicate another type of self-repair in line 11, where a word is abandoned in mid-production. But the dots after the word 'so' in line 7 are not a self-repair, but look like they indicate a pause in talk, a 'trailing off' of the utterance. But given that Russ's next turn is described as interruptive, and interruptive talk is — by definition — produced at the same time as the turn to which it is interruptive, we are invited to infer that that turn occurs in overlap with the turn in line 7 (a transcript with overlap included would have clarified this matter). So, just in this short segment there is ambiguity as to what exactly is being represented by the dots; furthermore, the same symbol is used to capture an activity initiated by the speaker (self-repair) and an activity initiated by the interviewer (interruptive overlapping talk). Similar concerns are relevant to Petitmengin's transcript, where the use of dots is extended to indicate not just a spate of silence, but (presumably) the absence of one participant's turn (line 54). The transcripts are important data in scientific analysis; yet these two examples illustrate how standard orthographic transcription can engender a degree of imprecision in the representation of what actually happened in the interview.

There are some more technical considerations. In the Hurlburt transcript, there are five turns that are described as interruptive (lines 8, 23, 26, 31 and 36). Presumably, this is because they to some degree intersect an ongoing turn (although this is not clear from the transcript). In conversation analytic research, the term 'interruption' is not used to refer to all moments where one speaker starts during another's ongoing turn as it implies a mildly aggressive act: an attempt to seize the floor at a point where turn transfer is not normatively undertaken. But research has shown that much of overlapping talk is not an attempt to appropriate speakership, or evidence of a departure from turn exchange practices, but is affiliative, or displays a clear understanding of the norms of turn taking. For example, in her study of the organisation of overlap, Jefferson (1983) showed how some overlaps can occur because a next speaker, orienting to the propriety of speakership change at a forthcoming turn transfer place, begins to talk at the same time that the current speaker, in some way, extends the current turn. This kind of transition overlap may be occurring in lines 7 and 8 of the Hurlburt transcript: Russ' turn in 8 may be at the same time as Sandy's in 7, but only because Russ anticipates that it is normatively appropriate to initiate a turn at the end of the word 'voice', at the same time that Sandy tacitly recognise that it is also normatively appropriate to extend her turn at that point, as she does — albeit momentarily — with 'so'.

This kind of recognitional overlap (Jefferson, 1983) occurs when the next speaker's start is designed to display their understanding of some aspect of the turn in production. In the following section, Sandy's turns in lines 23 and 26 that are described as interruptive might be better described as recognitional overlap, in that—if they do indeed occur at some point during the ongoing turn—they provide confirmation prior to the turn in which the detail to be confirmed is completed.

22 R 4:	OK. So the, so there's like a black background…
23 S 4:	(Interrupts) Yes.
24 R 5:	…and the word "life" is printed somehow sort of on the left side of
25	this image, and…
26 S 5:	(Interrupts) Yes…yes (gestures again with left thumb and forefinger
27	"C" just as before)
28 R 6:	…and, and, and is it possible to answer the question what kind of
29	letters are these printed in? Is it like written-out letters or printed
30	letters or typewritten letters…
31 S 6:	(Interrupts) Lower case

In line 31, Sandy's turn 'lower case' is described as an interruption. Presuming that her turn momentarily overlaps with the prior turn, there are good grounds to argue that this is a clear case of recognitional overlap. Russ's prior turn poses two questions, and the second offers examples of the kind of answer Sandy might provide. It offers three examples: written out letters, printed letters and typewritten letters. It is a three part list of possibilities.

Three part lists are common feature of everyday interaction (Jefferson, 1990). Evidence suggests that there is a normative expectation that lists in conversation should be produced in threes. So, lists that extend beyond three parts are vulnerable to overlapping and interruptive talk from a next speaker. When a list is clearly in production but it is apparent that the speaker is having trouble locating a suitable third, next speakers may offer a candidate third item. Finally, if a suitable third is not found, speakers often use general phrases such as 'and so on', 'etcetera' and 'that kind of thing', to ensure that the list is completed in three parts.

One key task for a speaker in conversation is to monitor ongoing talk to anticipate when a point will be reached when turn transfer may be normatively appropriate, and achieved with minimal dysfluency, such as gaps between turns or periods of overlapping talk. Jefferson argues that lists in three parts exhibit completeness, and because of this, they are a resource in the management of turn taking; once a possible next speaker recognises a list is in production, she can (tacitly) anticipate when it will end, and can therefore prepare to initiate a turn at that point. This is illustrated in the following extract from Jefferson's analysis of conversational listing.

(8.4) (From Jefferson, 1990: 74)

Matt: The good actors are all dyin out.
Tony: They're all- they're all dyin out [yeah.
Matt: [Tyrone Po:wuh. Clark Gable
           Gary Cooper,
Tony: Now all of 'em are dyin.

The list of good but dead actors could easily have been extended, as it is not the case that there are only three names that legitimately fall into this category. Thus, Tony's decision to start talking at the end of the third item displays his tacit understanding of the norm that lists are produced in threes, and therefore, that a normatively appropriate place to initiate turn transfer arrives at the end of the third. (And insofar as no further names are added to the list, it would appear that he was right.)

Now compare this sequence to the one in Hurlburt's data that was identified as interruptive.

28 R 6:   ...and, and, and is it possible to answer the question what kind of
29   letters are these printed in? Is it like written-out letters or printed
30   letters or typewritten letters...
31 S 6:   (Interrupts) Lower case

There are some clear structural similarities. An ongoing turn is constructed out of a list; the next speaker begins a turn at the end of the third item; and the list is not continued. Sandy's turn in line 31, then, is not interruptive: it merely anticipates the imminent arrival of a point at which it is normatively appropriate for a next turn to be launched. Even if its start does encroach on the phrase 'typewritten letters', it is still transparently a case of recognitional overlap.

Standard orthographic transcripts that focus on the spoken words, and not on the detail or dynamics of the ways in which they were uttered, are of limited use in the analysis of verbal data. They tend to exclude a range of non-lexical conduct that may be important to our understanding of the way that participants offer their reflections on their inner experience, such as, for example, the way that alignment and affiliation may be managed in the co-production of laughter. Moreover, without fine grained attention to the details of interaction, it is not clear how exactly a transcript corresponds to those exchanges of which it is being used as a record – and, importantly, a record produced for the benefit of scientific analysis. For example, what exactly does '...' represent? This problem is compounded when it becomes clear that this symbol is used to represent a range of phenomena. Finally, orthographic transcriptions routinely tend to gloss over or exclude features of talk-in-interaction, such as periods of overlapping speech. In the absence of fine-grained transcription, empirically unsupported claims may be made. So, Hurlburt's annotations describe participants as interrupting each other. This is a claim about the way that participants are conducting themselves in relation to each other. But there is no empirical warrant for this claim: careful examination of his transcript in the light of findings from conversation analytic studies of talk-in-interaction suggests that what is happening is recognitional overlap, which is a more affiliative kind of action. A transcript that captured the organisation and exact moments of overlap — when, where and how it is done — would have acted as a safeguard against this unwarranted account of participants' conduct in the retrospective interview.

The missing interactional context

Conversation analytic research has shown that turns at talk are built to perform an activity that 'fits' with, or is relevant to, the producer's tacit understanding of its context, usually the activity performed by the prior turn. So, if we interpret a prior turn as doing 'questioning', we infer that 'answering' (or accounting for why we cannot answer) is a relevant next activity; if we interpret a prior turn as performing an invitation, we produce an acceptance (or rejection), and so on. There are two important implications from this feature of the moment-by-moment unfolding of interaction. First, it provides a mechanism by which intersubjective understanding can be monitored, negotiated and corrected in the real time of interaction (Heritage, 1984a). The design of a turn will display how its producer interpreted the prior turn; that interpretation is then publicly exhibited for the prior speaker, and subject to ratification, amendment or correction. To illustrate this, consider the following data extract that comes from Terasaki's (2005) analysis of pre-announcements in conversation. These exchanges come from a recording of a family discussion about a forthcoming parent-teachers meeting

(8.5) (From Terasaki, 2005: 202)

```
1   Mother:   Do you know who's going to that meeting?
2   Russ:     Who?
3   Mother:   I don't know!
4   Russ:     Ouh:: prob'ly: Mr Murphy an' Dad said prob'ly
5             Mrs. Timpte en some a' the teachers.
```

Mother's turn is ambiguous in that it could either be a question seeking information about attendees, or a pre-announcement of news about someone attending. Russ's next turn is a minimal, one word question that passes the floor immediately back to Mother, thereby exhibiting to Mother that he analysed the prior turn to be doing pre-announcement. Mother's next turn exhibits her understanding that Russ has made an interpretive error. And this in turn allows Russ to infer the error and do 'answering', the activity that Mother's original turn was intended to elicit. The participant's intersubjective knowledge of what-is-going-on-right-now is managed on a turn-by-turn basis. In this, sense the serial unfolding of interaction through paired sequences are the building blocks of intersubjective understanding (Heritage, 1984a: see also Schegloff, 1982).

The second implication is methodological, in that

> while understandings of other turns' talk are displayed to co-participants, they are available as well to professional analysts who are thereby afforded a proof criterion (and search procedure) for the analysis of what a turns' talk is occupied with. Since it is the parties' understandings of prior turns' talk that is relevant to their construction of next turns, it is their understandings that are wanted for analysis. The display of those understandings in the talk of subsequent turns afforded both a resource for the analysis of prior turns and a proof procedure for professional analysis of prior turns — resources intrinsic to the data themselves. (Sacks *et al.*, 1974: 729.)

The next turn proof procedure made available in the turn-by-turn development of interaction means that analytic claims can be anchored in close description of the data, and can also act as a safeguard against premature interpretation.

In the literature on the use of interviews in consciousness research, there is no discussion of the way that interviews proceed via a series of discursive activities. This is not a criticism of researchers like Vermersch, Petitmengin and Hurlburt — empirical research on the action orientation of language in interaction emerged from an entirely different academic discipline and was concerned with interactional dynamics of ordinary communication, not conscious experience. However, it is important, and something of which consciousness researchers should be aware. The retrospective interview is used to generate introspective descriptions that are subsequently examined for what they can tell us about nature of inner experience; they become the data for scientific analysis. But what people say is inextricably related to the interplay of discursive actions that constitute the immediate context in which — and for which — descriptions of inner experience are produced (Wooffitt and Widdicombe, 2007).

We can illustrate this by examining the implications of the way interviewer turns are designed. Early in the extract from the Petitmengin interview, there is the following sequence. (We appreciate that the interview was conducted in French and then translated into English; however, the analytic points we make here are quite broad, and thus are relevant despite any subtle transformations of sense or meaning that can occur in even the most careful translations.)

14 J At the moment I said to you "Think of an elephant", what did
15   you do, what happened?
16 C The first thing that happened is blackness, that is the screen was not lit. Or
17   rather it had reset itself, it had been erased, as in fact I was not prepared
18   for evoking an elephant.

There are two possible turn transition points in the interviewer's turn: the first arrives at the end of 'do' in that it is only at this point that a syntactically fully formed question has been constructed; the second arrives after the additional phrase, 'what happened'. Because there are no timings of periods of silence, it is not clear if the additional component is produced in response to the interviewee's silence. But the upshot is that the interviewee has been asked two questions: 'what did you do?' and 'what happened?'. These questions invite very different kinds of responses: the first invites the respondent to consider their own involvement in a process or events (even those occurring in consciousness), whereas the second formulates events as objective phenomena that occurred independent of the respondent's agency (Widdicombe and Wooffitt, 1995; Wooffitt, 1992). The most obvious impact of the interviewer's turn design is that it seems to shape the interviewee's response, which is designed to match or fit with the most recent additional component of the prior turn: she forms her answer in terms of events that 'happened'. But this in itself has implications for any record of what the interviewee's experiences turns out to be. She goes on to report her inner awareness as a series of events to which she was merely a witness — 'what happened is blackness', 'the screen was not lit', and 'it had reset itself' — events in which she is depicted as having no participation or intervention. By building her turn to fit with the last component of the prior question, the interviewee portrays her experiences as objective events in which her agency is diminished or absent. Insofar as her turn is designed to mesh with the last component of the prior turn, the content of interviewee's account of her experiences — the raw data for subsequent scientific analysis — can be said to be interactionally generated.

On occasions, the interviewer repeats part of the interviewee's prior turn: that is, they formulate a version of what the interviewee had just said. Here are two examples from the Petitmengin interview.

28 J Let's go back in time. You were saying to me: 'There is
29   this screen, there is blackness.' How does it reset itself, this screen?
30 C (...) I think...gradually.
31 J Gradually...
32 C The images fade away to leave something new behind.

40 C (...) When you told me it was not objects, that is some objects of which I
41   had vaguely thought, well they had to be erased.
42 J They had to be erased.
43 C That's why I pulled across a screen.

In the first instance, in response to a question about how the screen reset itself, the interviewee says 'I think...gradually'. The interviewer's next turn is a one word utterance: 'gradually'. In the second case, the interviewee's turn is quite complex, in that it retraces her recollections of interviewer instructions and their impact on her inner experience; this turn ends with the phrase 'well they had to be erased', a version of which is then repeated in the interviewer's next turn. In both cases, the interviewer's subsequent turn deletes a component of the prior turn. In the first case, the phrase 'I think' is not repeated; and in the second, the interviewer only repeats 'they had to be erased'. The interviewer is designing her next turn to repeat a selected component of the prior turn. This can have important interactional consequences, which in turn can impact on what the experience transpires to be.

Repeating what someone else has just said invariably has interactional consequences. It can be used to identify a turn design error and allow the producer to make a correction. For example, in the following examples from ordinary conversational interaction, partial repeats of prior turns are used to identify basic word selection errors.

(From Schegloff, Jefferson and Sacks, 1977: 370)

A: Hey the first time they stopped from sellin cigarettes was this morning
        (1.0)
B: From selling cigarettes
A: From buying cigarettes.

(From Schegloff, Jefferson and Sacks, 1977: 377)

K: 'Ee likes that waider over there.
A: Wait-er?
K: Waitress, sorry,
A: 'Ats bedder.

In both cases, the producer of the error recognises that the partial repeat of their turn identifies a problematic component, and, insofar as no correction is offered, invites them to execute the correction, which they do with the correct phrase or word in their next turn. In this sense, the partial repeat of the prior utterance acts as a next turn repair initiator (Schegloff, Jefferson and Sacks, 1977). Repeating another's words, then, can make them *accountable* for that turn (Antaki and Leudar 2001; Goodwin, M.H., 1980, 1990).

In the extracts from the Petitmengin interview, the way that the inter-viewee responds to the interviewer's partial repeat of their prior turns suggests that she too infers that in some sense, she is being called to account for that turn. In the first instance, in response to the interviewer's 'gradually' the interviewee says 'The images fade away to leave some-thing new behind'. This is an expansion and elaboration of her earlier report of the way the image of a screen reset itself. This demonstrates that she heard the interviewer's turn not as a neutral repeat of what she said, but as recasting her description as somehow inadequate or incomplete, and thereby constituting an invitation to say more. A related interactional dynamic plays out in the second instance. The interviewer's turn is 'They had to be erased', which is a formulation of the prior turn, in that it pre-serves some components and deletes others (Heritage and Watson, 1979). The interviewee does not treat this as the interviewer merely clarifying just that component of her utterance; she does not say 'yes' or 'that's right', for example. Her next utterance is 'That's why I pulled across a screen', which is an explanation for subsequent (mental) activity. This exhibits her inference that the interviewer treats the report of the imperative — 'they had to be erased' — as requiring a further account of the agency by which that imperative was met. The account of that agency is now part of the experience — a feature of the raw data of inner experience — but it was interactionally generated in the turn-by-turn unfolding of the interview.

Discussion

Interviews are a routine form of data collection in the social sciences; a large proportion of qualitative analysis is based on verbal accounts elic-ited in informal or semi-structured interviews. It is no surprise that con-sciousness researchers have adopted interview techniques, especially on those occasions when they might be interested in conscious phenomena that occur in everyday life away from the laboratory or researcher's office. However, interviews are not neutral data gathering instruments; they are periods of social interaction that rely on the participants' use of everyday communicative competences. In this chapter we have examined data from studies by Hurlburt and Heavy and Petitmengin, first to illustrate the way that consciousness researchers are using retrospective interviews to gen-erate data about inner experience, and second, to sketch some of the prob-lems that arise if the interactional dimensions of interviews are not taken into account. In particular we focused on the way that an overriding concern with the *content* of interviewees' accounts is reflected in the use of orthographic transcriptions which capture the words that were said but which obscure or ignore a range of detail that can be important in understanding how the interview proceeds. We also argued that in the absence of a more formal and detailed transcription of the interactional dynamics of an interview it is often unclear what orthographic transcriptions actually represent, which can in turn lead to questionable empirical claims about the nature or significance of participants' utterances.

If consciousness researchers are to use retrospective interviews, then the accounts and descriptions of inner experience that are generated during interviews are, essentially, the raw data for analysis of those participants' inner experience. In subsequent analysis, there is a temptation to focus on participants' accounts as more or less adequate descriptions of inner experience, and to forget that they were elicited during periods of social interaction. This a seems to be a default analytic procedure in qualitative social science that relies on interview data: it is routine to see academic papers in which participants' accounts are reproduced in the text, and the focus of analytic work, but it is rare to be presented with the interviewer's prior turns that elicited those accounts in the first place. This default analytic and presentational practice can also be found in the consciousness studies literature. In their examination of the experience of sounds, for example, Petitmengin and her colleagues use excerpts from explicitation interviews, but the interviewer's talk is noticeably absent (Petitmengin, Bitbol , Nissou, Pachoud, Curallucci, Cermolacce and Vion-Dury, 2009). It is as if the accounts emerge fully formed in an interactional vacuum.

But interviews *are* periods of social interaction, and it is important to recognise that any descriptions of imagery and sensations, and any reflections on inner experience, are inextricably rooted in and shaped by the immediate interactional context in which they were generated, and for which they were designed to be responsive. In the second part of this chapter, we have begun to sketch how the participants' tacit understanding of immediate interactional dynamics during the interview can inform the design of their utterances, thereby directly shaping the reports, descriptions and reflections that constitute the primary data for the researchers' subsequent analytic efforts. We explore this further in the next chapter.

Chapter Nine

Interaction in retrospective interviews

The mentation reviews

The mentation review is a form of interview to clarify the research participants' experience of the contents of their conscious awareness. In the ganzfeld procedure, it functions first, to allow the experimenter to confirm, clarify or correct their hand written notes of the prior mentation, and thereby lead to a final record of the mentation narrative; and second, to ensure that the participants' imagery is fresh in their mind prior to beginning the judging phase of the experiment. The review is a retrospective interview about conscious experience, and it has similar objectives to the kinds of interviews conducted by introspection researchers in which accounts of inner experience are retrospectively elicited, and the participants' experience of their subjective awareness is clarified, expanded, and the subject of further probing and investigation.

The key feature of the review is the step wise progression through the experimenter's notes: after repeating their record of a particular imagery report, the experimenter will allow time for the participant to affirm that report, or offer a correction. Sometimes participants remain silent after the report of their imagery, and this is taken to be a confirmation that the experimenter's record was correct. On other occasions the participant's confirmation is produced as a minimal turn, such as 'mh hm', or variants thereof. Once the report has been confirmed, the experimenter moves to the next item in their record. There are few departures from this format. The experimenter may explicitly seek confirmation or clarification of their record by explicitly drawing the participant's attention to some ambiguity in their record. Alternatively, participants may intervene in the step wise procedure to draw the experimenter's attention to an otherwise unidentified error in their record. Participants may also volunteer further information about the imagery: recollection of more information triggered by the experimenter's report, or some comment or reflection on the imagery that

they have just confirmed. Finally, and much less frequently, experimenters may comment on mentation imagery, especially if it was particularly
striking, unusual or humorous. These activities of expansion, clarification
and correction constitute a momentary suspension of the step wise procedure; therefore the final activity of the review is the *resumption* of the imagery by imagery review of the experimenter's notes.

The mentation review, then, is a period of social interaction that is characterised by a limited range of activities. The way that experimenters and
participants manage these activities, however, can have an impact on not
only the smooth progression of the review, but can also inform the final
record of the participants' imagery. This is because participants' imagery
reports are mediated with respect to ongoing interactional requirements
of the review. In this chapter we illustrate this by examining some consequences attendant on two routine activities: the ways in which experimenters introduce discrete imagery items into the review; and the ways in
which experimenters receipt or acknowledge participants' reflections on
their imagery, or their provision of further detail.

Imagery prefaces and 'you said' reports

There are various ways by which the experimenters introduced their
report of the participants' imagery into the review The following extract,
which is a complete record of this participant's mentation review, illustrate some regular features of the experimenters' turns.

(9.1) (01-09: E3/M)

```
1    E:   O:ka:y (0.6) ˙hh first one wuz: uh::, (.) ˙h uh sense of heat or melting,
2         (1.4)
3    E:   thh then::: deep and distant
4         (1.0)
5    P:   °°mhm°°
6    E:   (tk) uniform:, (1.3) ˙hh dark shadow:: (1.8) waves: (1.3) deep dark tunnel
7         (1.7) spots of light (1.3) °°hhh°° uh::, and then I'm not sure what you said
8         next- >I think it was< ho::le
9         (0.6)
10   P:   mm (.) °I think so°
11   E:   °o::kay° (.) ˙hhh then ever (.) ever decreasing circles:?
12   P:   mm,
13        (0.6)
```

```
14   E:    °o::kay:,° (0.7) (tk) ˙hh uh: space:: (1.0) ° ˙h° stroking, (0.5) so:ft
15   P:    (°°mhm[m°°)
16   E:              [ °m-m-° bubble (.) cloud, (1.7) diffus:e (0.5) ˙hhh and then:,
17         shadows in::::- I'm not sure what you said °is° i °°thi-°° >it sounded a bit
18         like< shadows in a: >in a< clipped; (.) sce:ne:
19   P:    °mm,° (0.5) eclipse I think?
20   E:    oh an eclipse: (.) o:kay, (2.6) ˙h aw:ri:ght, (0.6) uh::, slow:: (1.0) ˙h
21         penetrate (1.3) constant (1.3) ˙h bubbling,=swirling,=growing, (2.0) flames
22         (1.1) ˙h rapid movement=reaching=upwards, (1.7) lava, (1.5) engulfing
23         (1.8) ˙h undulating (1.6) ˙h whirlwind, (.) rapidly moving away:, (.) further
24         and further (1.0) ˙h blue, (1.2) ˙h absorption (1.3) sinking (.) or floating,
25         (1.2) ((sound of pages being turned))
26   E:    ˙h pa:tterns (0.5) °m°cycles (.) °or° circles. (0.8) ˙hhh(a) (1.1) RA:Ndom
27         (1.3) e::ven (2.1) ˙h meandering (1.5) s:pee:d (0.9) ° ˙h°
28         swirling,=shaking,=moving,=round and round. (.) spin (1.0) ˙h change of
29         direction (1.1) a::nd then that was °so::: when I came in, was there
30         anything else? uh
```

The experimenter can simply report the imagery or sensation, for example, 'uniform' (line 6) or 'spots of light' (line 7). The experimenter may report the mode of perception or awareness by which the imagery was apprehended by the participant, as in 'sense of heat or melting' (line 1). Imagery may be introduced in relation to its location in the stream of imagery reported by the participant, for example: 'then::: deep and distant' (line 3) and 'then ever (.) ever decreasing circles:?' (line 11). Finally, the experimenter can use a reported speech marker, 'you said', for example, 'and then I'm not sure what you said next- >I think it was< ho::le (lines 7 and 8).

There may be various reasons why experimenters introduce imagery or sensations in the way they do, and these may be interactionally uninteresting: it may simply be matter of variation to avoid tedious repetition. Alternatively, introductions may try to capture some aspect of the participant's original mentation (for example, an explicit statement that an image can be clearly heard or seen in the mind's eye might result in the experimenter saying 'and then you heard/saw/'). But there are some considerations that suggest an interactional organisation at play with respect to 'you said' prefaces. First, as the mentation narrative is the participant's verbal description of their experience of their own consciousness, logically *every* item in the review could be introduced with a 'you said' preface. The relative absence of 'you said' prefaces, then, is analytically interesting, as it points to a degree of selectivity in their use. The selective use of a 'you said' preface in this extract is even more notable given that for much of the review the experimenter actually uses direct reported speech to introduce the participant's prior imagery. The experimenter employs the appropriate syntax and tenses which would have been used by the participant in the original mentation, for example, 'bubbling,=swirling,=growing, (2.0) flames (1.1) 'h rapid movement=reaching=upwards, (1.7) lava, (1.5) engulfing (1.8) 'h underlining (1.6) 'h whirlwind, (.) rapidly moving away' (lines 21 to 23). These periods of direct reported speech explicitly index the participant's authorship of the imagery descriptions, and consequently, the absence of 'you said' prefaces seems conspicuous.

The use of a 'you said' preface seems to be tied to a particular activity. In extract 9.1 there are two instances, and both occur in turns in which the experimenter is initiating repair (Schegloff *et al.*, 1977), in that he explicitly seeks the participant's assistance to clarify an ambiguity in the record of the mentation. The two 'you said' prefaces occur in relation to the imagery of a hole (line 8) and a clipped scene/eclipse (line 18), and engender a change in the participant's participation. This is because the experimenter's uncertainty or doubt about their record constitutes a procedural difficulty in the review, in that progression through the remaining imagery can not resume until the participant has had the opportunity to resolve the uncertainty. However, the experimenter does not issue an explicit request for clarification from the participant. Instead, the turn in which the problematic item is introduced establishes the relevance of participant intervention, and initiates or invites clarification, confirmation or correction.

In both cases the experimenter's turns project the trouble source while at the same time establishing his uncertainty: in lines 7 and 8 the utterance 'and then I'm not sure what you said next' identifies that the experimenter's difficulty concerns the immediately following imagery; and in line 17 the report of the imagery is temporarily abandoned just prior to the problematic component, and the experimenter announces 'I'm not sure what you said'.

The experimenter offers candidate hearings of the participant's report, and these are produced with epistemic doubt markers that establish the experimenter's equivocality about the accuracy of his record. In the first instance a candidate item is introduced with the doubt marker, 'I think (it was hole)'; while in the second case the experimenter's report of what the imagery *sounded like* ensures the conditional status of the subsequent candidate item. Finally, the 'you said' formulations explicitly identify the participant as the source of the imagery of which the experimenter's notes now stand as an uncertain record, and this in turn licences their participatory role as arbiter. For the first 'you said' formulation, the participant produces a mitigated alignment to the candidate version 'hole': 'I think so' (line 10). In relation to the second, the participant corrects the experimenter's candidate 'shadows in a clipped scene' with 'eclipse' (line 19).

The 'you said' preface, then, is a component of a form of repair device by which to initiate other repair. 'You said' prefaces explicitly identify the recipient as author of what follows, and thereby their accountability as arbiters for the accuracy of the experimenter's record becomes relevant.

The use of 'you said' prefaces to initiate repair is routine in the mentation review corpus.

(9.2) (01-88: E1/F)

```
1   E:  ·h >kay< when you started off you sai:d (.) ·h it felt warm (0.6) ·h like the
2       light of the sun giving out heat (0.9) it could be the wa:ves or it could be
3       wi:nd (0.9) I think its waves (0.9) its very ca:lm despite the sound of
4       the wa:ves (0.9) there's a very still atmosphere=in the air (1.7) now it
5       appears da:rk (0.9) it could be under water (1.2) and there are waves crashing
6       above my head (.) ·h but its very still underneath (1.3) on a boat (1.4) I see a
7       movement (0.9) a very gentle movement (0.8) like waves lapping on a shore
8       (1.6) my arms are tingling (1.3) I see patches of white light sometimes (0.8)
9       and it's not red anymore (2.0) °·h° I can hear above the noise of the wa:ves
10      children's voices (.) ·h there are children's voices=they sound like happy
11      voices (1.9) ·h arms are still tingling, (0.5) h and the light keeps changing
12      from bla:ck (.) to re:d (0.8) ·h sometimes it mo:ves (.) like the wa°ves°
13      (1.2) it feel (.) >I feel< like I:'m moving (.) like my body is twisting slo:wly
14      to the left ·h like I'm slo:wly: turning (0.5) >an I< can't seem to lie straight.
15      (1.3) you could hear music (0.4) very distant (.) ·h a sort of ba:nd (.) maybe of
16      bra:ss instruments (0.7) °·h° not classical music ·h but more folk like. (1.3)
17      perha:ps a salvation army type of band. (1.7) and now it feels like you're
18      turning and like you're tilted again on to one side. (1.4) the span °u- th-° >I'm
19      sorry< the ba:nd were still go:ing, (1.3) and the colours were still changing (.)
20      and sometimes shapes (0.4) kind=of=like wa:ve crests
21      (3.2) ((sound of paper turning))
22  E:  now it felt like, (0.6) you could hear an airplane going overhea:d ·h a big jet,
23      (0.4) ·h it sou:nds, (.) just like being in heathrow airport. (0.8) ·h this reminds
24      me of friends who live near, (.) the airport (.) ·h and of a concord=jet, I once
25      saw going over their house (0.7) the noise of the jet is fading now. (1.5) I still
26      feel tilted °°m°°like I'm turning: and tilting slowly. (0.8) almost like being on
27      a rollercoaster, (.) ·h a:nd, (.) slow:ly: °°m-°° (0.5) moving and going around
28      the bends? (1.1) ·hh the chair is: (0.4) the chair feels like it's tilting, (.) and
29      like its turning ve:ry slo::wly °·h° (0.5) tilting over (1.5) °·h° again, turning
30      slo:wly (0.9) °·h° my arms are tingling (1.5) now I'm in- up in the air now: (.)
31      looking down at trees ·h like a birds eye view: (1.3) its still quiet. (1.2) I can
32      still feel turning=like I'm turning ·h but now I'm turning back the other wa:y
33      (0.5) ·h the light seems to be moving (1.7) see a train going into a tunnel (0.5)
34      °·h° (0.5) a brick tunnel (2.1) °·ha see a small ↑dot of li:ght, °·h° (.) and I can
35      hear the band playing:: very distant=can still hear it. (1.4) ·h I still feel like
36      I'm turning, I'm flipping over (0.6) °·h° and my legs are now flipping up,
```

37   (0.6) ° h° the tingling feeling has moved to my legs now rather than the a:rms
38   (1.5) 'h now it seems like I'm near a ro:ad=a very busy road like- (0.6) em
39   twenny fi:ve (1.8) which is the: road from: >your home,< to::, the
40   airport.=gatwick airport. (0.9) ° h° you could see hi:lls and tree:s (.) but only
41   the view to the right (1.6) 'h a bright white li:ght (.) in the top of your view
42   (0.7) 'h seems to be moving ha:s=a jagged edge (1.1) 'h profile of a person,
43   (1.6) ° h° and then I think you said a picture of cha:rles working at his de:sk?
44   (0.5)
45 P: gi:les
46 E: jarles 'h and that made you laugh: bec[ause you knew he wa[sn't
47 P: [hhhhh   [°huhu°
48   (2.3)
49 E: 'hh oka:y? (0.9) 'hhhh um, >a view< of: pollock halls,
50   (1.6)
51 P: yeah
52 E: and the noise there, and there were people walking around. (1.4) 'h
53   victoria falls:=that's the noise that I he:ar…

In this review, the participant is entirely silent until the experimenter uses a 'you said' preface to invite clarification: 'and then I think you said a picture of cha:rles working at his de:sk?' (line 43). In response to this, the experimental subject's participation in the review changes, in that instead of confirming the experimenter's record by withholding talk at a point at which correction could occur, she explicitly clarifies the experimenter's expressed doubt about one component of the imagery. This is acknowledged by the experimenter, who repeats the participant's clarification of the name (albeit with an unusual pronunciation), and who then introduces a further component of the imagery related to the now correctly named individual. This further component reveals that the participant was amused by the disjuncture between the image and her expectations and knowledge of the person in the imagery. The participant laughs briefly (line 47), acknowledging the humorous aspect of the original image. There is then a gap (of greater duration than the majority of other periods of silence, during which time it is likely that the original incorrect record was being amended), and then the experimenter speaks again. The experimenter says 'okay', with a questioning intonation, and withholds further talk for about a second before proceeding with the next imagery.

The selective use of reported speech markers is starkly apparent in this extract. From the start of the review, the experimenter actually uses direct reported speech to introduce the participant's prior imagery, and employs the appropriate syntax and tenses which would have been used by the participant in the original mentation: for example 'my arms are tingling (1.3) I see patches of white light sometimes (0.8) and it's not red anymore (2.0) °°h° I can hear above the noise of the wa:ves' (lines 8 and 9), and 'I can still feel turning=like I'm tur<u>ning</u> 'h but now I'm turning back the other wa:y (lines 31 and 32). This degree of direct reported speech is extremely unusual in the corpus, as, in mentation reviews in other trials, imagery is indirectly reported or paraphrased. Yet explicit acknowledgment of the participant's authorship of the imagery occurs only twice: in a turn that initiates the review (hinting at a procedural or organisational function), and in a turn that initiates repair.

There are various ways in which experimenters can display that they have some doubt over the accuracy of their record. Phrases such as 'I think' or I'm not sure' routinely occur in turns in which a 'you said' reported speech marker prefaces imagery about which there is experimenter uncertainty. The presence of these epistemic doubt markers ensure that the imagery subsequently described is heard as a candidate description, provisional upon confirmation or correction by the experimenter. Alternatively, epistemic doubt markers may be placed after a report, thereby retrospectively constituting the provisional or candidate status of the prior image description. In the following extract, the experimenter introduces the imagery 'boardwalk' without any explicit indication of uncertainty about the item (although it is said louder than surrounding talk, which may constitute some signal of its special status relative to other imagery). After a 0.4 second gap, the experimenter then reports uncertainty about the accuracy of the written record.

(9.3)(01-42: E3/M)

```
1    E:   two figures (.) someone walking away in the distance (0.8) 'h TA:pping: =
2         footsteps (0.5) 'h BOARDwalk (0.4) °I think you said.° (0.4) no wasn't
3         sure I think you said boardwa:lk and [then both of us:=
4    P:                                         [(°no°)
5    P:   = isn't a word that I:=I use, ah:: (.) [boardwalk
6    E:                                          [°hm°
```

Experimenters may also insert general references at that point in the turn where a specific description would be expected, thereby signalling the location of problematic items, and aiding participant recall for correction. In the following case the experimenter uses the word 'something' in that part of the earlier sequence of imagery in which a word appears over which there is uncertainty. She then offers a candidate description.

(9.4)(01-69: E2/M)

```
1    E:   and then a train again
2    P:   uh huh
3         (1)
4    E:   'hh and now I missed something you said people (in a) something (.)
```

5   and I think you said writing on the ha::t?
6   (1.0)
7   P: (oh::[::)
8   E: [the people in ha:[ts?
9   P: [>people in <u>hard</u> hats<

It is clear that 'you said' formulations are strongly associated with turns in which experimenters explicitly seek the participants' assistance with respect to ambiguities or possible errors in their record of the mentation narrative. Used in conjunction with explicit markers of experimenter uncertainty, they invite a more active involvement from the participant, thus changing — albeit only momentarily — the interactional landscape of the review. This, then, is an institutional use of 'you said' prefaces, in that it allows the participants to engage in activities necessary for the smooth progression of the experimental procedure.

However, there are wider cultural conventions associated with 'you said' reported speech markers, and these may have consequences for their use in this particular setting

'You said' prefaces: ambiguity and accountability

As we noted earlier, direct reports of the others' speech, such as those prefaced by 'you said' formulations, tend to occur in circumstances in which participants are engaged in argument or accusation; or situations in which the recipient is being called to account for something they are reputed to have said. For example, Goodwin's study of the 'he said-she said' organization of gossip disputes amongst young Black American females (Goodwin, M.H., 1980, 1990) examined the culturally based, communicative skills by which young girls organise participation in disputes, and provides numerous instances of the way that another's utterances may be used as a component of an accusatory turn, and as evidence in warranting the legitimacy of an offence or complaint. In the more institutional context of UK parliamentary debates, Antaki and Leudar (2001) have shown how an MP's exact words (as recorded in Hansard, the official record of parliamentary proceedings) can be recruited by debaters as a rhetorical strategy to undermine their opponent's credibility. Evidence of the way that 'you said' reported speech prefaces can be used to point to the accountability of another's utterances comes from Bell's (1998) study of the pragmatics of second language teaching. Her data come from a recording of Korean students taking a class in English. In a discussion of the use of 'too many/too much', one of the male students reports his understanding that 'too many' can be used pejoratively (he says 'too' can mean 'so bad'). The teacher agrees, saying 'Oh, yes, that "too" means bad.' The student then says, 'You said too many Koreans here…' thereby reporting and partially repeating a prior statement from the teacher. The teacher clearly feels that she is being called to account for her utterance, because, as Bell reports, the teacher 'goes into an explanation intended to reassure that [it is] the makeup of the class [which] is difficult, not the students themselves' (Bell, 1998:32). There is, then, a wider, culturally-based understanding that, in mundane inter-action, 'you said….' makes relevant some form of account (or defence) of what is then reported.

In the context of the ganzfeld experiment (as in other more traditional psychology experiments), interaction is not confrontational or adversarial in any way; indeed, both experimenters and participants collaborate to accomplish the experiment as a joint activity. Even in this non-adversarial, collaborative context, however, participants' conduct may be informed by broader cultural understanding that a 'you said' reported speech preface calls a co-participant to account for some prior utterance. And this in turn may have consequences for the unfolding trajectory of the experimental procedure, in that, on occasions, an unmarked 'you said' preface — that is, one produced in the absence of epistemic doubt markers or other repair initiation components — may generate further talk from the participant. Moreover, that further talk has a cautiously reflective character. Consider the following case.

(9.5) (01-80: E1/M)

```
1    E:   ˙hh and now the do:g again it's the same one ˙hh with
2         skinny straight legs (.) [and it's black and white
3    P:                            [uh huh
4    P:   uh huh
5         (0.6)
6    E:   ˙hh and then you said it looks like (0.3) tall tall
7         tree. ˙hh bro[wn
8    P:                [oh that was odd. (.) ye [:s that was odd=
9    E:                                         [yeah.
10   P:   =that looked like a telegraph pole with little green stumps sticking
11        out li [ke that=I- I can't imagine
12   E:          [(CH)uh::huh huh hu
13   P:   that being in do you?
14        (.)
15   E:   (h)okay? (.) ˙hh ehrm shapes again.
```

The 'you said' preface in line 6 is not a component of a turn that initiates repair. It does, however, preface imagery about which the participant pro-vides more information. This is not, though, a neutral report of further fea-tures of the imagery. The participant emphasises its strangeness, 'oh that was odd. (.) ye:s that was odd', and offers some further information about the image to illustrate how unusual it was: 'that looked like a telegraph pole with little green stumps sticking out like that'. Upgrading the strangeness of the imagery would suggest that the participant infers he has been called to account for the report of the imagery, the emphasis on its strangeness standing as warrant for its inclusion in the original review. The participant then assesses the likelihood that this image appeared in the target materials: 'I- I can't imagine that being in do you?'.

In this context, this is significant: the experiment is designed to investigate if communication can occur mentally, without the use of the normal communication channels. The logic of the experiment, then, leads to ambiguity about the provenance of one's inner mental life. This is because, as we noted in an earlier chapter, during the sending period, the participant's imagery may have been projected into their consciousness as a consequence of the sender's volition. The imagery the participant experiences, then, *may not be their own*. The participant's assessment, however, implicitly articulates a position on the origin of the imagery: that it was not part of the experimental procedure, and therefore, that it does not stand as evidence of anomalous communication. Effectively, this utterance normalises his experience, thus undermining its possible institutional significance as a possible indicator of the operation of parapsychological processes.

Similar work appears to be going on in the participant's utterance in the following extract; again this turn is a response to locally selective but unmarked 'you said' prefaces.

(9.6) (01-18: E1/M)

```
1     E:    ˙mhh and you were wobbling from si:de to side
2     R:    mm
3           (0.5)
4     E:    and then you said cycling=cycl[ing down north bri[dge]
5     R:                              [yeah              [˙hh]>I
6           (th)ink th's I'd li(k)- th-< that made me (.) made me
7           think of (.) ˙hh of y'know being blown about on the
8           wi:nd on a bike
9           (0.8)
10    E:    mm hm,
11    R:    ˙hh (y'know) the whole whole (.) chair felt like
12          it was s't've wobbling in fact
13          (1.2)
14    E:    °'kay° (0.6) and then you said the wi:nd and the cold.
```

Here the experimenter introduces the imagery of 'cycling down North Bridge' via a (then) 'you said' preface (line 4). Although the participant's subsequent talk is unclear, he goes on to establish that that imagery brought to mind a more general experience: being 'blown about' while riding a bike in wind. This is a more vivid characterisation than the initial formulation 'cycling down North Bridge'. After a minimal confirmation from the experimenter, the participant relates the experience to physical experiences at the time of the sending period, when he was producing his mentation narrative: 'the whole whole (.) <u>chair</u> felt like it was s't've wobbling in fact'. This suggests a non-parapsychological, or mundane account for the imagery: the sense of movement experienced as cycling was a consequence of his perception of the movements on the chair in which he was sitting at the time.

'You said' prefaces can be heard as making the imagery they introduce somehow accountable. If they are heard this way, participants address the call to account for the report in two ways: they upgrade the unusualness of the imagery; then they offer an explanation or account that indexes mundane, non-parapsychological causes.

There is, then, an ambiguity about the function of 'you said' prefaces in these data. They are clearly used in turns in which the experimenter articulates some doubt or hesitancy about the accuracy of their record; and participants routinely treat these turns as initiating some form of clarification or correction. However, unmarked 'you said' prefaces may also facilitate further description in which participants normalise their imagery by offering non-parapsychological or mundane explanations, or in which they articulate their own doubt about its parapsychological provenance.

The ambiguity of unmarked 'you said' formulations may rest on the lag between the initial report of the imagery in the mentation and its introduction in the subsequent review. Consider the case of the 'you said' report from Bell's study of Korean students taking an English class. The student's utterance 'You said too many Koreans here...' is heard by the teacher as requiring a defensive explanation. To a degree, this reflects the wider cultural understanding that 'you said' speech markers are (mildly) hostile acts. But there may be another factor in play. The student's observation comes in close proximity to the teacher's discussion of the use of 'too'. The teacher's subsequent defensive explanation is in part generated out of the way that the student's utterance relates to something she has just said. It is hearably challenging because it is immediately responsive. Indeed, the proximity of the 'you said' formulation to the utterance being reported may be a resource by which participants in interaction can infer the degree of hostility or challenge being mobilised by the reference to what they had said.

In the ganzfeld procedure, however, that resource is not available: imagery items are introduced some time after their initial report in the mentation. Moreover, it is a review of *all* their imagery: it is not that the experimenter has selected this report for special attention, and that that itself accounts for the use of the 'you said' preface. The fact that the experimenter uses an unmarked 'you said' preface, then, is not explicable in terms of proximity nor inferably motivated selection. There are grounds for ambiguity about what a 'you said' preface may be doing; it is not surprising, then, that sometimes participants hear it as a call to account; and sometimes, they do not. And the grounds for ambiguity about the kind of action invited by an unmarked 'you said' preface may be institutionally provided for, in that they emerge from the organization of the interaction to realise experimental — that is, institutional — goals.

Doubt marked receipts of further imagery information

In chapter three we noted how, in the mentation review, after each item is introduced the experimenter is momentarily silent, thus providing for a 'slot' in the interaction in which the participant can expand upon their imagery, or correct or clarify the experimenter's understanding, and so on. Some participants offer further comment on every item; however, this degree of participation is rare. It is more common to find that participants pass on the opportunity to speak, for example, by not saying anything after the introduction of each item, or by offering minimal confirmations, such as 'yeah' or 'mm hm'. This is illustrated in the following extract, in which the subject uses a 'mm hm' to confirm the imagery 'boat in the water leaving a wake'. The next imagery item, 'a pile of something?' does, however, generate further participation, and there follows an *imagery expansion sequence*.

(9.7) (01-05: E3/F)

```
1    E:    hh boat in the water leaving a wake,
2    P:    m:m::
3          (0.6)
4    E:    (tk) hh a pile of something?
5          (1.1)
6    P:    > h yeah< it was like a pile of pla:tes or:: ' (0.7) um::
7          (1.1) °something like that°
8    E:    °okay:?° (0.5) h a fro:g(h) >a big one?<
```

There is an ambiguity about this extract, in that the experimenter may not have heard what the pile consisted of during the participant's earlier report of her imagery, in which case the turn is a form of repair initiation, in that 'something' exhibits the basis of experimenter's confusion and guides the requirements of any subsequent clarification. Alternatively, the experimenter may be accurately reporting what the participant had said during the sending phase, but that now in retrospect the participant has a clearer understanding of the earlier imagery. Either way, this extract illustrates some common features of imagery expansion sequences. There is an initial and emphatic (although not immediate) confirmation followed by further information. The participant makes an attempt to provide more detail, identifying the objects in the pile. She then says 'something like that' more quietly than the preceding talk, which marks the 'general adequacy' of the prior description and stands a closing component of the expansion turn. This closing component is matched by the experimenter's immediate 'okay' produced with a rising or 'questioning' intonation. The absence of any further participant contribution in response to the question marked 'okay' is treated by the experimenter as licence to return to the stepwise progression through the mentation imagery, and he introduces the next item (the frog). The absence of further participant talk after a question-marked 'okay' is common throughout the corpus, and it routinely stands as the end of an expansion sequence and marks the progression to the next imagery item to be considered.

Extract 9.8, which comes from a ganzfeld experiment with a more vocal participant, provides further evidence of this use of 'okay'. However, it also illustrates another recurrent feature of expansion sequences: that the participants' further description of or talk about imagery occupies a single turn. That is, when the experimenter receipts an expansion turn, the participant does not subsequently continue to speak on that item, and a new item is introduced.

(9.8) (01-81: E1/M)

```
1     E:   and then teeth (.) sharp teeth
2          (0.8)
3     E:   ˙hh [ y-
4     P:       [yeah: that one came back (.) that was a (0.5) °>but it from that
5          one<° the beginning it was like on the inside (.) the second time it
6          came around it was like (.) looking from the outside. ˙hh [h
7     E:                                                              [mkay
8     P:   °s(h)o°
9     E:   ˙hh then you saw the back of someone's hand >with< °w-°with light
10         reflected on their faces (.) ˙h as if the=light was from a tee vee screen,
11    P:   (reckon) that was like (.) a cartoon. (0.4) like a picture instead of a (.)
12         real life °thing°
13    E:   mkay (.) ˙hh a tree a
```

In this extract, the experimenter initially introduces the imagery of sharp teeth. After a gap, and at the same time as the experimenter begins to speak again, the participant talks about this imagery, and although his utterance is somewhat confusing, he seems to be claiming that this was a recurrence of earlier imagery, and tries to mark the differences between the two instances. At the recognisable end of the turn, the experimenter acknowledges the expansion with 'mkay'. Note that the participant then says 'so', which could be taken as projecting some final concluding talk on the teeth imagery. However, the experimenter does not withhold his talk to see if the participant does go on to offer further comment, but moves immediately to the next item, 'the back of someone's hand'. The participant provides further information about this item, establishing the cartoon-like quality of the image. Again this is receipted with "mkay' and the experimenter moves to the next item in the review.

In these extracts, item expansion turns tend to have an unequivocal and declarative design. In extract 9.11, for example, the participant's expansion turn is unequivocal, in that he clarifies the properties of the 'pile of something' with '>yeah< it was like a pile of pla:tes', although he does subsequently go on to offer a more equivocal description, °something like that°. Similarly, in extract 9.12, the participant's expansion turns relate two appearances of the same image, or offer further characterisation of the phenomenological quality of an image. In neither does the participant question the image, or express doubt about its properties. Participants' expansion turns exhibit a degree of epistemic confidence in their recall of the imagery or the information they go on to provide.

There is, though, a class of expansion sequences that exhibits different properties.

On occasions, instead of using ' okay' to receipt expansion turns, experimenters produce minimal utterances, such as 'mm hm'.

(9.9) (01-21: E3/M)

```
1     E:    °° ˙(n)hh°° °o:kay,° (tk). ˙hh and then I think the final thing you said was
2           uh:: (.) ˙h something like a chair (.) >in< in a pyramid?
3     P:    °(n)hh° yeah, >saw the< (.) the triangle thing again and then (.) ° ˙h°
4           >something< which reminded me of like, (.) um, (0.5) ˙h an upright
5           chair like um:, (1.5) °(n)hhh° (.) um:? >°so-°< like a black chair,
6           (1.4)
7     E:    m:hm
8           (0.5)
9     P:    not like the one I'm sitting on or °anything° jus:::t °uh:° (3.5) >I don't
10          know,< it was >sort of< °uhm:(h)° (2.1) >like a s-< like a sort of
11          padded chai(hh)r or something ° ˙h° >it was just< from the side that
12          I saw it, so >it was like< an ell shape (.) ° ˙h° [that =
13    E:                                                      [°mhm°
```

14   P: = suggested a chair:

In this extract the experimenter introduces the last imagery from the participant's report of their experiences during the earlier sending phase of the experimenter, the 'chair in a pyramid'. The participant immediately produces an unequivocal confirmation 'yeah,' and then provides more information: there is a report of the immediately prior imagery 'the triangle thing again' and then the participant tries to detail the imagery by drawing on an associated everyday object '>something< which reminded me of like, (.) um, (0.5) 'h an upright chair'. At this point in the turn the participant says 'like um:,' which would suggest that the turn at that point is incomplete. There is a gap of 1.5 seconds and then after some non-lexical contributions the participant says '>°so-°< like a black chair,', thereby establishing how the report of the chair was related to the imagery. When this final component of the turn is complete, the participant stops speaking, and there are good grounds for assuming that the participant has completed his expansion turn. He has provided further detail, and the final part of the turn was designed as an upshot or conclusion to prior talk, thereby signalling the terminal status of that component. Moreover, in the subsequent 1.4 second gap the participant does not initiate further talk, or take a pronounced inbreath, which routinely signals the onset of participatory status. There is no immediate response to the completion of the expansion turn. Moreover, when the experimenter does speak, he does not use 'okay' to exhibit his recognition of the likely completion of the expansion turn, but offers instead 'm:hm' (line 7).

Non-lexical contributions such as 'mm hm' and 'uh huh' might seem intuitively inconsequential; and it is common to find social science research papers which use verbal data in which such items are deliberately omitted from transcripts. But in everyday interaction, though, minimal continuers do particular kinds of work. Speakers use them to pass on opportunities in which turn transfer could be initiated, thereby publicly displaying their producer's continued recipiency and passive status within the interaction (Jefferson, 1984; Schegloff, 1982). Routinely, then, minimal continuers are taken to exhibit the expectation that there is more to come in the prior speaker's talk. As such, they are resources by which co-participants to interaction can facilitate another's production of an extended turn (such as telling a joke or a lengthy anecdote).

We might, then, expect these kinds of non-lexical items to occur in the mentation review: it is designed to elicit further information, and we know that minimal continuers are a device to facilitate further talk from a co-participant. It is no surprise, then, to see that this is precisely how the experimenter's 'mm hm' works in extract 9.13: the participant continues to talk about the 'chair-in-a-pyramid' mentation item. However, compare the kind of talk produced in response to the introduction of the mentation item with that turn elicited by the experimenter's minimal continuer. The first is broadly positive: it expands upon and clarifies the original mentation report. But the post-continuer turn is different, in that the subsequent talk about the imagery is now more circumspect or hesitant than the initial expansion. There are various ways in which this circumspection is manifest.

The turn starts with an account of what the imagery *is not* like (line 9). There is an explicit doubt marker 'I don't know'. 'I dunno/ I don't know' formulations have some interesting interactional properties. They are used in occasions when speakers are making sensitive or slightly controversial claims, and have grounds for assuming that co-participants may be unsympathetic to or dissatisfied with the kind of report or account they are making. They display speakers' awareness that recipients may not align with the position they take (Potter, 1997; Widdicombe and Wooffitt, 2006). 'I don't know' formulations can be used to exhibit a position of uncertainty, caution or scepticism about a specific claim; in this, they allow the speaker to align with, or at least suggest the absence of opposition to, an anticipated sceptical response. Moreover, compared to the pre-continuer expansion, there is increased use of words and phrases that suggest uncertainty, such as 'sort of'. The post expansion turn is marked by perturbations and hesitations (such as intra turn gaps, word stretching, and so on). Finally, the participant's report reveals that the imagery was perceived in his consciousness from a side view; he also explicitly states that the image was of an 'L' shape which *suggested* a chair. This turn then, is designed to exhibit his limited or partial perspective on this experience.

There are, then, two ways in which experimenters can receipt expansion turns, but they seem to have very different properties and outcomes. 'Okay' is produced soon after a recognisable terminal point in the expansion turn; it seems to mark the experimenter's understanding that the expansion turn is complete, and tends to come immediately before progression to the next item in the review. 'Mm hm', however, is produced after a delay, and precedes a further turn from the participant in which they provide a more hesitant or cautious report or reflection on the imagery which was the subject of the initial expansion turn. This shift in the speaker's stance or implied confidence in the imagery is not a unique case. Here is another example, which comes from an earlier stage of the mentation review from which extract 9.9 was taken. Following the experimenter's minimal continuer, the participant's talk is marked by expressions of doubt or hesitation.

(9.10) (01-21: E3/M)

```
1     E:    m:hm (0.6) ˙h °ri:ght° o:kay and then I think the: ˙h the
2            first regular impression you had was something like
```

3   images of a pyramid?
4   (1.0)
5   P: yeah:, it's like (0.5) hills or a pyramid °or something°
6   E: m:h [m
7   P: ['(n)hh uhm hh (.) >everything seems to be like<
8   moving, (0.5) you know, °it wasn't° (.) static °or
9   anything so it kept° °°>sort of<°°
10   (.)
11   E: [mm
12   P: ['h dunno it's just my eyes were moving or::

There is an important difference in the production of the experimenter's minimal continuer, in that, unlike the instance in extract 9.9, in this case it is produced without delay, immediately after the expansion turn. However, the design of the expansion turn allows the experimenter to anticipate its completion and thereby 'cues in' the start of the experimenter's expansion receipt. This is because the expansion turn is produced as a three part list of two specific items, 'hills', and 'a pyramid', completed by a more general reference, the quietly spoken 'or something'. As we noted in the previous chapter, Jefferson (1990) has studied listing in everyday conversational interaction, and has shown that speakers orient to lists as being complete upon the provision of a third part. The normative convention that lists should come in three parts allows speakers to anticipate the onset of turn transition spaces in interaction, and is therefore one of a range of tacit inferential resources by which speaker transition is managed (Sacks *et al.*, 1974). The participant's expansion turn in line 5, then, has the properties of a list, the three parted character of which is established via a generalised list completer. This is relevant, in that it warrants the claim that the experimenter was aware that the participant's expansion turn was complete upon the provision of the third item. Indeed, the precision timed 'mm hm' exhibits the experimenter's understanding that this was a space in the interaction in which a contribution would be normatively appropriate.

Immediately after the 'mm hm', the participant begins a further turn. Initially there is an in audible breath, which indicates preparation for speaking, a hesitation marker, and the report that '>everything seems to be like< moving, (0.5) you know', which suggests the basis for uncertainty about or lack of confidence in the nature of the imagery. The participant goes on to employ another explicit doubt marker when he proposes an explanation for this sense of movement: 'dunno it's just my eyes were moving or:::'.

What we have, then, is an emerging rationalisation of the participant's depiction and displayed understanding of the image. In the first expansion turn he merely reports factually what the imagery was like: hills or pyramids. But in the subsequent post-continuer expansion turn there is marked doubt about the basis of his understanding of the imagery because of general movement, and this movement is itself explained in terms of normal causes: minor oscillations of the eye during the mentation phase of the procedure.

The expression of doubt or uncertainty about imagery, as illustrated in extract 9.9, and the incremental rationalisation of imagery, as illustrated in extract 9.10, are discursive phenomena which seem to be intimately connected to the experimenter's use of a minimal continuer to receipt an initial period of expansion, rather than 'okay'. There seems, then, to be an interactional basis for the production of *doubt marked expansion sequences*. This seems to be a robust phenomenon. In the following extract there are two further instances.

(9.11) (01-28: E2/F)

```
1    E:   and you said you felt you could see for mi:les (.)
2         across countryside,=
3    P:   =yea°f-s°, ( ) ˙hh like I was flying across it
4         (0.5 )
5    E:   (h) m↑hm
6    P:   ˙hh looking down over (0.5) ˙hhh hhh fields a- >I don't
7         know:< it was very odd hh yeah,
8    E:   °m°↑hm
9    P:   °° ˙hhhh hhhh°°
10        (0.3)
11   P:   (°mus:-°) >I'd-< hh (.) ˙h ↑I'M NOT VERY GOOD
12        AT DESCRIBING IT it's a very weird >sort of<
13        va:gue (. ) ˙hh (1.2 ) >°it°< just felt like (>sort of
14        you<) so::: (0.3) ˙hh body's just: (1.2) taking off
```

The imagery is the participant's sensation that she could 'see for miles across countryside', and she expands upon this in various ways. She reports initially that the view in her mind was similar to that facilitated by flight. The experimenter produces the first minimal continuer expansion receipt, and in response, the participant continues to expand upon the imagery, reporting that she was 'looking down over (0.5) ˙hhh hhh fields'. She then says '>I don't know:< it was very odd hh yeah' (lines 6 and 7), which offers a doubt marker and explicitly points to the unusual nature of the imagery. It also acts as a summary formulation suggesting that, at that point, the participant's expansion turn had finished. However, there is another experimenter continuer (line 8) and after a spate of audible breathing and a 0.3 second gap, the participant speaks again. The first component ('I'd') is abandoned and the turn is re-launched, and she reports '↑I'M

NOT VERY GOOD AT DESCRIBING IT'. This turn, both in its design and delivery at greater volume than previous talk, unambiguously fore-grounds the participant's uncertainty in her account of the imagery. The expansion turns are concluded with further references to the strangeness of the experience, and a (somewhat disjointed) attempt to convey that it was like 'a body taking off'.

Finally, in the following extract, the participant responds to the intro-duction of the imagery item by correcting the experimenter's description, rather than volunteering an expansion. However, the sequential trajectory of this spate of interaction follows the pattern identified in earlier extracts: the corrective turn provides clarification of and further detail about the imagery, it is (eventually) receipted by a minimal continuer, and then the participant produces a further turn which exhibits a relatively greater degree of circumspection.

(9.12)(01-31: E3/M)

```
1    E:   °°m,°° (0.5) °okay,° (0.5) .hhhh (0.4) then you said at
2         one stage feels like it's uh:: °°n-°° >I- I< ↑thought you
3         said? something like a rolling uh:, °°mm°°=uh::, ˙h
4         head? (.) but did you mean like a rolling field?
5         or:, [°( )°
6    P:        [ no:: °a-° I remember at one (.) point, (0.7) eh::,
7         (1.1) it seemed as if there was somebody rolling over
8         the ground? ° ˙hh°
9    E:   m: [hm,
10   P:        [>and,< (0.2) tha:t was when I started (.) thinking
11        about this person ˙hh
12   E:   [mhm,
13   P:   [°and° (0.3) it was as if he was: like? (1.1) °hh° he was
14        rolling over towards:: °°>uh<°°a kinda? ˙hhh wee
15        (.) °°u°°=hi:ll or lump or something in the
16        ground and then? ° ˙hh almost° like burrowing
17        under it
18        (1.3)
19   E:   m:°hm°
20        (1.0)
21   P:   °°e:h it-°° °>it was all very,<° it was very kinda, i- (.)
22        you know, (0.7) indistinct but, °u° (.) that was the
23        kind of feeling that I was getting,
```

Here the participant's expansion turn corrects the experimenter's report of the mentation imagery (lines 6 through to 17). During this turn the experi-menter produces two minimal continuers. In each case, the participant continues to talk, and uses 'and' to establish that the turn had not been complete at those points at which the experimenter produced the minimal continuers. Eventually, there is a 1.3 second gap (line 18), and then the experimenter issues another minimal continuer, this time clear of any surrounding participant talk. This use of a minimal continuer to receipt the correction again elicits further information about the imagery. In the first component of this turn the participant explicitly describes how indistinct the imagery was (lines 21 and 22). He then characterises his understanding of the imagery as a feeling, which markedly downgrades the expressed or implied certainty compared to the prior correction.

In this section we have focused on two ways in which the experimenter can proceed after an initial expansion turn, and the implications of the different sequential outcomes initiated by the two forms of expansion receipt. 'Okay' seems to exhibit the experimenter's understanding that the expansion turn is complete, and precedes a return to the stepwise progression through the experimenter's record of the participant's imagery. 'Mm hm' however, generates further talk about the imagery, and the return to the item-by-item progression through the record of the imagery is delayed. Moreover, this subsequent turn exhibits caution, uncertainty or circumspection about the imagery, and the participant's degree of confidence in its properties or apprehension. There are explicit references to how vague or indistinct the imagery was; there are reports of its strangeness (thus acknowledging the difficulty of accurate description); there are explicit formulations of doubt, 'I don't know'; there are phrases such as 'sort of', which modulate or conditionalise the attempt at description; and there are speech perturbations and dysfluencies, such as relatively long pauses, hesitation markers, and instances of turn components abandoned or terminated in mid-production.

Discussion

The mentation review is characterised by a limited range of interactional activities: introducing the imagery into the review, clarification and correction (if required), acknowledgement of any further information, and then a return to the stepwise progress of the review. In this chapter we have examined two routine activities, and considered the interactional consequences that follow from the ways these tasks may be accomplished. So, from the range of ways that imagery items might be introduced into the review, we focused on 'you said' reported speech markers. And we have examined occasions when experimenters use 'mm hm' receipts, as opposed to 'okay', to acknowledge the participant's provision of further information about their imagery. It is important to be clear that we are not suggesting that experimenters intentionally used these utterances to achieve the interactional consequences identified in this chapter. Rather, we have examined mentation review data to highlight how participants' inferences about a prior turn will be informed by an intersection of culturally available knowledge of the way turn components are used in everyday interaction, and tacit understanding of the normative expectations and conventions that inform their use in any particular institutional setting. In this, we illustrate the kinds of interactional and normative practices that underpin all kinds of institutional or work related talk, such as that which characterises retrospective interviews in introspection research.

In everyday interaction, 'you said' prefaces are routinely used in circumstances in which the recipient may be being called into account for what they had said. This is reflected in the way that they function in the review: even in the absence of any indications of explicit epistemic uncertainty, unmarked 'you said' prefaces may be interpreted by the participant as exhibiting the experimenter's expectation that further talk about the imagery so introduced should be forthcoming. Similarly with 'mm hm' type turn receipts. Studies of conversational interaction show how these kinds of minimal utterances can act as continuers, in that they exhibit the producer's understanding that there is more to come in a co-interactant's turn. As such, they are resources by which speakers collaboratively facilitate extended periods of one party talk. In the context of an experimental situation, the participants seem to hear minimal continuers produced in the clear of ongoing talk and after their initial expansion turn as exhibiting the experimenter's understanding that the prior expansion is incomplete, and that more description is expected or required.

But it is not just that participants speak more when presented with imagery with a 'you said' preface, or their when their prior expansion is receipted with an 'mm hm' preface. Their turns exhibit that they infer they are required to do a particular kind of work with their subsequent talk. So, if participants hear a reported speech marker as inviting them to say more about their imagery, they reflect cautiously on the likely parapsychological provenance of their imagery; or their subsequent reports normalise their imagery, and cast doubt as to its parapsychological status. In so doing, they offer a reassessment of the relevance of their imagery in relation to the core goals of the experimental procedure. And with respect to expansion acknowledgements, it is clear from the design of subsequent turns that participants infer that the experimenters' 'mm hm' displays some level of scepticism about the implied certainty of their initial expansion turn; or that it orients to an expectation that they should temper or downgrade the degree of expressed certainty, or at least exhibit an awareness of the contingencies which may effect clear recall of conscious imagery initially experienced at an earlier phase of the experiment.

In both cases, then, mundane discursive practices in the interview are interpreted in such a way that participants offer some form of revised assessment of their imagery with respect to what it was, its relevance to the experiment, or their epistemic confidence in their own earlier reports.

This may be significant. The now revised account of the imagery will be recorded by the experimenter in the production of the 'final record' of the mentation—records that may be examined in subsequent attempts to explore the interaction of mundane and parapsychological processes (or indeed, which may be used as data in a non parapsychological investigation of inner experience). Moreover, the ganzfeld experiment is designed to investigate whether or not images in one person's consciousness can be transmitted by volitional thought alone into the consciousness of someone else. The logic of the experiment, then, means that participants are aware of the possibility that the images they experience and report during the sending phase of the experiment are not their own; or at least, they do not originate in their own consciousness, or arise from their own cognitive procedures. It is highly likely that the participant's assessment of the parapsychological significance of their imagery will be informed by their assessment or understanding of its inferable source. And this in turn may be significant when the participant moves to the judging phase of the experiment and has to select which of four candidate film clips was the object of the sender's mental projections based on their conscious imagery during the sending phase. Imagery which seems transparently to reflect the routine circumstances of the experiment, or which is manifestly the epiphenomenon of mundane physiological events, or about which there is doubt and uncertainty, is unlikely to be interpreted as originating from an external source. How the participant reflects on his or her imagery, then, may be consequential for the way in which they make decisions in the judging phase of the experiment, which in turn, of course, influences the degree to which this particular experiment—and the ganzfeld procedure more generally—stands as a convincing and replicable demonstration of parapsychological processes.

The analysis of the mentation review data allows us to highlight some key issues that are relevant to research on consciousness that relies on retrospective interviews to capture inner experience, or refine an already existing report of that experience. The research interview is a period of social interaction in which everyday communicative competences are mobilised with respect to specific task related requirements. The use of these communicative competences will both reflect their wider use in their home environment, mundane conversational interaction, and their specific use in this setting, in relation to the activities they manage and, more importantly, with respect to the participant's tacit inferences about their on going involvement in the setting, and their normative understanding as to what counts as appropriate participation. This complex interpretative nexus impacts in every detail of the interview. It inhabits the very weave of the setting as an unnoticed but ever present *'interactional substrate'* — the 'basic skills for engaging meaningfully' in interviews (Maynard and Shaeffer, 2002: 9). And it shapes not only how people act, but also what they say.

Chapter Ten

Introspection, Description, Consciousness, Action

The key argument of this book is very simple. The practices of description are practices of social action. Introspection and retrospective accounts of inner experience generated in interviews are descriptive activities, conducted through language, in a social context, that address interpersonal and inferential contingencies relevant to that setting. Our argument is based on a view of language use that has emerged from empirical social science research on the organisation of talk-in-interaction, in which analytic priority is given to the ways in which people use talk to perform social actions. This invites an empirical investigation of the practices of introspection; and the analyses presented in this book are the first step in that direction.

Our data, though from the unusual setting of a parapsychology experiment, consist of two types of introspective data: monologues on inner experience, or mentation narratives; and retrospective interviews in which participant and experimenter review the prior mentation narrative to allow for clarification or correction of the experimenter's record of their mentation, and to provide an opportunity for the participant to offer more detail about their imagery and experiences. Our empirical analyses make three broad points. Analysis of the ways in which participants report how they apprehended conscious imagery, and examination of periods of silence in mentation narratives, exposed the way in which the design of talk, and the organisation of its withholding, exhibited the participants' tacit sensitivity to features of the setting of their participation in a (para)psychological experiment and its (inferred) attendant requirements. In two chapters on the poetics of introspective reports, we argued, first, that communicative competences through which mentation narratives are produced can exhibit quite complex properties, and second, that participants' orientation to the production of poetic phenomena can significantly shape what is reported. And in the final two empirical chapters, we examined social interaction in retrospective interviews. Our analyses identified how ostensibly mundane interactional activities can generate trajectories of social action in which the participants' accounts of their experience, and their stance towards their experience, may be revised, amended and negotiated. So, whether participants are reporting out loud whatever came to mind, or subsequently discussing their recollections of their inner experience prompted by the experimenter, their descriptions of inner experience are a series of discursive acts through which they pragmatically address institutional, interpersonal and inferential contingencies of the setting. What counts as 'inside the head', then, is a product of the discursive management of the social outside. And it is hard to imagine how the elicitation of verbal reports of consciousness in *any context*, via *any method*, can side-step this range of issues. Wherever and however we may attempt to capture consciousness — to paraphrase William James, to catch the snowflake of experience in the warm hand of observation before it becomes a drop of liquid (James, 1892) — socially organised discursive practices will be inextricably implicated in our understanding of the nature of our phenomena. For this reason, it seems inescapable to us that recognition of introspection as communicative social action should be foundational in research in consciousness studies, or any other cognate discipline that uses as data reports of inner experience. To proceed as if this were not the case is, at best, to overlook a fundamental property of descriptions of consciousness; at worst, it is essentially to misconstrue the nature of introspective data, with significant ramifications for our understanding of lived experience.

The analyses presented here suggest that it is extremely unwise to assume that people's reports of their inner experience somehow unproblematically capture aspects of that phenomenological reality that are independent of their descriptions. It is important to stress, however, that this is a methodological argument, not an ontological one; the empirical approach we have developed is not committed to a particular view as to what inner experience consists of. It does not endorse the kind of philosophical critiques of cognitivism found in Wittgenstein (1953), Ryle (1949) or the ethnomethodological critiques of Coulter (1979, 1989) or Watson, R. (1998), or the critiques of cognitivism in discursive psychology (Billig, 1987; Edwards, 1997; Edwards and Potter, 1992, 2005; Potter, 2000). Neither is our position a form of ontological social constructivism of the kind exemplified by Burns and Engdahl's argument that individual consciousness is constituted through the interplay of 'culture, language, institutions, collective representations, social interaction and communication' (Burns and Engdahl 1998b: 183; see also, Burns and Engdahl, 1998a). Although we appreciate that the kinds of findings presented here are more likely to be recruited in support of a social constructionist argument, rather than one that asserts the determinant primacy of cognitive and mental phenomena, the empirical approach we have adopted is agnostic as to the ultimate reality and nature of inner experience.

In this, our approach broadly parallels the position taken by some sociologists of scientific knowledge in their study of scientific disputes, who argued that it was necessary to suspend common sense, culturally available or scientifically accepted versions of what was true or false in order to expose and investigate the ways in which knowledge claims were socially produced, negotiated, ratified or contested (Bloor, 1976). It was not that sociologists denied the existence of an objective world that could be explored through the scientific method. The argument was primarily methodological: that in order to understand the social processes that underpinned scientific research, it was necessary to bracket off commitment to the scientific output of those scientists whose activities were being studied (Collins, 1975, 1981, 1985; Collins and Pinch, 1982; Pinch, 1985). This agnosticism is reflected in our position on the relationship between introspective description (in which we include retrospective interviews) and consciousness and inner experience. The study of how communicative competences are marshalled in the situated production of descriptions of inner experience does not deny that inner experience exists. It is more that the empirical approach suspends assumptions about the nature of inner experience to focus on the dynamic and action oriented properties of descriptions that constitute the raw data for empirical inquiry into consciousness.

Apart from encouraging a view of introspection as a social activity, where does this research take us? What is gained from this kind of detailed study of introspective discourse? To conclude, we consider the implications of our approach for three issues: the concept of demand characteristics, the way that methodological discussions of introspection are often conduced without reference to actual examples of descriptions of inner experience, and the largely negative view of language that informs many commentaries on introspective discourse.

Orne's (1962) articulation of demand characteristics focuses on two broad social psychological processes that occur in laboratory (or therapeutic) settings. First, he argues that it is necessary to recognise that experimental participants pick up cues about the purpose of the experiment during the procedure. Second, he discusses the importance of expectations attached to the roles of experimenter and research participant: '[T]he experimental situation is one which takes place within the context of an explicit agreement of the subject to participate in a special form of social interaction known as "taking part in an experiment." Within the context of our culture the roles of subject and experimenter are well understood and carry with them well-defined mutual role expectations' (Orne, 1962: 777). For Orne, then, key features of the social psychology of the psychology

experiment are role expectations and cues via which the research participant may attempt to understand the significance of the tasks they have
been asked to perform. His account does not, however, consider the
interactional and normative basis of communication between experimenter and participant. This may be highly significant, for the following
reasons.

First, a general point: the notion of social role is problematic, in that it
traditionally draws upon a static notion of contextually relevant identities,
and fails to provide an adequate account of the ways in which role or identity expectations are managed and negotiated in actual spates of interaction. There are now numerous studies in conversation analysis and
discursive psychology that have revealed the ways in which the relevance
of characterisations and attributions of identity are interactional achievements (for example, Antaki, Condor and Levine, 1996; Antaki and
Widdicombe, 1998; Benwell and Stokoe, 2006; Edwards, 1991; Sacks, 1979,
1984; Widdicombe, 1993; Widdicombe and Wooffitt, 1990; 1995). What
these and other studies have demonstrated is that detailed analysis of
talk-in-interaction associated with conversation analytic research offers
an empirically-grounded account of the communicative mechanisms by
which participants in interaction orientate to social roles or social identities as their relevance is interactionally occasioned. Second, and more
important: consider the claim that the research participant picks up on
cues in experimental procedures that expose the experimenter's intentions
or interests. In Orne's account, the research participants' interpretation of
the significance of an act or event seems to occur in an interactional vacuum, in that it is not grounded in the flow and development of interpersonal activities which constitute a social encounter. Yet it is highly likely to
be the case that the kind of events or activities that may be significant will
be communicative acts: things that the experimenter says.

In the previous chapter we examined interaction between experimenter
and participants in which they reviewed the experimenter's record of the
immediately prior introspective mentation narrative. We noted that
experimenters use two types of turn to acknowledge or receipt participants' turns in which they expand upon their imagery, or provide more
information about their inner experiences. Ostensibly, 'okay' and 'mm
hm' seem broadly similar kinds of expressions: simply two ways to
acknowledge a prior turn. However, the analysis provided strong evidence that these two types of utterance appear to generate very different
interactional trajectories in the subsequent talk. On the basis of the kind of
turns they go on to produce, it is clear that participants draw specific inferences about what kind of discursive activity is next expected of them by
virtue of the experimenter's use of 'mm hm' to receipt their initial expansion turn. And, insofar as these next activities display a particular stance

towards the participants' conscious imagery — perhaps the most important element in the ganzfeld experimental procedure — their production
may have a systematic bearing on the participants' subsequent behaviour
in the experiment. These analytic observations show how interpretations
as to what is appropriate activity is managed on a turn-by-turn basis; the
participants' inferences about the ongoing interaction are informed by
their tacit analysis of the kind of activity the experimenter's prior turn was
designed to perform. Moreover, it suggests that tacit inferences which a
participant may draw about the implications of the experimenter's turns
are related to the wider normative expectations relevant to the setting. So,
the participants' production of circumspect or doubt-marked expansion
turns following a 'mm hm' receipt display their inference about the kind of
turn which is expected and normatively appropriate at that moment in the
interaction.

The notion of cues in experimental practice is important, as it directs our
attention to participants' inferences about the significance of events in laboratory procedures. But to develop an empirically grounded appreciation
of the ways in which participants draw inferences from the experimenters'
activities, it is necessary to examine the normative properties of those communicative practices through which the experiment as a form of social
interaction is produced. And at that point, the concept of demand characteristics is not only limited, but also it becomes redundant. This is because
we can see that highly complex inferential work is inextricably woven into
the very fabric of the moment-by-moment and turn-by-turn unfolding of
interaction. It is not necessary to retain the concept of demand characteristics to point to systematic inferential and interpretative work that people
perform in laboratory settings; it is sufficient to study talk-in-interaction
through which the work of that setting is accomplished. This is as true for
introspective description produced in the service of research on consciousness and inner experience as it is for any talk in any formal psychological
research setting.

The perspective we have developed throughout this book offers a sustained and rigorously empirical investigation of introspective reports.
People's descriptions of their inner experience are not glossed, categorised
into themes, interpreted in terms of theoretical positions or philosophical
theories, or transformed via orthographic transcription practices. Working with recordings and transcripts that capture in detail what participants actually said, we have instead tried to identity the communicative
competences that inform the way that descriptions of inner experience are
designed and organised, and to explicate the work that these descriptions
do.

To researchers working in or familiar with conversation analytic methods (and other research traditions in linguistics and related disciplines),

sustained analysis of the detail of actual talk is routine. It is, however, in stark contrast to the tenor of methodological debates in consciousnesses studies, where it is routine to encounter lengthy discussion of approaches to introspective data and their merit, which do not contain reference to actual instances of introspective description. For example, in a recent issue of the *Journal of Consciousness Studies* celebrating an earlier publication exploring phenomenological and introspective methods (Varela and Shear, 1999), there are thirteen separate articles and replies, each of which contributes to broader methodological debates about introspection (Petitmengin, 2011). But only one of these articles, by Russel Hurlburt, presents any actual data (Hurlburt, 2011). The other contributions are, essentially, theoretical or philosophical arguments about introspection. It is in keeping with Hurlburt's approach to the investigation of everyday experience that his contribution to this collection is grounded in consideration of an example of introspective description. It is, though, still somewhat surprising that, as in most debates about introspection, no other examples of introspection are presented in the other contributions, let alone given the kind of systematic examination illustrated in this book.

The conspicuous absence of extensive engagement with introspective data in methodological discussions may reflect the disciplinary heritage of attempts to use introspection to examine inner experience. Most methodological discussions of introspection and introspective data are couched in terms of phenomenological philosophy or psychological issues. This has had a negative impact on sustained study of the *practices* of introspective description. A phenomenologically oriented understanding of introspection directs attention to the realm of subjective experience and what we can say about it, and the extent to which we might trust what we say about it as method for exploring underlying experiential substrates (for example, Depraz, 2009; Vermersch, 2011; Zahavi, 2011). Psychologically motivated discussion of introspection tends to focus on its performance in terms of considerations that resonate with the experimental laboratory: accuracy, bias, control, measurement, validity, reliability, standardisation, and so on (for example, Froese, Gould and Seth, 2011; Hendricks, 2009; Klinger, 2011). Neither perspective acknowledges the primary feature of introspective description: that it is, in all instances, a situated moment of discursive social action. It is hardly surprising, then, that actual practices of introspective description rarely receive sustained attention in the literature.

There may another reason. In debates about introspection, language and description are, essentially, treated with caution, if not suspicion. It is not difficult to find instances of a more general suspicion of language in the literature on introspection. There are, of course, the widely recognised and rehearsed arguments that people's accounts may be distorted by confabulation, belief based reconstruction, a desire to impress or please the researcher, foibles of memory and so on. But there is, underlying these recognised issues, a deeper mistrust of language and description. So for example, in a discussion of language and introspection, Zahavi outlines Bergson's claim that 'all language is able to capture are lifeless shadows' (Zahavi, 2011:14). Moreover, in their study of reports of the onset of epileptic episodes, Petitmengin and her colleagues assert that participants require intervention and assistance from the experimenter to 'enable [the participant] to put his experience into words, the main difficulty being the *paucity of vocabulary* for describing these subtle sensations' (Petitmengin, Navarro and Quyen, 2007: 751, emphasis added. See also, Pettitmengin, 2006: 238-239). And to support their arguments about the inherent deficiencies of language, Petitmengin and Bitbol quote William James ('We find ourselves in continual error and uncertainty so soon as we are called upon to name and class, and not merely to feel') and Hurlburt and Schwitzgebel ('We almost completely lack the concepts and competencies that would allows us to parse, think about, talk about, and remember the complexities of experience') (Petimengin and Bitbol, 2009: 370). As support for the general distrust of description in introspection, it has even been claimed that 'the process of description itself has been little studied and described' (Petitmengin and Bitbol, 2009:387).

However, description has been studied, and studied extensively. Conversation analytic research (as well as research in discourse analytic approaches informed by conversation analytic methods and findings) has systematically examined how descriptions are designed, the work they do, and their relationship to the trajectory of talk and interaction in which they occur and which they progress. Descriptions have been studied in mundane conversational activities, such as asking and answering questions, offering, endorsing or qualifying assessments, in making and accepting or rejecting complaints, in offering accounts and explanations for behaviour, in seeking and providing information, in arguments, in requests, in jokes, in the telling of stories and in responses to those stories — in short, in all discursive activities that constitute social life. Descriptions of events, of people, of things, of desires, of wants, wishes and intentions — of experience itself — are part of the fabric of talk-in-interaction, which is the focus of conversation analytic investigations. To say that description has been little studied is to ignore half a century's worth of sustained and increasingly influential empirical research, a cumulative body of knowledge that can be drawn upon in the investigation of descriptions of consciousness and inner experience.

In the literature on introspection, there is an unfortunate corollary to the view that language must be treated with suspicion: it is that people are, in some way, deficient in their abilities to report their experience. Consequently, it is argued that research participants require close attention of experimenters in iterative or focused interviews; or that they need some form of training to provide accounts of experience suitable for the researchers' goals. This view of the participant as deficient is directly at odds with the view of the human actor in studies of talk-in-interaction, which attends to, and thereby exposes, everyday communicative competences and skills through which social interaction is conducted. Research findings from studies of how people produce talk, and exploration of the detail with which social interaction is enacted, is sustained and substantial testament to the extraordinary range of tacit communicative, interpretative and inferential skills that underpin social interaction. But perhaps the most striking illustrations of this perspective come from studies of interaction in which one of the participants is understood to be impeded from fully interacting with others for medical reasons. For example, Schegloff (1999) has examined video and audio recordings of a clinical session in which a patient with surgically separated brain hemispheres is tested by a researcher. His conversation analytic investigation of turn taking in the encounter revealed that the patient exhibited a range of subtle interactional capacities, some of which, according to current neuroscientific knowledge, would not be expected given the nature of the patient's impairment. Similarly, Maynard (2005) has examined interaction between researchers and children diagnosed with autism, in which the children are administered psychological tests designed to record their 'interpersonal difficulties'. His analysis shows that the children's interaction with the researchers during the administration of the test exhibits an otherwise unnoticed degree of interactional orderliness and sophistication. And there is the irony that psychological tests of interpersonal problems require for their completion reliance on precisely those kinds of communicative competences that underpin and facilitate interpersonal relationships.

The detailed study of how people actually use language, whether in everyday life, or in the production of introspective reports of inner experience, reveals unanticipated competences and skills, and invites not caution and suspicion, but renewed appreciation of those communicative capacities that define us as social — and conscious — beings.

References

Adams, W. (2000) *Introspection reconsidered.* Presented at: "Towards a science of consciousness", April 10-15, 2000, Tuscon Convention Center, Tuscon, AZ. Retrieved in January 2008 from https://sites.google.com/site/billadamsphd/publications/publications-docs.

Alcock, J. E. (1981) *Parapsychology: Science or Magic?* Oxford and New York: Pergamon Press.

Alcock, J. E. (1987) Parapsychology: science of the anomalous or search for the soul? *Behavioural and Brain Sciences,* 10, 4: 553-565.

Antaki, C., Condor, S., and Levine, M. (1996) Social identities in talk: speakers' own orientations. *British Journal of Social Psychology,* 35, 473-492.

Antaki, C. and Leudar, I. (2001) Recruiting the record: using opponent's exact words in parliamentary argumentation. *Text,* 21(4), 467-488.

Antaki, C. and Widdicombe, S. (Eds.) (1998) *Identities in Talk.* London: Sage.

Armstrong, D. (1968) *A Materialist Theory of Mind.* New York: Humanities Press.

Atkinson, J. M. (1984) *Our Masters' Voices: The Language and Body Language of Politics.* London: Methuen.

Atkinson, J. M. and Drew, P. (1979) *Order in Court: The Organisation of Verbal Interaction in Judicial Settings.* London: Macmillan.

Atkinson, R. and Shiffrin, R. (1971) The control of short-term memory. *Scientific American,* 225, 82-90.

Austin, J.L. (1962) *How to Do Things with Words.* Oxford: Oxford University Press.

Baars, B. (2009) Is feeling pain just mindreading? Our mind-brain constructs realistic knowledge of ourselves. *Behavioural and Brain Sciences,* 32, 139-140.

Bailey, A. R. (2000) Beyond the fringe; William James on the transitional parts of the stream of consciousness. In F. Varela and J. Shear (eds.) *The View from Within: First Person Approaches to the Study of Consciousness.* Exeter: Imprint Academic, 141-145.

Barnes, R., and Moss, D. (2007) Communicating a feeling: the social organisation of 'private thoughts'. *Discourse Studies,* 9, 123-148.

Barrett, L. F, Robin, L., Pietromonaco, P. R. and Eyssell, K. M. (1998) Are women the 'more emotional' sex? Evidence from emotional experiences in social context. *Cognition and Emotion,* 12, 4, 555-578.

Basso K.H. (1972) To give up on words: silence in Western Apache culture In P.P. Giglioli, (ed.), *Language and Social Context.* Harmondsworth, UK, Pelican, 67-85.

Bell, N. (1998) Politeness in the speech of Korean ESL learners. *Working Papers in Educational Linguistics*, 14, 1: 25-47.

Bem, D. (2011) Feeling the future: Experimental evidence for anomalous retroactive influences on cognition and affect. *Journal of Personality and Social Psychology*, 100(3), 407-425.

Bem, D. and Honorton, C. (1994) Does psi exist? Replicable evidence for an anomalous process of information transfer. *Psychological Bulletin*, 115, 4-18.

Bentall, R. (1990) The illusion of reality: A review and integration of psychological research on hallucinations. *Psychological Bulletin*, 107, 82-95.

Benwell, B.M. and Stokoe, E. (2006) *Discourse and Identity*. Edinburgh: Edinburgh University Press.

Billig, M. (1987) *Arguing and Thinking: A Rhetorical Approach to Social Psychology*, Cambridge: Cambridge University Press.

Binswanger, L. (1958) Existential analysis and psychotherapy. *Psychoanalysis Review*, 45, 79-83.

Bloor, D. (1976) *Knowledge and Social Imagery*. London: Routledge and Kegan Paul.

Boden, D. and Zimmerman, D. (Eds) (1991) *Talk and Social Structure*. Cambridge: Polity Press.

Bolger, N., Davis, A., and Rafaeli, E. (2003) Diary methods: Capturing life as it is lived. *Annual Review of Psychology*, 54, 579-616.

Boring, E. (1929) *A History of Experimental Psychology*. New York: Appleton-Century-Crofts.

Boring, E. (1953) A history of introspection. *Psychological Bulletin*, 50, 169-189.

Brentano, F. (1874/1960) The distinction between mental and physical phenomena. In R. M. Chisolm (Ed.), *Realism and the Background of Phenomenology*. Glencoe, Ill.: Free Press, 39-61.

Brewer, H., Eatough, V., Smith, J., Stanley, C., Glendinning, N. and Quarrell, O. (2008) The impact of Juvenile Huntington's Disease on the family: The case of a rare childhood condition. *Journal of Health Psychology*, 13, 5-16.

Brock, A. (1991) Imageless thought or stimulus error? The social construction of private experience. In W. Woodward and R. Cohen (Eds.), *World Views and Scientific Discipline*. Dordrectht, The Netherlands: Kluwer, 97-106.

Broughton, R. (1991) *Parapsychology: the Controversial Science* . London and Sydney: Rider.

Brown, R. and Kulik, J. (1977) Flashbulb memories. *Cognition* 5: 73-99.

Bruneau, T.J. (2008) How Americans use silence and silences to communicate. *China Media Research*, (4) 2, 77-85.

Burns, T., and Engdahl, E. (1998a) The social construction of consciousness, Part 1: Collective consciousness and its socio-cultural foundations. *Journal of Consciousness Studies*, 5, 67-85.

Burns, T., and Engdahl, E. (1998b) The social construction of consciousness, Part 2: Individual selves, self-awareness and reflectivity. *Journal of Consciousness Studies*, 5, 166-184.

Cardeña, E. (1994) Introspection is alive and well: Current methodologies to study conscious experience. *Proceedings of the 5th Simpósio da Fundaçao Bial*. Porto, Portugal: Bial, 43-54.

Carpenter, J. C. (2004) Implicit measures of participants' experiences in the ganzfeld: Confirmation of previous relationships in a new sample. *Proceedings of the 47h Annual Convention of the Parapsychological Association*. New York: The Parapsychological Association, 112-127.

Carruthers, P. (2009) How we know our own minds: the relationship between mindreading and metacognition. *Behavioral and Brain Sciences*, 32, 121-182.

Carter, R. and McCarthy, M. (2004) Talking, creating: Interactional language, creativity and context. *Applied Linguistics, 25* 62-88.

Castro, M., Buyrrows, R. and Wooffitt, R. The paranormal is (still) normal: towards the sociology of exceptional human experiences. (in preparation).

Chalmers, D. (1996). *The Conscious Mind*. Oxford and New York: Oxford University Press.

Chalmers, D. (1999) First-person methodologies in the science of consciousness. *Consciousness Bulletin*, University of Arizona, June 1999. Retrieved in May 2007 from: http//consc.net/papers/firstperson.html.

Chalmers, D. (2004) *How can we construct a science of consciousness*. Retrieved in May 2007 from: http//consc.net/papers/scicon.html.

Clayman, S.E. (2002) Disagreements and third parties: dilemmas of neutralism in panel news interviews. *Journal of Pragmatics*, 34, (10/11), 1385-1401.

Clift, R. (2006) Indexing stance: reported speech as an interactional evidential. *Journal of Sociolinguistics*, 10, 5, 569-595.

Cohen, W. (1957) Spatial and textural characteristics of the ganzfeld. *American Journal of Psychology*, 70, 403-410.

Collins, H.M. (1975) The Seven Sexes: a study in the sociology of a phenomenon, or the replication of experiments in physics. *Sociology, 9*, 205-24.

Collins, H.M. (1981) Son of Seven Sexes: the social destruction of a physical phenomenon. *Social Studies of Science* 11, 33-62.

Collins, H.M. (1985) *Changing Order: Replication and Induction in Scientific Practice* Chicago: University of Chicago Press.

Collins, H.M. and Pinch, T.J. (1979) The construction of the paranormal: nothing unscientific is happening'. In R. Wallis (ed.) *On the Margins of Science: The Social Construction of Rejected Knowledge*. University of Keele, Sociological Review Monograph no. 27, 237-270.

Collins H.M. and Pinch, T J. (1982) *Frames of Meaning: the Social Construction of Extraordinary Science*. London: Routledge and Kegan Paul.

Conner, T., Barrett, L., Tugade, M., and Tennen, H. (2007) Idiographic personality: The theory and practice of experience sampling. In R. Robins, R. Frayley, and R. Kreuger (eds.), *Handbook of Research Methods in Personality Psychology.* New York: Guilford Press.

Coon, D (1993) Standardizing the subject: Experimental psychologists, introspection, and the quest for a technoscientific ideal. *Technology and Culture*, 34, 757-783.

Corallo, G., Sackur, J., Dehaene, S., and Sigman, M. (2008) Limits on introspection: Disotorted subjective time during the dual-task bottleneck. *Psychological Science*, 19, 1110-1117.

Costall, A. (2006) 'Introspectionism' and the mythical origins of scientific psychology. *Cognition and Consciousness*, 15, 634-654.

Cotton, D., and Gresty, K. (2005) Reflecting on the think-aloud method for evaluating e-learning. *British Journal of Educational Technology*, 37, 45-54.

Coulter, J. (1979) *The Social Construction of Mind: Studies in Ethnomethodology and Linguistic Philosophy.* London: Macmillan.

Coulter, J. (1989) *Mind in Action*. Oxford: Polity.

Crain-Thoreson, C., Lippman, M., and McClendon-Magnuson, D. (1997) Windows on comprehension: Reading comprehension processes as revealed by two Think-aloud procedures. *Journal of Educational Psychology*, 89, 579-591.

Crick, F. (1994) *The Astonishing Hypothesis: The Scientific Search for the Soul*. London: Simon and Schuster.

Dallenbach, K. M. (1913) The measurement of attention. *American Journal of Psychology*, 24, 465-507.

Damasio, A. (1992) The selfless consciousness. *Behavioral and Brain Sciences*, 15, 208-209.

Danziger, K. (1998). *Constructing the Subject: Historical Origins of Psychological Research*. Cambridge: Cambridge University Press.

Davis, W. L. (2003) Better a Witty Fool than a Foolish Wit: the art of Shakespeare's chiasmus. *Text and Performance Quarterly*, 23, 311-330.

Delamillieure, P., Doucet, G., Mazoyer, B., Turbelin, M., Delcroix, N., Mellet, E., Zago, L., Crivello, F. Petit, L., Tzourio-Mazoyer, N. and Joliot, M. (2010) The resting state questionnaire: An introspective questionnaire for evaluation of inner experience during the conscious resting state. *Brain Research Bulletin*, 81, 565-573.

Dennett, D. (1991) *Consciousness Explained*. London and New York: Penguin Books.

Dennett, D. (2003) Who's on first? Heterophenomenology explained. *Journal of Consciousness Studies*, 10, 19-30.

Dennett, D. (2007) Heterophenomenology reconsidered. *Phenomenology and the Cognitive Sciences*, 6, 247-270.

Depraz, N. (2009) The 'failing' of meaning: a few steps into a 'first-person' phenomenological practice. In C. Petitmengin (ed.) *Ten Years of Viewing From Within: The Legacy of E.J. Varela*. Special Issue, *Journal of Consciousness Studies*, 16, 10-12, 90-116.

Depraz, N., Varela, F. and Vermersch, P. (2000) *On Becoming Aware: A Pragmatics of Experiencing*. Amsterdam: John Benjamins.

Dersley, I. and Wootton A.J. (2000) Complaint sequences within an antagonistic argument. *Research on Language and Social Interaction* 33, 4, 375-406.

Dersley, I. and Wootton A.J. (2001) In the heat of the sequence: interactional features preceding walkouts from argumentative talk. *Language in Society* 30, 4, 611-38.

Dixon, N. (1971) *Subliminal Perception: The Nature of a Controversy*. London and New York: McGraw-Hill.

Drew, P. (1989) Recalling someone from the past. In D. Roger and P. Bull, (eds.) *Conversation: an Interdisciplinary Perspective*. Clevedon and Philadelphia: Multilingual Matters, 96-115.

Drew, P. (2006) When document 'speak': Documents, language and interaction. In P. Drew, G. Raymond and D. Weinberg, (eds), *Talk and Interaction in Social Research Methods*. London: Sage, 63-80.

Drew, P. and Heritage, J. (1992a) *Talk At Work: Interaction in Institutional Settings*. Cambridge: Cambridge University Press.

Drew, P. and Heritage, J. (1992b) Analyzing talk at work: an introduction. In P. Drew, P. and J. Heritage, (eds.) *Talk At Work: Interaction in Institutional Settings*. Cambridge: Cambridge University Press, 3-65.

Eckartsberg von, R. (1998) Existential-phenomenological research. In R. Valle (ed.), *Phenomenological inquiry in psychology: Existential and transpersonal dimensions*. New York: Plenum Press, pp. 21-61.

Edelman, G., and Tononi, G. (2001) *Consciousness: How Matter Becomes Imagination*. London: Penguin Books.

Edge, H. L., Morris, R. L., Palmer, J., Rush, J. H. (1986) *Foundations of Parapsychology: Exploring the Boundaries of Human Capability*. Boston: Routledge and Kegan Paul.

Edwards, D. (1991) Categories are for talking: on the cognitive and discursive bases of categorisation. *Theory and Psychology*, 1 (4), 515-42.

Edwards, D. (1997) *Discourse and Cognition*. London: Sage.

Edwards, D. and Potter, J. (1992) *Discursive Psychology*. London and Thousand Oaks, Ca.: Sage.

Edwards, D. and Potter, J. (2005) Discursive psychology, mental states and descriptions. In H. teMolder and J. Potter (eds.) *Conversation and Cognition*. Cambridge: Cambridge University Press, 241-259.

Engelbert, M. and Carruthers, P. (2010) Introspection. *Wiley Interdisciplinary Reviews: Cognitive Science*, 1, 245-253.

Ericsson, K. (2002) Toward a procedure for eliciting verbal expression of nonverbal experience without reactivity: Interpreting the verbal overshadowing effect within the theoretical framework for protocol analysis. *Applied Cognitive Psychology*, 16, 981-987.

Ericsson, K. (2003) Valid and non-reactive verbalization of thoughts during performance of tasks: Towards a solution to the central problems of introspection as a source of scientific data. *Journal of Consciousness Studies*, 10, 1-18.

Ericsson, K., and Simon, H. (1980) Verbal reports as data. *Psychological Review*, 87, 215-251.

Ericsson, K., and Simon, H. (1993) *Protocol Analysis: Verbal Reports As Data*. Cambridge, MA: MIT Press.

Evans, J. (2009) Introspection, confabulation and dual-process theory. *Behavioural and Brain Sciences*, 32, 142-143.

Festinger, L. and Carlsmith, J. (1959) Cognitive consequences of forced compliance. *Journal of Abnormal and Social Psychology*, 58, 203-210.

Forer, B. R. (1949) The fallacy of personal validation: a classroom demonstration of gullibility. *Journal of Abnormal and Social Psychology*, 44, 118-123.

Fox, B., Hayashi, M. and Jasperson, R. (1996) Resources and repair: a cross-linguistic study of syntax and repair. In E. Ochs, E.A. Schegloff and S.A. Thompson (Eds), *Interaction and Grammar*. Cambridge: Cambridge University Press, 134-184.

French, C. (2003) Fantastic memories: The relevance of research into eyewitness testimony and false memories for reports of anomalous experiences. *Journal of Consciousness Studies*, 10, 153-174.

Frith, C., and Lau, H. (2006) The problem of introspection. *Consciousness and Cognition*, 761-764.

Froese, T., Gould, C. and Seth, A.K. (2011) Validating and calibrating first and second person methods. In C.Petitmengin (ed.) *Ten Years' Viewing From Within: Further Debate*. Special Issue, *Journal of Consciousness Studies*, 18,2, 38-64.

Garfinkel, H. (1967) *Studies in Ethnomethodology*. Englewood Cliffs: Prentice Hall.

Gazzaniga, M. (1992) *Nature's Mind*. London: Basic Books.

Gertler, B. (2001) Introspecting phenomenal states. *Philosophy and Phenomenological Research*, 63, 305-328.

Gilbert, N. and Mulkay, M. (1984) *Opening Pandora's Box: A Sociological Analysis of Scientists' Discourse*. Cambridge: Cambridge University Press.

Ginsburg, C. (2005) First-person experiments. *Journal of Consciousness Studies*, 12, 22-42.

Giorgi, A., and Giorgi, B. (2003) Phenomenology. In J. Smith, (ed.), *Qualitative Psychology: A Practical Guide to Research Methods*. London: Sage, 25-50.

Goffman, E. (1961) *Encounters*. New York: Bobbs-Merrill.

Goffman, E. (1971) *Relations in Public*. New York: Basic Books.

Goffman, E. (1981) *Forms of Talk*. Oxford: Blackwell.

Gold, P.E (1992) A proposed neurobiological basis for regulating memory storage for significant events. In E. Winograd, and U. Neiser (eds.) *Affect And Accuracy in Recall: Studies of 'Flashbulb Memories'*. Cambridge, Cambridge University Press, 141- 161.

Goodwin, C. (1987) Forgetfulness as an interactive resource. *Social Psychology Quarterly*, 50: 115-30.

Goodwin, M.H. (1980) He-said-she-said: Formal cultural procedures for the construction of a gossip dispute activity. *American Ethnologist*, 7:4, 674-695.

Goodwin, M.H. (1990) *He-Said-She-Said: Talk as Social Organisation among Black Children*. Bloomington: Indiana University Press.

Gould, S.J. (1995) Researcher introspection as a method in consumer research: applications, issues and implications. *Journal of Consumer Research*, 21, 719-722

Greeley, A. M. (1975) *The Sociology of the Paranormal: A Reconnaissance*. Beverly Hills and London: Sage.

Greeley, A. (1991) The paranormal is normal: a sociologist looks at parapsychology. *Journal of the American Society for Psychical Research* 85, 367-374.

Greenfield, S. (1995) *Journey to the centers of the mind: Toward a science of consciousness*. New York: W. H. Freeman and Co.

Gregory, R., and Gombrich, E. (eds.). (1973) *Illusion in Nature and Art*. London: Duckworth.

Gross, R. (1996) *Psychology: The Science of Mind and Behaviour*. London: Hodder and Stoughton.

Grothe, M (1999)*Never Let a Fool Kiss You or a Kiss Fool You:?Chiasmus and a World of Quotations ThatSay What They Mean and Mean What They Say*. New York: Viking Penguin.

Gummesson, E. (2005) Qualitative research in marketing: Road-map for a wilderness of complexity and unpredictability. *European Journal of Marketing,* 39, 309-327.

Hanlon, J. (1974) Uri Geller and science. *New Scientist*, 17th October, 170-185.

Haraldsson, E. (1985) Representative national surveys of psychic phenomena: Iceland, Great Britain, Sweden, the United States of America and Gallup's multinational survey. *Journal of the Society for Psychical Research*, 53, 145-158.

Haraldsson E., and Houtkooper, J. M (1991) Psychic experiences in the multinational human values study: Who reports them? *Journal of the American Society for Psychical Research*, 85, 145-165.

Harré, R. (1995) Agentive discourse. In R. Harré and P. Stearns (eds.) *Discursive Psychology in Practice*. London and Thousand Oaks: Sage, 120-136.

Harré, R. (1999) Social construction of consciousness. In M. Velmans (Ed.), *Investigating Phenomenal Consciousness: New Methodologies and Maps*. Advances in Consciousness Research, Volume 13. Amsterdam and Philadelphia: John Benjamins, 233-254.

Harvey, J., Richards, J., Dziadosz, T., and Swindell, A. (1993) Misinterpretation of ambiguous stimuli in panic disorder. *Behavioral Science*, 17, 235-248.

Hatfield, G. (2005) Introspective evidence in psychology. In P. Achinstein (Ed.), *Scientific Evidence: Philosophical Theories and Applications*, pp. 259-286. Baltimore and London: John Hokins University Press.

Haybron, D. (2007) Do we know how happy we are? On some limits of affective introspection and recall. *Noûs*, 41, 394-428.

Heavey, C. and Hurlburt, R. (2008) The phenomena of inner experience. *Consciousness and Cognition*, 17, 798-810.

Hektner, J., Schmidt, J., and Csikszentmihalyi, M. (2006) *Experience Sampling Method: Measuring the Quality of Everyday Life.* London: Sage Publications.

Hendricks, M. (2009) Experiencing level: an instance of developing a variable from a first person process so it can be reliably measured and taught. In C. Petitmengin (ed.) *Ten Years of Viewing From Within: The Legacy of E.J. Varela.* Special Issue, *Journal of Consciousness Studies*, 16, 10-12, 129-155.

Heritage, J. (1978) Aspects of the flexibilities of language use. *Sociology* 12, 1: 79-104.

Heritage, J. (1984a) *Garfinkel and Ethnomethodology*. Cambridge: Polity Press.

Heritage, J. (1984b) A change of state token and aspects of its sequential placement. In J.M. Atkinson and J. Heritage (eds.) *Structures of Social Action: Studies in Conversation Analysis*. Cambridge: Cambridge University Press, 299-345.

Heritage, J. (1997) Conversation analysis and institutional talk: analysing data. In D. Silverman, (ed.) *Qualitative Research: Theory, Method and Practice*. London and Thousand Oaks: Sage.

Heritage, J. (2005) Cognition in discourse. In H. te Molder and J. Potter (eds.) *Discourse and Cognition*. Cambridge: Cambridge University Press, 184-202.

Heritage, J. and Clayman, S.E. (2010) *Talk in Action: Interactions, Identities, Institutions*. Chichester: Wiley-Blackwell.

Heritage, J. and Greatbatch, D. (1991) On the institutional character of institutional talk: the case of news interviews. In D. Boden and D.H. Zimmerman (eds.) *Talk and Social Structure: Studies in Ethnomethodology and Conversation Analysis*. Berkely: University of California Press, 93-137.

Heritage, J. and Raymond, G, (2005) The terms of agreement: indexing epistemic authority and subordination in talk-in-interaction. *Social Psychology Quarterly*, 68:1, 15-38.

Heritage, J. and Watson. D.R. (1979) Formulations as conversational objects. In G. Psathas (ed.) *Everyday Language: Studies in Ethnomethodology*. Irvington: New York, 123-162.

Honorton, C. (1993) Rhetoric over substance: the impoverished state of scepticism. *Journal of Parapsychology*, 57, 191-214

Hopper, R. (1992) Speech errors and the poetics of conversation. *Text and Performance Quarterly*, 12:3, 113-124.

Houtkoop-Steenstra, H. (2000) *Interaction and the Standardized Survey Interview*. Cambridge: Cambridge University Press.

Hull, C. (1920) Quantitative aspects of the evolution of concepts. *Psychological Monographs*, 123.

Hurlburt, R.T. (1979) Random sampling of cognitions and behavior. *Journal of Research in Personality*, 13, 103-111.

Hurlburt, R.T. (1990) *Sampling Normal and Schizophrenic Inner Experience*. New York: Plenum Press.

Hurlburt, R.T. (1993) *Sampling Inner Experience in Disturbed Affect*. New York: Plenum Press.

Hurlburt, R. T. (2009) Iteratively apprehending pristine experience. In C. Petitmengin (ed.) *Ten Years of Viewing From Within: The Legacy of E.J. Varela*. Special Issue, the *Journal of Consciousness Studies*, 16, 10-12, 156-188.

Hurlburt, R.T. (2011) In response to Froese, Gould and Seth. In C.Petitmengin (ed.) *Ten Years' Viewing From Within: Further Debate*. Special Issue, *Journal of Consciousness Studies*, 18,2, 65-78.

Hurlburt, R., and Heavey, C. (2001) Telling what we know: Describing inner experience. *Trends in Cognitive Sciences*, 5, 400-403.

Hurlburt, R., and Heavey, C. (2002) Interobserver reliability of descriptive experience sampling. *Cognitive Therapy and Research*, 26, 135-142.

Hurlburt, R. T. and Heavey, C. L. (2004) To beep or not to beep: Obtaining accurate reports about awareness. *Journal of Consciousness Studies*, 11, 113-128.

Hurlburt, R., and Heavey, C. (2006a) *Exploring Inner Experience: The Descriptive Experience Sampling Method*. Advances in consciousness research, Volume 64. Amsterdam and Philadelphia: John Benjamins.

Hurlburt, R, and Heavey, C. (2006b) *Descriptive experience sampling manual of terminology*. Retrieved in May 2007 from: http://www.nevada.edu/~russ/codebook.html.

Hurlburt, R., Heavey, C., and Bensaheb, A. (2009) Sensory awareness. *Journal of Consciousness Studies*, 16, 231-51.

Hurlburt, R., and Schwitzgebel, E. (2007). *Describing Inner Experience? Proponent Meets Skeptic*. Cambridge, MA.: MIT Press.

Hutchby, I. (1996a) *Confrontation Talk: Arguments, Asymmetries and Power on Talk Radio*. Malwah, NJ.: Lawrence Erlbaum.

Hutchby, I. (1996b) Power in discourse: the case of arguments on a British talk radio show. *Discourse and Society*, 7, 481-497.

Hutchby, I. and Wooffitt, R. (2008) *Conversation Analysis*. (Second edition), Oxford: Polity Press.

Hyman, R. (1977) 'Cold reading': how to convince strangers that you know all about them. *Skeptical Enquirer*, 2, 18-37.

Hyman, R. (1995) Evaluation of the program on anomalous mental phenomena. *Journal of Parapsychology* 59:4, 321-352.

Hyman, R. and Honorton, C. (1986) A joint communique: The psi ganzfeld controversy. *Journal of Parapsychology*, 50, 351-364.

Hymes, D. (1977) Discovering oral performance and measured verse in American Indian narrative. *New Literary History*, 8(3), 431-457.

Irwin, H. J. (1999) *An Introduction to Parapsychology*. Jefferson, NC., and London: McFarland. (Third edition.)

Jack, A., and Roepstorff, A. (2003) Why trust the subject? *Journal of Consciousness*, 10, v-xx.

Jack, A. and Roepstorff, A. (Eds.) (2004) 'Trusting The Subject: Part 2' Special issue, *Journal of Consciousness Studies*, Vol. 11 (7-8).

Jack, A., and Shallice, T. (2001) Introspective physicalism as an approach to the science of consciousness. *Cognition*, 79, 161-196.

Jacobson, E. (1911) On meaning and understanding. *American Journal of Psychology*, 22, 553-577.

James, W. (1890) *The Principles of Psychology*. New York: Holt.

James, W. (1892/1955) *Psychology (Briefer Course)*. South Bend, Indiana, University of Notre Dame Press.

James, W (1897/1979) *The Will to Believe*. Cambridge, Massachusetts: Harvard University Press.

James, W. (1902/1985) *The Varieties of Religious Experience*. New York and London: Penguin Books.

Jaworski, A. (1993) *The Power of Silence: Social and Pragmatic Perspectives*. London: Sage.

Jaworski, A. and Stephens, D. (1998) Self-reports on silence as a face-saving strategy by people with hearing impairment. *International Journal of Applied Linguistics* (8) 1, 61-80.

Jefferson, G. (1983) Notes on some orderliness of overlap onset. *Tilburg Papers in Language and Literature No. 28*. Department of Linguistics, Tilburg University.

Jefferson, G. (1984) Notes on the systematic deployment of the acknowledgement tokens "yeah" and "hm mm". *Papers in Linguistics*, 1,7 197-206.

Jefferson, G. (1989) Notes on a possible metric for a standard maximum silence of approximately one second in conversation. In D. Roger and P. Bull, (eds.) *Conversation: an Interdisciplinary Perspective*. Clevedon and Philadelphia: Multilingual Matters, 166-96.

Jefferson, G. (1990) List construction as a task and resource. In G. Psathas (ed.) *Interaction Competence*. Washington DC: University Press of America, 63-92.

Jefferson, G. (1996) On the poetics of ordinary talk. *Text and Performance Quarterly* 16, 1-61.

Jefferson, G., Sacks, H. and Schegloff, E. A. (1987) Notes on laughter in pursuit of intimacy. In G. Button and J.R.E. Lee (eds), *Talk and Social Structure*. Clevedon: Multilingual Matters, 152–205.

Jensen, J.V. (1973) Communicative functions of silences. *ETC: A Review of General Semantics*, (30), 249-257.

Jodelet, D. (1991) *Madness and Social Representations*. London: Harvester Wheatsheaf.

Johannesen, R. L. (1974) The functions of silence: a plea for communication research. *Western Speech*, (38), 25-35.

Johansson, P., Hall, L., Silkström, S., Tärning, B., and Lind, A. (2006) How something can be said about telling more than we can know: On choice blindness and introspection. *Consciousness and Cognition*, 15, 673-692.

Johnstone, B. (1987) An Introduction. in B. Johnstone (ed.) Special issue on 'Perspectives on repetition' *Text*, 7, 205-214.

Jones, W. H. and Russel, D. (1980) The selective processing of belief disconfirming information. *European Journal of Social Psychology*, 10, 309-312.

Kelly, M. (1996) Using the think-aloud protocol to study the effects of test anxiety on spatial task performance. *Dissertation Abstracts International Section A: Humanities and Social Sciences*, 56(10-A), 3889.

Klinger, E. (2011) Response organization of mental imagery, evaluation of DES and alternatives. In J. Weisberg (ed.) *Describing Inner Experience: A Symposium Debating Descriptive Experience Sampling (DES)*. Special issue, *Journal of Consciousness Studies*, 18, 1, 92-101.

Kosslyn, S. M., Segar, C., Pani, J., and Hillger, L. A. (1990) When is imagery used in everyday life? A diary study. *Journal of Mental Imagery*, 14, 131-152.

Kroker, K. (2003) The progress of introspection in America: 1996-1938. *Studies in History and Philosophy of Biological and Biomedical Sciences*, 34, 77-108.

Külpe, O. (1895/1973) *Outlines of Psychology*. New York: Arno Press.

Kurtz, P. (Ed.) (1985) *A Skeptic's Handbook of Parapsychology*. New York: Prometheus Books.

Lachman, R., Lachman, J., and Butterfield, E. (1979) *Cognitive Psychology and Information Processing: An Introduction*. Hillsdale, NJ: Lawrence Erlbaum.

Lakatos, I. (1978) *The Methodology of Scientific Research Programmes*. Philosophical Papers Vol, I, Cambridge: Cambridge University Press.

Lambie, J., and Marcel, A. (2002) Consciousness and the varieties of emotion experience: A theoretical framework. *Psychological Review*, 109, 219-59.

Lamiell, J. (1981) Toward an idiothetic psychology of personality. *American Psychologist*, 36, 276-289.

Langdridge, D. (2007) *Phenomenological Psychology: Theory, Research and Method*. Harlow: Pearson.

Laplane, D. (1992) Use of introspection in scientific psychological research. *Behavioural Neurology*, 5, 199-203.

Lerner, G. H. (2005) *Conversation Analysis: Studies from the First Generation*. Amsterdam/Philadelphia: John Benjamins.

Levine, J. (1983). Materialism and qualia: The explanatory gap. *Pacific Philosophical Quarterly*, 64, 354-361.

Levinson, S. C. (1983) *Pragmatics*. Cambridge: Cambridge University Press.

Libet, B., Wright, E. W., Feinstein, B., and Pearl, D. (1979) Subjective referral of the timing for a conscious sensory experience: A functional role for the somatosensory specific projection system in man. *Brain*, 102, 193-224.

Lloyd, M. (2007) Rear gunners and troubled privates: wordplay in a dick joke competition. *Journal of Sociolinguistics*, 11, 5-23.

Locke, E. (2009). It's time we brought introspection out of the closet. *Perspectives on Psychological Sience*, 4, 24-25.

Loftus, E. (1996) *Eyewitness Testimony*. Cambridge, Mass.: Harvard University Press.

Luff, P., Gilbert, N. and Frohlich, D. (Eds) (1990) *Computers and Conversation*. London: Academic Press.

Lutz, A. (2007) Neurophenomenology and the study of self-consciousness. *Consciousness and Cognition*, 16, 765-767.

Lutz, A., and Thompson, E. (2003) Neurophenomenology: Integrating subjective experience and brain dynamics in the neuroscience of consciousness. *Journal of Consciousness Studies*, 10, 31-52.

Lutz, A., Lachaux, J., Martinerie, J. and Varela, F. (2002) Guiding the study of brain dynamics by using first-person data: Synchrony patterns correlate with ongoing conscious states during a simple visual task. *Proceedings of the National Academy of Sciences*, 99, 1586-1591.

Lyons, W. (1986) *The Disappearance of Introspection*. London and Cambridge, MA: MIT Press.

McClenon, J. (1982) A survey of elite scientists: their attitudes towards ESP and parapsychology. *Journal of Parapsychology*, 46, 127-152.

McQuarrie, E. F., and Mick, D.G. (1996) Figures of rhetoric in advertising language. *The Journal of Consumer Research*, 22, 424-438.

Magnusson, L. (2006) 'Donne's language: the condition of communication' in A. Guibbory (ed.) *The Cambridge Companion to John Donne*. Cambridge: Cambridge University Press: 183-200.

Maltz, D.N. (1985) Joyful noise and reverent silence: the significance of noise in Pentecostal worship. In D. Tannen and M. Saville-Troike. (Eds.) *Perspectives on Silence*. Norwood, NJ.: Ablex, 113-137.

Mandler, G. (2007) *A History of Modern Experimental Psychology: From James and Wundt to Cognitive Science*. Cambridge. MA.:: MIT Press.

Manen, van, M. (1990) *Researching Lived Experience: Human Science for an Action Sensitive Pedagogy*. New York: Barnes and Noble.

Martia, S., Sackurd, J., Sigman, M, and Dehaene, S. (2010) Mapping introspection's blind spot: Reconstruction of dual-task phenomenology using quantified introspection. *Cognition*, 115, 303-313.

Maurel, M. (2009) The explicitation interview: Examples and applications. In C. Petitmengin (ed.) *Ten Years of Viewing From Within: The Legacy of E.J. Varela*. Special Issue, *Journal of Consciousness Studies*, 16, 10-12, 58-89.

Mayer, A., and Orth, J. (1901) Zur qualitativen untersuchung der assoziation. *Zeitschrift für Psychologie und Physiologie der Sinnesorgane*, 26, 1-13.

Maynard, D.W. (2005) Social actions, gestalt coherence and designations of disability: Lessons from and about Autism. *Social Problems*, 52,4, 499-524.

Maynard. D.W. and Shaeffer, N.C. (2002) Standardization and its discontents. In D.W. Maynard *et al.* (eds.). *Standardization and Tacit Knowledge: Interaction and Practice in the Survey Interview*. New York: Wiley, 3-46.

Merleau-Ponty, M. (1945). *Phenomenology of Perception*. London: Routledge and Kegan Paul.

Mill, J. S. (1882) *Auguste Comte and Positivism*. London: George Routledge and Sons.

Miller, G. (1952) The magical number seven, plus or minus two: Some limits on our capacity for processing information. *Psychological Review*, 63, 81-97.

Moerman, M. (1988) *Talking Culture: Ethnography and Conversation Analysis*. Philadelphia: University of Pennsylvania Press.

Moran, D. (2000) *Introduction to Phenomenology*. London and New York: Taylor and Francis.

Morris, B. (1991). *Western Conceptions of the Individual*. New York and Oxford: Berg.

Morris, R.L., Dalton, K., Delanoy, D. and Watt, C. (1995) Comparison of the sender/no sender condition in the ganzfeld. In *Proceedings of Presented Papers, 38th Annual Parapsychological Association Convention*, edited by N.L. Zingrone. Fairhaven. MA., the Parapsychological Association, 244-259.

Murdock, B. (1962) The serial position effect of free recall. *Journal of Experimental Psychology*, 64, 482-488.

Nagel, T. (1974) What is it like to be a bat? *Philosophical Review*, 83, 435-50.

Nahmias, E. (2002) Verbal reports on the contents of consciousness: Reconsidering introspectionist methodology. *Psyche*, 81: http://psyche.cs.monash.edu.au/v8/psyche-8-21-nahmias.html.

Nakane, I. (2008) Silence and politeness in intercultural communication in university seminars. *Journal of Pragmatics* (38), 1811-1835.

Nanny, M. (1994) Textual echoes of echoes. In A. Fisher (ed.) *Repetition (Swiss Papers in English Language and Literature*. Narr: Tubinggen,115-144

Natsoulas, T. (1987) The six basic concepts of consciousness and William James' stream of thought. *Imagination, Cognition and Personality*, 6, 289-319.

Natsoulas, T. (1991) The concept of consciousness – the interpersonal meaning. *Journal for the Theory of Social Behavior*, 21, 63-89.

Neisser, R and Fivush, R. (Eds.) (1994) *The Remembering Self*. Cambridge and New York: Cambridge University Press.

Neisser, U. and Harsch, N. (1992) Phantom flashbulbs: false recollections of hearing the news about the Challenger. In E. Winograd, and U. Neisser (eds.) *Affect And Accuracy in Recall: Studies of 'Flashbulb Memories'* . Cambridge: Cambridge University Press, 9 -31.

Neisser, U and Winograd, E. (eds.) (1988) *Remembering Reconsidered: Ecological and Traditional Approaches to the Study of Memory*. Cambridge and New York: Cambridge University Press.

Nisbett, R., and Wilson, T. (1977) Telling more than we can know: Verbal reports on mental processes. *Psychological Review*, 84, 231-259.

Norrick, N.R. (2000/2001) Poetics and conversation. *Connotations* 10, 243-26 .

Nye, R. (1986). *Three Psychologies: Perspectives from Freud, Skinner, and Rogers.* Monterey, CA: Brooks/Cole.

Orne, M. T. (1962) On the social psychology of the psychological experiment: with particular reference to demand characteristics and their implications. *American Psychologist*, 17, 776 -783.

Orne. M.T. and Whitehouse, W.G. (2000) Demand characteristics. In A.E. Kazdin (ed.) *Encyclopedia of Psychology*. Washington, DC.: American Psychological Association and Oxford University Press, 469-470.

Overgaard, M. (2006) Introspection in science. *Consciousness and Cognition*, 15, 629-633.

Overgaard, M., Gallagher, S., and Ramsøy, T. (2008) An integration of first-person methodologies in cognitive science. *Journal of Consciousness Studies*, 15, 100-120.

Parfit, D. (1989) Divided minds and the nature of persons. In C. Blakemore, and S. Greenfield (eds.), *Mindwaves*. Oxford: Basil Blackwell.

Pekala, R. (1991). *Quantifying Consciousness: An Empirical Approach*. New York: Plenum Press.

Pekala, R., and Cardeña, E. (2000) Methodological issues in the study of altered states of consciousness and anomalous experiences. In E. Cardeña, S. J. Lynn., and S. Krippner (eds.), *Varieties of Anomalous Experience*. Washington, DC: American Psychological Association, 47–81.

Petitmengin, C (2006) Describing one's subjective experience in the second person: an interview method for the science of consciousness. *Phenomenology and the Cognitive Sciences*, 5, 229-269.

Petitmengin,.C (Ed.) (2011). *Ten Years' Viewing From Within: Further Debate*. Special Issue, *Journal of Consciousness Studies*, 18, 2.

Petitmengin, C. and Bitbol, M. (2009) The validity of first person descriptions as authenticity and coherence. In C. Petitmengin (ed.) *Ten Years of Viewing From Within: The Legacy of E.J. Varela*. Special Issue, *Journal of Consciousness Studies*, 16, 10-12, 363-404.

Petitmengin, C,. Bitbol, M., Nissou, J-M., Pachoud, B., Curallucci, H.,Cermolacce, M. and Vion-Dury, J, (2009) Listening from within. In C. Petitmengin (ed.) *Ten Years of Viewing From Within: The Legacy of E.J. Varela*. Special Issue, *Journal of Consciousness Studies*, 16, 10-12, 252-284.

Petitmengin, C., Navarro, V., and Le Van Queyen, M. (2007) Anticipating seizure: Pre-reflective experience at the center of neuro-phenomenology. *Consciousness and Cognition*, 16, 746-764.

Petitmengin-Peugot, C. (1999) The intuitive experience. In F. Varela and J. Shear (eds.) *The View From Within: First Person Approaches to the Study of Consciousness*. Exeter: Imprint Academic, 43-78.

Philippot, P., and Segal, Z. (2009) Mindfulness based psychological interventions: Developing emotional awareness for better being. *Journal of Consciousness Studies*, 16 (10-12), 285-306.

Piccinini, G. (2003) Data from introspective reports: Upgrading from common sense to science. *Journal of Consciousness Studies*, 10, 141-56.

Piccinini, G. (2007) *Introspection as a source of public evidence.* Downloaded in May 2007 from http://www.umsl.edu/~piccininig/First-person%20Data%20short%202.htm.

Pillemer, D.B. (1984) Flashbulb memories of the assassination attempt on President Reagan. *Cognition,* 16, 63-80.

Pillemer, D.B. 1992 Remembering personal circumstances: a functional analysis. In E. Winograd, and U. Neiser (eds.) *Affect And Accuracy in Recall: Studies of 'Flashbulb Memories'* . Cambridge: Cambridge University Press, 236-264.

Pinch, T.J. (1985) Towards an analysis of scientific observation: the externality and evidential significance of observational reports in physics. *Social Studies of Science*, 15, 3-36.

Pinku, G., and Tzelgov, J. (2006) Consciousness of the self (COS) and explicit knowledge. *Consciousness and Cognition*, 15, 655-661.

Poland, B. and Pederson, A. (1998) Reading between the lines: interpreting silences in qualitative research. *Qualitative Inquiry*, (4) 2: 293-312.

Pomerantz, A.M. (1980) Telling my side: 'limited access' as a 'fishing' device'. *Sociological Inquiry*, 50L 186-98.

Pomerantz, A.M. (1984) Agreeing and disagreeing with assessments: some features of preferred/dispreferred turn-shapes. In J.M Atkinson and J. Heritage, J. (eds.) *Structures of Social Action: Studies in Conversation Analysis.* Cambridge: Cambridge University Press, 79-112.

Pomerantz, A. M. (1986) Extreme case formulations: a way of legitimizing claims. In G. Button, P. Drew, J. Heritage (eds.) *Human Studies* 9 (Special Issue on Interaction and Language Use), 219-229.

Potter, J. (1996) *Representing Reality*. London: Sage

Potter, J. (1997) Discourse analysis as a way of analysing naturally occurring talk. In D. Silverman (ed.) *Qualitative Analysis: Issues of Theory and Method.* London: Sage, 144-60.

Potter, J. (2000) Post-cognitive psychology' *Theory and Psychology*, 10(1), 31-37.

Potter, J. and Edwards, D. 91990) Nigel Lawson's tent: discourse analysis, attribution theory and the social psychology of fact. *European Journal of Psychology* 20: 405-24.

Potter, J. and Hepburn, A. (2003) "I'm a bit concerned": early actions and psychological constructions in a child protection helpline. *Research on Language and Social Interaction*, 36(3), 197-240.

Potter, J., and Wetherell, M. (1987) *Discourse and Social Psychology: Beyond Attitudes and Behaviour*. London: Sage publications.

Price, D., and Aydede, M. (2005) The experimental use of introspection in the scientific study of pain and its integration with third-person methodologies: The experiential-phenomenological approach. In Aydede, M. (ed.), *Pain: New Essays on its Nature and the Methodology of its Study*. Cambridge, MA: MIT Press, 243-274

Pronin, E. (2009). The introspection illusion. In M. Zanna (Ed.), *Advances in Experimental Psychology*. Vol. 41, pp. 1-67. Burlington: Academic Press.

Quattrone , G. (1985) On the congruity between internal states and action. *Psychological Bulletin*, 98, 3-40.

Radin, D. (1997) *The Conscious Universe: The Scientific Truth of Psychic Phenomena*. New York: HarperEdge.

Randi, J. (1988) *Flim-flam: The Truth About Unicorns, Parapsychology and Other Delusions*. New York: Prometheus Books.

Raymond, G. (2000) The voice of authority: the local accomplishment of authoritative discourse in live news broadcasts. *Discourse Studies*, 2, 354-79.

Raymond, G. and Heritage, J. (2006) The epistemics of social relations: owning grandchildren. *Language in Society*, 35, 677-705.

Rogers, C. (1951) *Client-Centered Therapy: Its Current Practice, Implications and Theory.* London: Constable.

Rudrauf, D., Lutz, A., Cosmelli, D., Lachaux, J., and le van Quyen, M. (2003) From autopoiesis to neurophenomenology: Francisco Varela's exploration of the biophysics of being. *Biological Research*, 36, 27-65.

Ryle, G. (1949) *The Concept of Mind.* London: Hutchinson.

Sacks, H. (1979) Hotrodder: a revolutionary category. In G. Psathas (ed.) *Everyday Language: Studies In Ethnomethodology.* New York: Irvington, 7-14. (Edited by G. Jefferson from unpublished lectures: Spring 1966, lecture 18.)

Sacks, H. (1984) On doing 'being ordinary'. In J.M. Atkinson and J. Heritage (eds), *Structures of Social Action.* Cambridge: Cambridge University Press, 413-29.

Sacks, H. (1992) *Lectures on Conversation.* (Volumes I and II), edited by G. Jefferson and E. A. Schegloff. Oxford and Cambridge, Mass.: Basil Blackwell.

Sacks, H., Schegloff, E.A. and Jefferson, G. (1974) A simplest systematics for the organisation of turn-taking for conversation. *Language* 50, 696-735.

Sajama, S., and Kamppinen, M. (1987) *A Historical Introduction to Phenomenology.* London and New York: Croom Helm.

Schachter, S. and Singer, J. (1962) Cognitive, social and physiological determinants of emotional state. *Psychological Review*, 69, 379-399.

Schegloff, E. A. (1968) Sequencing in conversational openings. *American Anthropologist*, 70, 1075-95.

Schegloff, E.A. (1972) Notes on a conversational practice: formulating place. In D. Sudnow (ed.) *Studies in Social Interaction.* New York: Free Press, 75-119.

Schegloff, E. A. (1982) Discourse as an interactional achievement: some uses of "uh huh" and other things that come between sentences. In D. Tannen (ed.) *Analysing Discourse: Georgetown University Roundtable on Languages and Linguistics.* Washington D. C.: Georgetown University Press, 71-93.

Schegloff, E.A. (1984) On some questions and ambiguities in conversation. In J.M. Atkinson and J. Heritage (eds.) *Structures of Social Action: Studies in Conversation Analysis.* Cambridge: Cambridge University Press, 28-52.

Schegloff, E.A. (1987) Between micro and macro: contexts and other connections. In J.C. Alexander, B. Giesen, R. Munch and N.J. Smelser (eds.) *The Micro-Macro Link.* Berkeley: University of California Press, 207-236.

Schegloff, E.A. (1988/9) From interview to confrontation: observations on the Bush/Rather encounter. *Research on Language and Social Interaction* 22, 215-240.

Schegloff, E. A. (1997) Whose text? Whose context? *Discourse and Society* 8, 165-187.

Schegloff, E. A. (1999) Discourse, pragmatics, conversation, analysis. *Discourse Studies*, 1, 405-435.

Schegloff, E.A. (2002) Survey interviews as talk-in-interaction. In D.W. Maynard, H. Houtkoop-Streenstra, N.C. Schaffer and J. van der Zouwen (eds), *Standardization and Tacit Knowledge: Interaction and Practice in the Survey Interview.* New York: Wiley, 151-157.

Schegloff, E.A. (2007) *Sequence Organization in Interaction: A Primer in Conversation Analysis, Volume 1.* Cambridge: Cambridge University Press.

Schegloff, E.A., Jefferson, G. and Sacks, H. (1977) The preference for self-correction in the organisation of repair in conversation. *Language*, 53, 361-382

Schegloff, E.A., Koshik, I., Jacoby, S. and Olsher, D. (2002) Conversation analysis and applied linguistics. *Annual Review of Applied Linguistics*, (22), 3-31.

Schegloff, E. A. and Sacks, H. (1973) Opening up closings. *Semiotica*, 7, 289–327.

Schenkein, J. (1978) Sketch of the analytic mentality for the study of conversational interaction.In J. Schenkein (ed.) *Studies in the Organisation of Conversational Interaction*. New York: Academic Press, 1-6.

Schooler, J. and Engstler-Schooler. T. (1990) Verbal overshadowing of visual memories: some things are better left unsaid. *Cognitive Psychology* 22, 36–71.

Schooler, J., and Schreiber, C. (2004) Experience, meta-consciousness, and the paradox of introspection. *Journal of Consciousness Studies*, 11, 17-39.

Schwartz, J.M. and Begley, S. (2002) *The Mind and the Brain: Neuroplasticity and the Power of Mental Force*. New York: Regan Books.

Schwitzgebel, E. (2008) The unreliability of naive introspection. *Philosophical Review*, 117, 245-273.

Searle, J. (1969) *Speech Acts*. Cambridge: Cambridge University Press.

Searle, J. (1997) *The Mystery of Consciousness*. London: Granta Books.

Shinebourne, P., and Smith, J. (2009) Alcohol and the self: An interpretative phenomenological analysis of the experience of addiction and its impact on the sense of self and identity. *Addiction Research and Theory*, 17,152-167.

Shoemaker, S. (1994) Self-knowledge and inner sense. *Philosophy and Phenomenological Research*, 54, 249-314.

Sinclair, U.B. (1930) *Mental Radio*. New York: Albert and Charles Boni.

Singer, B. and Benassi, V.A. (1981) Occult beliefs. *American Scientist*, 69, 49-55.

Singer, J. (1976) *Daydreaming and Fantasy*. London: George Allen and Unwin.

Smith, D. E. (1978), "K is mentally ill": The anatomy of a factual account. *Sociology*, 12, 23-53.

Smith, J. (2008) (Ed.) *Qualitative Psychology: A Practical Guide to Research Methods*. London: Sage.

Smith, J., and Osborn, M. (2003) Interpretative phenomenological analysis. In J. Smith (ed.), *Qualitative Psychology: A Practical Guide to Research Methods*. London: Sage, 25-50.

Smith, J., Flowers, P., and Larkin, M. (2009) *Interpretative Phenomenological Analysis: Theory, Method, Research*. London: Sage.

Sorjonen, M-L. (1996) On repeats and responses in Finnish conversations. In: E. Ochs, E.A. Schegloff and S.A. Thompson (eds.) *Interaction and Grammar*. Cambridge: Cambridge University Press, 277-327.

Sorjonen, M.L. and Heritage, J. (1991) Constituting and maintaining activities across sequences: and-prefacing as a feature of question design. *Language in Society*, 23,1, 1-29.

Spinelli, E. (2005) *The Interpreted World: An Introduction to Phenomenological sychology*. London: Sage.

Sternberg, R. (2009) *Cognitive Psychology*. Belmont, CA: Wadsworth.

Stevens, R. (1999) Phenomenological approaches to the study of conscious awareness. In M. Velmans (Ed.), *Investigating Phenomenal Consciousness: New Methodologies and Maps*. Advances in Consciousness Research, Volume 13. Amsterdam and Philadelphia: John Benjamins, 99-120.

Stivers, T. (2005) Modified repeats: one method for asserting primary rights from second position. *Research on Language and Social Interaction* 38:2, 131-158.

Stokoe, E.H. and Hepburn, A. (2005) "You can hear a lot through walls": noise formulations in neighbour complaints. *Discourse and Society*, 16, 647-73.

Storms, M. and Nisbett, R. (1970) Insomnia and the attribution process. *Journal of Personality and Social Psychology*, 2, 319-328.

Suchman, L. and Jordan, B. (1990) Interactional troubles in face-to-face survey interviews. *Journal of the American Statistical Association* 85, 232-41.

Tainio, L. (2003) "When shall we go for a ride?" A case of the sexual harassment of a young girl. *Discourse and Society*, 14, 173-190.

Tannen, D. (1987) Repetition in conversation: towards a poetics of talk. *Language* 63, 574-605.

Tannen, D. (1998) "Oh talking voice that is so sweet": The poetic nature of conversation. *Social Research*, 65(3), 631-651.

Tarnas, R. (1991) *The Passion of the Western Mind: Understanding the Ideas that Shaped our World View*. London: Pimlico.

Tart, C. (1975) *States of Consciousness*. New York: E.P. Dutton and Co.

Teasdale, J., Moore, R., Hayhurst, H., Pope, M., Williams, S., and Segal, Z. (2002) Metacognitive awareness and prevention of relapse in depression: Empirical evidence. *Journal of Consulting and Clinical Psychology*, 70, 275-287.

ten Have, P. (1999) *Doing Conversation Analysis: a Practical Guide*. London and Thousand Oaks: Sage.

Terasaki, A. (2005) Pre-announcement sequences in conversation. In G. Lerner (ed), *Conversation Analysis: Studies from the First Generation*, Amsterdam: John Benjamins, 171-224.

Thomas, N. (2010) *Founders of Experimental Psychology: Wilhelm Wundt and William James*. Retrieved in July 2010 from http://plato.stanford.edu/entries/mental-imagery/founders-experimental-psychology.html.

Thompson, E. (2007) Look again: Phenomenology and mental imagery. *Phenomenology and the Cognitive Sciences*, 6, 137-170.

Thompson, E., Lutz, A., and Cosmelli, D. (2005) Neurophenomenology: An introduction for neurophilosophers. In A. Brook and K. Akins (Eds.), *Cognition and the Brain*, pp. 40-97. Cambridge: Cambridge University Press.

Titchener, E. (1898) The postulates of structural psychology. *Philosophical Review*, 7, 449-465.

Titchener, E. (1912) The schema of introspection. *American Journal of Psychology*, 23, 485-508.

Tulving, E. (1972) Episodic and semantic memory. In E. Tulving and W. Donaldson (eds.), *Organisation of Memory*, London: Academic Press.

Utts, J.M (1995) An assessment of the evidence for psychic functioning. *Journal of Parapsychology*, 59, 289-320.

Valentine, E. (1998) *Conceptual Issues in Psychology*. London: Routledge.

Varela, F. (1996) Neurophenomenology: A methodological remedy for the hard problem. *Journal of Consciousness Studies*, 3, 330-349.

Varela, F. (1999) Present-time consciousness. *Journal of Consciousness Studies*, 6, 111-140.

Varela, F. and Shear, J. (Eds.) (1999) *The View From Within: First Person Approaches to the Study of Consciousness*. Exeter: Imprint Academic.

Velmans, M. (Ed.). (2000a) *Investigating Phenomenal Consciousness: New Methodologies and Maps*. Advances in Consciousness Research, Volume 13. Amsterdam and Philadelphia: John Benjamins.

Velmans, M. (2000b) *Understanding Consciousness*. London and Philadelphia: Routledge.

Velmans, M. (2007) Heterophenomenology versus critical phenomenology. *Phenomenology and the Cognitive Sciences*, 6, 221-230.

Vermersch, P. (1999) Introspection as practice. In F. J. Varela, F.J. and J. Shear (eds.) *The View From Within: First Person Approaches to the Study of Consciousness*. Thorverton: Imprint Academic, 17-42 (Originally published as *Journal of Consciousness Studies*, 6(2-3): 17-42.)

Vermersch, P. (2009) Describing the practice of introspection. In C. Petitmengin (ed.) *Ten Years of Viewing From Within: The Legacy of E.J. Varela*. Special Issue, *Journal of Consciousness Studies*, 16, 10-12, 20-57.

Vermersch, P. (2011) A reply to Zahavi. In C.Petitmengin (ed.) *Ten Years' Viewing From Within: Further Debate*. Special Issue, *Journal of Consciousness Studies*, 18,2, 20-23.

Wackermann, J., Putz, P. and Allefeld, C., (2008) Ganzfeld induced hallucinatory experience, its phenomenology and cerebral electrophysiology. *Cortex*, 44, 1364-1378.

Waismann, F. (1965) *The Principles of Linguistic Philosophy*. London: Macmillan. (Edited by R. Harre.)

Wales, K. (2009) Unnatural conversations in unnatural conversations: speech reporting in the discourse of spiritual mediumship. *Language and Literature*, 18(4), 347-356

Wallace, A. (2000). *The Taboo of Subjectivity: Toward a New Science of Consciousness*. New York: Oxford University Press.

Wallendorf, M. and Brucks, M. (1993) Introspection in consumer research: implementation and implications. *Journal of Consumer Research*, 20, 339-59.

Walsh, R. (1995) Phenomenological mapping. *The Journal of Transpersonal Psychology*, 27, 21-53.

Washburn, M. (1922) Introspection as an objective method. *Psychological Review*, 29, 89-112.

Watson, J.B. (1913) Psychology as the behaviorist views it. *Psychological Review*, 20, 158-177

Watson, R. (1998) Ethnomethodology, consciousness and self. *Journal of Consciousness Studies*, 5, 202-203.

Watson, W.G.E. (1981) Chiastic patterns in Biblical Hebrew poetry. In J. W. Welch (ed.) *Chiasmus in Antiquity: Structures, Analyses, Exegesis*. Provo: Research Press, 118-168.

Welch, J.W. (ed.) (1981a) *Chiasmus in Antiquity: Structures, Analyses, Exegesis*. Provo: Research Press.

Welch, J.W. (1981b) Introduction. In J. W. Welch (ed.) *Chiasmus in Antiquity: Structures, Analyses, Exegesis*. Provo: Research Press, 11-16.

Welch, J.W. (1981c) Chiasmus in ancient Greek and Latin literatures. In J. W. Welch (ed.) *Chiasmus in Antiquity: Structures, Analyses, Exegesis*. Provo: Research Press, 250-269.

Welch, J.W. (1981d) Chiasmus in the Book of Mormon. In J. W. Welch (ed.) *Chiasmus in Antiquity: Structures, Analyses, Exegesis*. Provo: Research Press, 198-210.

Wegner, D. (2002) *The Illusion of Conscious Will*. Cambridge, MA: MIT Press.

Weisberg, J. (2011) (Ed.) Describing Inner Experience: A Symposium Debating Descriptive Experience Sampling. *Journal of Consciousness Studies*, 18,1, 1-305

Whalen, J., Zimmerman, D. and Whalen, M.R. (1988) When words fail: a single case analysis. *Social Problems* 35, 4, 333-362.

White, P. (1988) Knowing more about what we can tell: introspective access and causal report accuracy 10 years later. *British Journal of Psychology*, 79, 13-45.

Widdicombe, S. (1993) Autobiography and change: rhetoric and authenticity of 'gothic' style'. In E. Burman and I. Parker (eds.), *Discourse Analytic Research: Repertoires and Readings of Texts in Action*, London: Routledge.

Widdicombe, S. and Wooffitt, R. (1990) "Being" versus "doing" punk: On achieving authenticity as a member'. *Journal of Language and Social Psychology*, 9, 257-77.

Widdicombe, S. and Wooffitt, R. (1995) *The Language of Youth Subcultures: Social Identity in Action*. Hemel Hempstead: Harvester Wheatsheaf.

Wiggins, S. (2001) Construction and action in food evaluation: conversational data. *Journal of Language and Social Psychology*, 20:4, 445-463.

Wiggins, S. and Potter, J. (2003) Attitudes and evaluative practices: category vs item and subjective vs objective constructions in everyday food assessment. *British Journal of Social Psychology*, 42, 513-31.

Wilkinson, R. (1995) Aphasia: Conversation analysis of a non-fluent aphasic person. In M. Perkins and S. Howard (eds), *Case Studies in Clinical Linguistics*, London: Whurr: 271-292

Wilkinson, R., Bryan, K., Lock, S., Bayley, K., Maxim, J., Bruce, C., Edmundson, A. and Moir, D. (1998) Therapy using conversation analysis: Helping coupes adapt to aphasia in conversation. *International Journal of Language and Communication Disorders*, 33: 144-148.

Wilson, T. (2002). *Strangers to Ourselves: Discovering the Adaptive Unconscious*. Cambridge, MA: Harvard University Press.

Wilson, T. (2003) Knowing when to ask: Introspection and the adaptive unconscious. *Journal of Consciousness Studies*, 10, 131-40.

Wilson, T., and Schooler, J. (1991) Thinking too much: Introspection can reduce the quality of preferences and decisions? *Journal of Personality and Social Psychology Bulletin*, 19, 331-9.

Wittgenstein, L. (1953) *Philosophical Investigations*. Oxford: Basil Blackwell. (Edited by. G. Anscombe.)

Woodside, A. G. (2004) Advancing from subjective to confirmatory personal introspection in consumer research. *Psychology and Marketing*, 21(12), 987-1010.

Wooffitt, R. (1992) *Telling Tales of the Unexpected: the Organisation of Factual Discourse*. Hemel Hempstead: Harvester Wheatsheaf.

Wooffitt, R. (2005) From process to practice: language, interaction and "flashbulb memory". In H. te Molder and J. Potter (eds.) *Discourse and Cognition*. Cambridge: Cambridge University Press, 203-225.

Wooffitt, R. (2006) *The Language of Mediums and Psychics: the Social Organisation of Everyday Miracles*. Aldershot: Ashgate.

Wooffitt, R., Fraser, N., Gilbert, G.N. and McGlashan, S. (1997) *Humans, Computers and Wizards: Conversation Analysis and Human (Simulated) Computer Interaction*. London: Routledge.

Wooffitt, R. and Widdicombe, S. (2006) Interaction in interviews. In P. Drew, G. Raymond and D. Weinberg, (eds), *Talk and Interaction in Social Research Methods*. London: Sage, 28-49.

Woolgar, S. (1980) Discovery, logic and sequence in a text. In K.D. Knorr, R. Krohn, R. Whitley, (eds.) *The Social Process of Scientific Investigation*. Dordrecht: Reidel, 239-268.

Wundt, W. (1897) *Outlines of Psychology*. Translated by C. H. Judd. Leipzig: Wilhelm Engelmann (Reprinted Bristol: Thoemmes, 1999). Retrieved in June 2010 from: http://psychclassics.yorku.ca/Wundt/Outlines/

Wundt, W. (1907/1958) From outlines of psychology (translated by C. Judd). In Reeves, J., *Body and Mind in Western Thought*. Glasgow: Penguin Books, 386-388.

Wundt, W. (2008). *An Introduction to Psychology*. London: Muller Press.

Young, A., and Block, N. (1996) Consciousness. In V. Bruce (Ed.), *Unsolved Mysteries of the Mind: Tutorial Essays in Cognition*, UK: Taylor and Francis, pp. 149-179.

Zahavi, D. (2011) Varieities of reflection. In C.Petitmengin (ed.) *Ten Years' Viewing From Within: Further Debate*. Special Issue, *Journal of Consciousness Studies*, 18,2, 9-19.

Zimbardo, P. G., Cohen, A., Weisenberg, M., Dworkin, L., and Firestone, I. (1969) The control of experimental pain. In E G. Zimbardo (ed.), *The Cognitive Control of Motivation*. Glenview, IL: Scott, Foresman, 100-122.

Zusne, L. and Jones, W.H. (1989) *Anomalistic Psychology: a Study of Extraordinary Phenomena and Experiences*. Hillside, N.J.: Lawrence Erlbaum Associates.

Index